ON ETHICS ECONOMICS

"To say I'm interested in ethics is probably just to say I'm a human being. You're brought up full of ethical concerns; these things are part and parcel of life. The real issue is whether you think about ethical concerns rather than just accept them."

So begins a remarkable conversation with Kenneth Arrow. Part intellectual autobiography and part exposition of complex yet contemporary economic ideas, this lively conversation with renowned scholar and public intellectual Kenneth J. Arrow focuses on economics and politics in light of history, current events, and philosophy as well. Reminding readers that economics is about redistribution and thus about how we treat each other, Arrow shows that the intersection of economics and ethics is of concern not just to economists but also for the public more broadly. With a foreword by Amartya Sen, this book highlights the belief that government can be a powerful force for good, and is particularly relevant in the current political climate and for the lay reader as well as the professional economist.

Kenneth J. Arrow is Joan Kenney Professor of Economics and Professor of Operations Research, Emeritus at Stanford University.

Kristen Renwick Monroe is Chancellor's Professor of Political Science at the University of California, Irvine.

Nicholas Monroe Lampros is an Associate at Covington & Burling LLP.

Praise for *On Ethics and Economics*

No one has done more than Kenneth Arrow to define what economic theory is today. His story is central to the modern history of economic thought. In this beautiful book, he has given a unique personal perspective on this great work which will be valued for ages to come.

Roger Myerson, *Nobel Laureate, University of Chicago*

Kenneth Arrow changed my life when, as a math major in college, I wandered into his course in the economics of information. The course showed me how economics can use mathematics and other technical tools to study important issues. He won me over and I ended up doing a PhD with him. This book should give readers some idea of why he was so persuasive.

Eric Maskin, *Nobel Laureate, Harvard University*

These interviews are a true delight to read, reminding us of Arrow's clear-headed intelligence, marvelous good sense, and how his broad views emerge from his pleasure in systematizing guided by ethical concern. Arrow provides cogent, common-sensical explanations of how economies work . . . and has a keen eye for what we don't grasp about economies, such as the role of non-market social networks and relations

Allan Gibbard, *University of Michigan*

Can you imagine having a conversation with one of the foremost social and economic thinkers in the world? Imagine no more. In this lively and engaging book, Kenneth J. Arrow—who continues to be productive well into his nineties—continues to enlighten us about the market economy, democracy, politics, social choice, and ethics. Few have done more to illuminate these fields, show how they're intimately connected, and why the connections are so important to understand.

Robert B. Reich, *University of California-Berkeley*

We are indebted to Kristen Monroe for a charming interview on ethics and economics with one of the great economists of our era. I enjoyed it thoroughly and am sure you will too.

Thomas C. Schelling, *Nobel Laureate, University of Maryland*

ON ETHICS AND ECONOMICS

Conversations with Kenneth J. Arrow

Kenneth J. Arrow

Kristen Renwick Monroe
Nicholas Monroe Lampros

With a foreword by
Amartya Sen

Routledge
Taylor & Francis Group

NEW YORK AND LONDON

Published 2017
by Routledge
711 Third Avenue, New York, NY 10017

and by Routledge
2 Park Square, Milton Park, Abingdon, Oxon, OX14 4RN

Routledge is an imprint of the Taylor & Francis Group, an informa business

Library of Congress Cataloging in Publication Data
Names: Arrow, Kenneth Joseph, 1921– author. | Monroe, Kristen
Renwick, 1946– editor. | Lampros, Nicholas Monroe, editor.
Title: On ethics and economics : conversations with Kenneth J. Arrow /
Kenneth J. Arrow ; edited by Kristen Renwick Monroe, Nicholas Monroe
Lampros ; with a Foreword by Amartya Sen.
Description: 1 Edition. | New York : Routledge, [2016]
Identifiers: LCCN 2015049666| ISBN 9781138676053 (hardback) |
ISBN 9781138676060 (pbk.) | ISBN 9781315560281 (ebook)
Subjects: LCSH: Arrow, Kenneth Joseph, 1921—Political and social views. |
Economics—Moral and ethical aspects.
Classification: LCC HB72 .A7677 2016 | DDC 174/.4—dc23
LC record available at https://lccn.loc.gov/2015049666

ISBN: 978-1-138-67605-3 (hbk)
ISBN: 978-1-138-67606-0 (pbk)
ISBN: 978-1-315-56028-1 (ebk)

Typeset in Bembo
by Florence Production Ltd, Stoodleigh, Devon

Printed and bound in the United States of America by Publishers Graphics,
LLC on sustainably sourced paper.

CONTENTS

FOREWORD

The Triumphs of Kenneth Arrow

Amartya Sen

I feel very privileged to have the opportunity of saying a few words about Kenneth Arrow, who is not only one of the greatest economists and political theorists of all time, but also an intellectual of exceptional vision, humanity, and generosity. It is wonderful that Kristen Monroe can share with us the really interesting conversations she has had with Arrow, covering a wide variety of subjects. The understanding of Arrow's thinking that we get from his answers to Monroe's well-chosen questions, combined with some passing remarks that Arrow makes, animate their conversations, and make them both lively and illuminating. On behalf of the readers of this engaging—and illuminating— volume, I would like to put on record our grateful appreciation.

Ken Arrow's genius found very early expression when he himself was only a graduate student. His doctoral dissertation completed in 1950, which was published the next year as a book, *Social Choice and Individual Values*, not only changed people's understanding of politics and economics, it also established Arrow as one of the foremost social thinkers in the world. Then came a series of foundational contributions on a wide range of fundamental problems in the social sciences. The subjects covered by him included the rationale, functioning and achievements of the market economy, the assessment of risk and uncertainty (including the operation of insurance as an activity), the role of information in general and of asymmetric information in particular, and the successes and failures of business relations and state intervention, among a hundred other brilliantly chosen problems to which Arrow brought exceptional illumination—transforming our understanding of them. With his general wisdom, combined with his logical power, his mathematical skills, and his sympathetic understanding of human relations, Arrow changed the subject of modern economics in a truly profound way.

For over 60 years this restless analyst has produced works of astounding importance in a variety of subjects, exploring some of the most fundamental issues of human relationships and social interactions. Arrow continues to be remarkably productive in his nineties. The world has benefited so immensely from Arrow's intellectual restlessness, it is interesting to ask what has been driving this restlessness. I think part of the answer can be found in the lines of the poet A.E Housman: "my two troubles they reave me of rest,/The brains in my head and the heart in my breast." Both brains and heart are immensely important in explaining Arrow's far-reaching productivity. Certainly, Arrow's extraordinary analytical power and penetrating insights have given him the capability to be so comprehensively productive. But, in addition, his dedication to clarifying the impact and implications of human decisions and their interactions, which can make a gigantic difference to the richness and poverty of human lives, has clearly been a constant motivation for Arrow.

Consider Arrow's early results on the working of the market economy. There is something quite remarkable in the fact that a collectivity of individually reasoned but uncoordinated choices of millions of people can somehow gel together to produce an equilibrium in the market economy, and that the equilibrium in some specifiable circumstances can achieve an efficiency that would be hard to attain through any other means. These absolutely central results, of the greatest importance not only to economic theory but also to the lives that we can lead in a modern economy, came almost at the same time as Arrow's spectacular breakthrough in social choice theory in his doctoral thesis, dealing with political relations and social evaluation that are of fundamental importance to our social existence.

If the subject of engagement in one exercise was the way the market economy can function, the theme of the other exercise was the role and reach of democratic systems and political relations. In his famous impossibility theorem, Arrow showed how a very plausible set of axioms for reasonable social choice can be impossible to meet simultaneously. This alerted social analysts to the fact that some demands on the reasonableness of social choice that look extremely plausible when seen individually can produce unexpected contradictions if they are combined together. Arrow's findings also led to a huge literature on seeing how the axiomatic requirements can be altered in a way that would allow consistent and reasonable social decisions.

Arrow's results, dependent on powerful logical and mathematical reasoning, were also of the deepest interest for the well-being and compatibility of human lives in relations with each other in modern society. Later on, Arrow would go on to investigate how the market economy can fail badly in delivering efficient and equitable health care, and have many other failures, which must invite supportive actions by the state and the society. He would also make it possible for people to understand how risks influence human lives, and how the market for insurances may be able to help people, and why it could sometimes fail to deliver what may be expected.

In these—and many other—far-reaching contributions on subjects of the greatest interest to humanity, Arrow made the world around us both better understood and better reformed. If the brains in Arrow's head allowed him to resolve these questions, it is his heart that firmly committed him to take up such daunting problems—of profound importance to our individual and social lives. It is interesting that in answer to Kristen Monroe's very first question, Arrow says, "To say that I am interested in ethics is probably just to say that I'm a human being." It is not just modesty that makes Arrow say that ethical concerns are "part and parcel of life"—there is a profound recognition there that is often ignored in mainstream economics—and yet there can be little doubt that Arrow has taken the responsibilities of being a human being in an exceptionally engaged way.

Arrow's series of engagement has continued over the decades with exploration—one after another—of foundational questions of deep human interest. And as new problems have emerged, or been identified as being crucially important, Arrow has risen to address those problems. For example, the new awareness in the world of the fragility of nature and the environment has led to some of the more recent intellectual engagements of Arrow, about which too he speaks with Monroe. Similarly, the need for reforming the banking system and the financial institutions has received careful attention from Arrow, as is well reflected in these conversations. Even when Arrow is clearly reluctant to go into the details of his thinking about financial regulations, he indicates the direction of his thought by noting that "we have to do something fairly drastic."

I must not overstay my welcome by going on and on about this exceptional economist, social scientist, and radical intellectual. But—aside for thanking Kristen Monroe again—I would like to say how fortunate the world is to have the benefit of Arrow's genius and of his sympathetic intellect, committed to understanding and solving problems that afflict humanity. This book can be seen as, among other things, a fine celebration of our good fortune.

INTRODUCTION

Chance Favors

Kristen Renwick Monroe and
Nicholas Monroe Lampros

Louis Pasteur famously observed that "chance favors the prepared mind."[1] This volume reflects that spirit insofar as it was not a book any of the three authors originally intended to write, but was instead the result of a felicitous encounter and a recognition of the great opportunity that particular encounter provided.

The book originated in an extended conversation which, in turn, arose after a visit by Professor Arrow to the University of California, Irvine Interdisciplinary Center for the Scientific Study of Ethics and Morality (hereafter Ethics Center). Founded by scholars dedicated to using scientific tools to examine issues that engage with ethical questions, the Ethics Center's regular program entailed the publishing of occasional talks. Arrow's talk was to be included in a volume with other scholars who had visited the Center.[2] For this particular volume, we thought it would be interesting to conduct short interviews with each of the contributors, asking them to tell us about the origin of their interest in the specific research topic for their chapter and in ethical issues more generally. Our interest in doing this was to flesh out the more personal route to intellectual work and to suggest what enables people to find original takes on topics that are both perennial and important.

The interviews we conducted were all quite interesting and are contained in *Science, Ethics, and Politics: Conversations and Investigations*

(2011, Paradigm Publishers). But even among these remarkable interviews, Arrow's stood out. I love interviewing people, am fascinated as they talk about their lives and construct meaning out of it all. After 20 years of interviews, I am by now prepared for people to surprise me, to take me in directions I had not thought about before, revealing thought patterns and linking ideas I would not have anticipated from initial conversations. What I was not prepared for in the Arrow interview was the incredible articulation and unusual weaving together of difficult concepts, many not usually thought of as closely related. This first became apparent as Professor Arrow responded to our first inquiry—a simple question: *How did you come to be interested in ethics?* His response was such an exceptionally erudite exposition, spoken uninterrupted, in what became 13 pages of edited text, and presented as if reading effortlessly from a prepared transcript. As will become obvious, the interview reveals a link between economics and ethics that is too often overlooked in a field that has become highly technical and specialized. Arrow's view on economics and ethics is refreshingly broadly based, and makes it clear how thinking about these issues is not just an economic concern but a topic of interest to all human beings. Arrow gives a heart and a voice to economics, a field that can too often be reduced simply to a head full of numbers. The conversation addresses difficult and complex economic topics in a straight forward manner that goes right to the essence of the problem.

Precisely because the conversation is so accessible to the general public and so pressingly relevant, given the current economic situation, both I and the Ethics Center intern who sat in on the interview, Nicholas Lampros, thought the interview deserved to have a broader venue than the usual chapter in an academic book. We thus began by condensing the interviews into a conversation, rather than a more formal exposition, a conversation we hope captures complex economic ideas in a format that can be shared with the general reading public. Our initial thinking was that the book would consist of our extended conversations with Professor Arrow, conducted initially in the summer of 2008, and supplemented with additional interviews throughout 2009 and 2010 and ending shortly after the mid-term election of 2010, an election in which economic policy and conditions—and the government's response to them and to the human suffering the economic downturn inflicted—played a major, if not dominant, role. Our conversations ask about Professor Arrow's own intellectual development and reveals his thoughts about why and how we got into the economic mess of 2008, and what can be done to avoid similar future economic downturns, considering both the needs of the market, the role of the government in the economy, the global economy, international regulation, and the ethics of economic policy. We edited the interviews to read as a conversation that is accessible to the general public, placing further identifying descriptions of critical concepts in the endnotes.

At the same time we conducted our interview with Professor Arrow, however, Stanford University's oral history project began a series of interviews on Arrow's life. With the kind permission of Jane Hibbard, who conducted these interviews in the fall of 2011, we added these interviews as Chapter 1 of this volume, to effectively outline Arrow's life in economics and constituting an intellectual biography, if you will. Chapter 1 thus is Arrow's intellectual autobiography, as told to a third person: Jane Hibbard. We are grateful to both Hibbard and Stanford University for allowing us to publish this interview. Chapter 2 presents Arrow's thoughts on the relation of economics to ethics, a linkage too often overlooked as economics increasingly becomes taught as a narrow and technical subject, void of any historical or philosophical context. Chapter 3 focuses on the 2008 economic meltdown and what Arrow believes should be done to prevent such a near-disaster in the future. Finally, Chapter 4 grew out of a question at the end of our interview, when we asked what Arrow might want to do still, what thoughts he had that he would like to revisit. I like to think this question triggered Arrow's interest in revisiting general equilibrium theory but, knowing how deep his intellect and curiosity remain, I suspect Arrow would have gotten to this project eventually without any of our questions. He did, however, write up his current thoughts on general equilibrium theory and presented them at a conference in Moscow in 2012. Chapter 4 presents the revised version of this paper. Finally, just as this book went into production, we added an Afterword since the 2016 presidential campaign seemed driven by public anger at some of the very economic policy failures Arrow discusses. This Afterword reveals how prescient Arrow's thought remains, and how important is his contribution to our public discourse.

This book thus contains both the past and the future. It describes Arrow's life in economics, and positions his thoughts about ethics and economics as a reminder that economics is about redistribution and thus about ethics and how we treat each other. It is a volume that reflects the thoughts of a senior economist hoping to influence and prod a new generation of economists to write and think about topics that take on a timeless importance. Our audience is not just other scholars and students of economics, but everyone interested in and affected by the current economic downturn that began in the fall of 2008 and those concerned with solutions that are both effective and ethical. It embodies the view that government can be a powerful force for good and should be utilized to work with market forces for the betterment of humanity.

We begin with a brief foreword by Amartya Sen to provide an overview of Kenneth Arrow's work and contribution to economics. We are grateful to Professor Sen for finding the time in an incredibly busy schedule to write this introduction. We are grateful to Professor Arrow for his generous favor, inspired by chance or otherwise, allowing us to spend time with a man of such erudition, intellectual curiosity, integrity, and such humanity. We are happy to be able to pass on the favor by sharing our conversations with others through this book.

Notes

1   The quotation is: *Dans les champs de l'observation le hasard ne favorise que les esprits préparés*. This quote, attributed to Pasteur's Lecture at the University of Lille on December 7, 1854, is translated differently by various authors, but the most frequently found translations include the following. "In the fields of observation chance favors only the prepared mind," "Chance favors the prepared mind," "Fortune favors the prepared mind," "In the field of observation, chance favors the prepared mind," and "Where observation is concerned, chance favors only the prepared mind."

2   The first volume produced by the Ethics Center comes from a conference on stem cell research, *Fundamentals of the Stem Cell Debate: The Scientific, Religious, Ethical, and Political Issues*. Co-edited with Ronald B. Miller and Jerome Tobis. University of California Press. 2007. For reviews see *Nature* or the *New England Journal of Medicine*. The second volume, produced in cooperation with the International Society of Political Psychology's Caucus of Concerned Scholars: Committee on Ethics and Morality, is *Benevolence in a Global Age*. New York: Oxford University Press, 2009. The third volume is *Science, Ethics, and Politics: Conversations and Investigations*, an edited volume with chapters by Francisco Ayala, Kenneth Arrow, Warren S. Brown, William Chiu, Joe DiMento, Gil Geis, Peter Hawkins, Jennifer Hochschild, Cheryl Koopman, Nicholas Lampros, Chloe Lampros-Monroe, Adam Martin, Rose McDermott, Kristen Renwick Monroe, Gregory Peterson, Bridgette Portman, Thomas Schelling, Michael Spezio, Kevin Reimer, James Van Slyke, and Nicole Wernimont. Paradigm Publishers. 2011. The most recent volume is *A Darkling Plain: Stories of Conflict and Humanity during War,* Cambridge University Press 2015. For further information on the Ethics Center or to receive copies of any of these books, please contact Marilu Daum at daumm@UCI.EDU, the Program Manager for the Ethics Center.

1

A LIFE IN ECONOMICS

Fall 2011

I was born in 1921 in New York City.[1] My parents were immigrants, although that statement is misleading because they were about two years old when they came.[2] Their English was different from other people's only in the fact that it was better. My mother graduated high school. She was the youngest of a large family. She was the first, I believe, to complete high school.

My father came from a very poor family, poorer than my mother's, but somehow he worked his way through college. He went to New York University School of Business. My mother had worked before marriage, secretarial work, but, as was normal then, did not work after marriage.

My father had a very up and down career. During the 1920s, he was working in a bank at some level of responsibility. The bank, however was in trouble during the Depression. He and most of the old officers were fired. For about seven years there was hand-to-mouth living. The Great Depression really hurt us. But my father finally did get a job as a manager of a middle-sized firm, a manufacturing firm making knit goods. His income was comfortable, but he had no accumulated wealth.

I was academically very good from an early age. Voracious reader, actually, probably before I went to school. I don't remember exactly.

My mother claimed that the first sign came very early. In those days, when people had a party, they would sing popular songs. We had a piano, and my mother played. The guests would sing from sheet music. It's incredible; today, everybody listens. But those days, the popular music could be sung by ordinary people. Somehow at some very early age, like four, she'd hold up a sheet of music, and I would read the titles. How I did it, I still to this day don't know.

In any case, in those days it was considered terrible to have a student working at a level below his ability. So people accelerated. "Skipping a grade" was the standard phrase. At one point, I went through four years of grades in two years. The school kept insisting I was under-challenged. So when I graduated high school, I was 14. Well, I was about to be 15. A lot of colleges wouldn't admit you at that point. But of course, it didn't matter because I couldn't afford to go to any paying college. So I went to the College of the City of New York, which was then free. Not anymore.

It was created in 1847 for precisely this purpose. Some leading merchants of the town decided it was important to educate the poor. They were able to persuade the public, and the City College came into existence. It is still there. It was a very good educational institution, though the buildings were under-maintained. The teachers were variable, but some of them were very good. I'd gone to a special high school, by the way—Townsend Harris High School, run by City College—where the students went through in three years instead of four. We had longer days. The high school had been created somewhere around 1900, when City College felt the ordinary high schools weren't getting students up to the level needed. My father had gone there. His teacher had told him about it. It turned out, according to the stories handed down, that this was a problem. You see, the local high school, there was no fare to get to school. But if you went to Townsend High, you had to pay a five cent fare. This was a significant drain on the family budget. My paternal grandfather was poor. Anyway, my father went to Townsend Harris, so he had the idea I should go to Townsend Harris, which was a very good idea. I developed in high school a great interest and skill in mathematics and became a mathematics major in college.

But I had very wide interests. I've always loved history. I kind of scattered my bets. The real problem I had when I was in college was what career to aim for. There was a lot of unemployment. You just had to read the papers and look at the newsreels—you've heard of newsreels, I hope. It's an archaic form now, truly archaic but common then. Unemployment was all around you. Other people in the family were similarly affected. A lot of them were small business people who were just barely eking out a living. So I was thinking. I was debating. I was a cautious type, and I was worried about how I could make a living. I was good in mathematics, but what good was mathematics for a career? The idea of being a professor simply wasn't on my mind, not even a bit. I came from a different world.

So I was debating with myself. One of the first things I thought of was to be a high school teacher in mathematics. As a result, I spent a fair fraction of my college taking education courses, which were required in order to qualify as a teacher. In fact, one of my training experiences didn't lead anywhere but it was in itself very memorable.

I was a practice teacher; this was part of the program. I would go into a high school and sit in the class, observe the teacher, and every now and then, she'd let me give a lecture. But one of the things that turned up was this: it was interesting, about American philosophy of education. New York is still unique, I think, in having statewide examinations. All high school students have to take what is called a Regents' Examination. The state has something called a Board of Regents, which is supposed to supervise all elementary and high school education. Or maybe it's only high school. Anyway, they set statewide examinations in a lot of fields. Plane geometry, algebra, history, whatever. Now, the high schools did not like to have people take the examination and fail. So they had evolved a system. Plane geometry was one of the central exams. The student was to take two one-term courses, Plane Geometry I and Plane Geometry II, and then take the Regents Examination. Well, suppose the student failed Plane Geometry I. He or she is required to take it over again.

But those who failed it so badly that it was felt that they'd never pass the Regents were encouraged to go on with a special course, Plane

Geometry II-X, with the understanding they would not take the Regents. This is what I thought was remarkable. They discovered over the years that some of the students in Plane Geometry II-X nevertheless were okay. They were better than their performance indicated. So they permitted a selected number to engage in a special tutorial, a class that met once a week. If the teacher in that class permitted it, the student could take the Plane Geometry examination, even though he or she had agreed not to. It was that last step where, I think, no European country would have gone. It's so distinctively American. And I was in charge of teaching this thing.

As a teaching experience, I've never had anything better. Let me tell you. I'm not a first-class teacher for various reasons. This was a success. First, motivation wasn't an issue. You didn't have any of the ordinary problems in teaching because the students were there voluntarily; they wanted it. They were very receptive, asked very good questions. Of course, I was giving tests along the way. I permitted about two-thirds of them to take the exam, and they all passed.

This had no bearing on my future career at all. When I graduated, I found that I couldn't become a high school teacher of math because there was no qualifying examination. They would only give an examination when all the people who had passed the previous exam, which had been administered seven years earlier, got jobs. They were on the waiting list. Everybody wanted to be teaching. People who had passed seven years earlier were doing something else. But teaching was still a better job than they had.

So here I am in 1940 with no exam, with no prospects as a high school teacher of math. Essentially, I decided to go to graduate school because I had nothing else to do. [Laughter]

While in college, I was smart enough to know that you don't put everything on one prospect. So what else? Well, I learned then about something called statistics, and it seemed like it had a practical application. Industry was hiring statisticians. It was not a big profession but there were some jobs. There was a course in the Math Department in Probability and Statistics. The teacher didn't know much of anything. In fact, most of the mathematics professors were very good, but he was not. There was one calculus teacher named Bennington Gill, who was absolutely marvelous. People who took his course ten years later would still talk about how good Gill was.

This is in college now, City College. The statistics teacher did have an excellent reading list. Starting with the reading list, I really got fascinated with statistics and started reading—actually, original literature. You know, reading the journals and current developments. The other thing I was fascinated by was logic. And that leads to Tarski. I read. There was no real course in logic, but I read by myself. There were a few other students with similar interests there and we'd have conversations.

Let me get this clear. In 1939, war breaks out. That was another thing. Of course, we were all terrified about the prospect of imminent war. I'm Jewish. I can remember back in 1930. I was with my mother in a car, and she stopped—somebody else was coming. Well, they had a conversation, I guess. They were both worried because the Nazis had gotten, I don't know, 30 percent of the seats, 25, 20 percent of the seats or something like that in the Reichstag election of 1930.[3] The idea that in this day and age, an anti-Semitic party could be getting near to power was frightening. Hitler didn't conceal what his views were and what he was going to do.

Then, of course, the Nazis came to power and all their programs followed. I can remember a very depressing day in 1939 when the Soviet Union and the Germans signed an agreement—I think it was on my birthday or the day after—because I thought this meant war, which did break out nine days later.[4] I thought of myself as a pacifist and believed that war was terrible. There were a lot of anti-war views then. My mother had always thought the idea of going to war was horrible, even though World War I had not been that striking for Americans. My father had been in the army, but he never got shipped overseas. I had a very anti-war attitude. On the other hand, there was Hitler. Then I first thought, "Well, you can't do anything about it. We should keep out of the war."

I can remember the election of 1940. My mother was a very strong Roosevelt lover. I remember there was a speech he gave over the radio in which he said, *"Mothers and fathers of America, I tell you. Your children will not fight in foreign wars."* My mother turned to me and said, "See? He said that." I said, "He's a liar." I was right but I was wrong on the basic issue. Roosevelt was right about the war. But he was lying.

So, back to my story. Alfred Tarski[5] was a Polish logician. Very famous. I mean I'd already heard of him. (His papers were beyond my ability.) But he got trapped. He came for a conference in New York and got caught with the outbreak of the war. So City College, the Philosophy Department had a vacancy. They had money, so they hired him for a year. He didn't speak any English. He said he would start teaching in February in the second term. He studied English apparently at that time. In his first couple of lectures, we couldn't understand what he was talking about. So we used to have little conferences afterwards to try to put together his lectures. We realized it was a question of how he stressed things more than anything else. His English actually was perfectly all right once you understood what he was saying. Anyway, it was a course on a subject called Calculus of Relations, which was rather technical. His was certainly one of the finest minds I have ever encountered.

In fact, I did well in his course. In the summer of 1940, he asked me to proofread for him. A book of his had been written in Polish, I guess, originally, but it was a German version which was now being translated into English. He wanted me to proofread it. Of course, he obviously didn't feel capable of proofreading in English.

It was to be translated by a German refugee, who I therefore met. I met him again later under interesting circumstances. His name was Olaf Helmer.[6] Tarski had a very good sense of language and he kept on asking me, "Is this a correct translation." Not so much." "Is it correct?" But "Is this the way you would say it?"

Helmer's English was pretty stilted, and Tarski could tell even though he'd just learned English himself. Tarski was very sensitive to the nuance. I was really quite impressed with his feel for the language. So we reworded it a little bit.

I wanted to study statistics. Now, statistics was not a recognized subject, in the sense there was no Department of Statistics anywhere.

You couldn't get a PhD in statistics. So I enrolled as a PhD candidate in mathematics because it was the closest thing to what we now think of as statistics, and I would take the statistics courses. There were not very many in the Unites States. The most important theoretical statistician was a man named Harold Hotelling.[7] He was my sponsor in a great many ways. My sponsor in graduate school.

Now we're talking graduate school because I graduated in 1940. That summer I had a job. I got it by pure chance, which turned out to be interesting. I was looking for something that might help me financially. I thought that a department store might need a clerk. They weren't hiring, it turned out but there was an insurance company across the street. I figured that my mathematics and statistics should be of some use in insurance. I walked in and, as it turned out, they hired me as a clerk calculating premiums on some novel kind of policy. I really learned a lot about the practical aspects of the insurance business in that place.

I think I'm receptive. I had entertained the thought of a third career choice. A high school teacher in math was looking pretty dead at that moment. But there was the statistics graduate degree. And there was the possibility of becoming an actuary, a life insurance actuary, which was somewhat related to statistics. To be an actuary, you had to take examinations. Actuaries were licensed by a private organization. I think it was called the American Society of Actuaries, or something like that.

They gave examinations, which were very hard. So I studied those. I took a couple of them but I never got very far down the road. I wanted to study statistics, and I figured, "Well, what PhD program would I go for?" Mathematics seemed closest. When I actually got to attending Columbia in the fall of 1940, I found out Hotelling[8] was a Professor of Economics. He also had a funny career. He was interested in journalism at some point. He got a master's degree in journalism. But he then went on to study for a PhD in mathematics at Princeton and worked on some very abstract sort of things for his dissertation. Somehow, after he finished it, he got involved in statistics. He came to Stanford, to the Food Research Institute, which is no longer in existence. Their first director wanted a broad approach. I don't know how exactly the connection was made.

But Hotelling developed new statistical methods. Columbia University had had one economist who was using statistical methods. The fellow had to be institutionalized. He had some mental breakdown. They decided to try to get another person like this. Hotelling had shown an interest in economics and had written one very good paper in economics. So they hired him. But his real campaign was to create a Department of Statistics. Not economics, but statistics. He wrote a number of papers, one very famous, and all of us students were all pushing for his ideas, of course. You create statistics as a separate discipline with contributions to psychology or to economics, and there are special problems in each one. So there should be a statistician in these departments. There should be a department that just taught statistics. There was a heading in the catalogue called Statistics. There was a course called Statistics 101 but there was no department associated with it. Hotelling is in the Economics Department. It turned out he had a course in Economics, in Mathematical Economics, which was completely out of kilter with the rest of the Economics Department. But it was an anarchic place where essentially professors decided what they wanted to teach. It was very poorly run at the time. There was no central thing.

It wasn't as stratified or organized as most places. Columbia's was the exception. Most places were much better organized. So Hotelling gave a course in Mathematical Economics. I took it out of curiosity and I got really fascinated by it. But still I thought of myself primarily as a statistician. Hotelling taught courses, he and other people, including another very famous statistician named Abraham Wald.[9] I was taking math courses as part of meeting my math requirements. I went to Hotelling to tell him that I wanted to continue to study but I needed financial support. (My father had borrowed money to pay for my first year's tuition. Since it was Columbia, I could live at home.) I asked him if he would write a letter of recommendation for a scholarship or fellowship in mathematics.

Hotelling said he had no influence in the Mathematics Department but he was sure he could be helpful with the Economics Department. I had already impressed him because of a solution I had found for a very minor problem in economic theory that he was interested in.

So I switched my PhD field from mathematics to economics. When people asked me, "How did I get in economics?" I was bought. They get shocked. I say, "Well, you're economists. Are you surprised that I would pick something for my financial advantage?" [Laughter] It's very practical to look for where you fit in or where you could get a job as well.

Okay. At that point, I switched my field from mathematics to economics, applied for admission to the Economics Department and for a scholarship, and I got a scholarship to cover my tuition, and a few hundred dollars extra. That was a significant amount then. Of course, prices are much higher now. But academic costs have gone up far more than anything else. Tuition was 400 dollars a year. The money my father had to borrow was 400 dollars, which today would be 40,000. Anyway, I got this scholarship. This was now 1941.

The next year, when I was really in the Economics Department was 1941–42. Now I studied economics. I learned that a good part of the department was quite anti-theoretical. I was a theorist. Mathematical methods in economics and formal statistical methods were not standard anywhere, but much of the department was even more anti-theoretical than most other places. Harvard or Princeton or Chicago were much more standard, as I learned later. They differed from each other but they were much closer to each other than to Columbia. Part of the situation at Columbia was the presence of a professor there who had been there for a long while. He'd been at Berkeley before that. He was named Wesley Mitchell, and he was opposed to all theory.[10] In his view, the only way to study economics was to collect a lot of data. Of course, as a statistician, I thought you should collect a lot of data but then you have to do something with it.

You need theory to exemplify it, to illuminate it. So I figured as long as I'm studying economics in this department, I'll take a course with Mitchell. He gave an annual course in what was then called Business Cycles. You know depressions and recessions. Well, it turned out he was on leave that year.

He had created an organization called The National Bureau of Economic Research, which still exists, although its functions are rather different than they used to be. It was a private organization for the purpose essentially of research, especially data collecting. Indeed, some extremely important series to our national statistics derive from work done at the National Bureau.

Mitchell's deputy at the Bureau had gotten a PhD at Columbia about 1932 and was then a professor at Rutgers. His name was Arthur Frank Burns.[11] He later became Nixon's economic advisor and later head of the Federal Reserve System. Burns, whom I'd never heard of, was going to take over Mitchell's course. I was a little disappointed but some older students told me, "You don't know how lucky you are. Mitchell's the dullest speaker in the world, and Burns is very lively."

I was coming from this formal statistical point of view and with some economic theory. So we had a lot of discussions. I want to say he was one of those brilliant people whose research accomplishments didn't measure up to their abilities. I mean fundamentally his ideas led nowhere. In terms of accomplished in economics, he would not rank high. That's one thing I've learned over the years. On the whole, intelligence is correlated with accomplishment but there are an awful lot of exceptions. Some very brilliant students never amounted to anything in terms of what work they produced, and there are some students who just by sheer persistence and industry have accomplished more than you would reasonably expect of them. So it's not as simple. Anyway, Burns and I developed a mutual respect.

In the middle of a year of studying economics, of course, was December '41. I'm sitting in the family living room on Sunday listening, as I always did, to the Philharmonic broadcast, when it was interrupted with news bulletins. I had favored pacifist ideas. How ridiculous they now seemed. I was clearly meant to go into the armed forces. I decided to look around for a program which would at least use some of my talents, and I found there was a weather training program which involved essentially being sent to a university for what amounted to a master's degree in meteorology.

Meteorology, then and now, is not widely taught. There are only a few institutions that teach it. In fact, there may be less now than there were then and at that point, there were only four or five places you could study it. I applied and got to take some tests. They were in science. Physics was the biggest disaster in my academic program at City College. I had gotten a C. There is a lot of math in physics but that's the point. They weren't using the math. They were trying to teach it in a non-mathematical order. If they had used calculus, I would have done much better. Also, I was very clumsy in my lab experiments.

So as part of my military service, I go into a program and study. You could enlist this way. I didn't wait to be drafted. I was just enrolled. I had to wait to be called up. Of course, there we were going on academic terms. So I completed my economics program through the year 1941–42, and took my oral examinations. The department chairman encouraged me to write a thesis before being called up. I was already marked as a very good student because of my orals for my economics degree. But it's not connected with a thesis, just a general examination. I remember the department chair, who (I happened to have taken a course with him) was urging me to try to finish a thesis before I got called up. But I felt I had to do something important. I started something but it was too ambitious. It was not something one person could do. Finally, in October, I was called up and sent to New York University.

They put us up in dormitories, which they called barracks. They tried to have some army discipline. They'd come and inspect your things, make sure your beds were made properly. Everything was dusted. I remember we were in a group—well, four of us, I guess, occupied some set of rooms there. They were clean and ready. One of us looked at a chandelier and said, uh-oh, and we dusted the chandelier. The officer who was inspecting put on a white glove and ran it over the chandelier. And we drilled. We had a drill sergeant. It was a little funny for a bunch of us students. We were carrying something most readers probably have never seen: slide rules. We used to carry them in our belts. Of course, meteorology was a perfectly serious course. The education was quite serious. I remember an early lecture, by a professor who later became head of the department at UCLA. The professor was named Hans Panofsky. You've heard of Wolfgang Panofsky? Well, this was his twin brother, although there's absolutely no physical resemblance. They must have been fraternal twins. Hans Panofsky was trying to explain something about the atmosphere and how it relates to heat. He said that oxygen and nitrogen let light in from the sun, and the heat out from the earth without obstacle. So it's only the gasses that are present in small quantities that cause the Earth's temperature to be above that of outer space.

They were called the trace gases. Of these, the two dominant ones were water vapor and carbon dioxide. He remarked that, since carbon dioxide has been accumulating, and since we've burnt so much more in the last 200 years, we can expect the Earth to get warmer.

He wasn't saying this to urge action. It was more to motivate the rather technical discussion. This was in 1942. 20 years later, we began to hear about global warming. I remembered that lecture and thought, "Oh, yes! That's what Dr. Panofsky said."

Meteorology was interesting. But when I was graduated, they sent me to research. I've always attributed this to their view that my forecasting abilities weren't too good.

I never left the United States. The idea was to try to improve forecasting. In part, I was just one member of a large group, checking how accurate the forecasts being made are. They weren't very good. I mean essentially a three-day forecast was worthless. Even at 36 hours, there may be a little bit of predictability but that depends on the skill of the forecaster. The main part of my job was to try to make two-week forecasts. I was trying to apply statistical methodology. I don't think I contributed much to the war effort, to be perfectly candid with you. Our office was moved around a lot. When I graduated from the training program, forecast research was in the Pentagon. So I went down to Washington and lived there for a year and a half. Then the authorities decided Washington was overcrowded, and there was no particular reason why our group should be in Washington. So we moved to Ashville, North Carolina, which is absolutely the opposite of a hell hole. It couldn't have been more beautiful. One thing from that period stayed with me for a long time: hiking. I got into the local group of hikers, The Wilderness Hikers of Ashville. Every Sunday we'd go out hiking the Blue Ridge. Sometimes, we went to the Great Smokies, although there was a problem with gasoline rations. About 15 or 20 years ago, I was invited to spend a week at the University of North Carolina, which is not there, but in the Piedmont. What I did was go a day early, go to Ashville, and hike to one of the peaks I remembered, Grandfather Peak, right outside Ashville. This led later on to hikes in the high country above Yosemite. You know, around Tuolumne Meadows. There's a whole bunch of camps there that you have to reserve on the 2nd of January because otherwise you can't get in.

I was finally transferred to Langley Field, Virginia. I did have occasion to write a paper. The Air Force had received from a contractor some proposal about how to use the winds when navigating. That was a simple idea and there was nothing particularly wrong with it but it struck me that they didn't ask the right question. I think the real question was how to get an airplane from one place to another faster, as fast as possible, if you know the winds.

How to use the winds. That led to a rather interesting mathematical problem, and I had to read papers in German, which I happen to know a little bit. I'd taken German in college, mainly to read mathematical literature since at that point a lot of mathematical literature was available only in German. I can't read a newspaper, but a mathematical journal is a lot easier to read than a newspaper. I made an important innovation, and that resulted in my first published paper, in the *Journal of Meteorology*. But it had nothing to do with economics. Just a year ago I got a communication from an American working in Japan. He had a question about arranging an orbit around an asteroid. So the question was how to maneuver that body. He had run across my paper in Houston.

It's a small triumph but I thought that was something out of the ordinary. Anyway, it was a good paper. I'm proud of it. It had nothing to do with anything that came later.

I was in Virginia until the end of the war. In fact, the war had ended before the transfer to Langley Field. I was waiting to be discharged. I had one taste of the future there. I was doing a lot of computing because I was using statistical methods. One of the problems which Hotelling was already worried about was that as soon as the problem got at all big, the computing was a problem. We used to have these desk calculators. They sat on your desk. They cost about 600 dollars. So it'd be like 6,000 or 7,000 dollars. What they could do was add, multiply, subtract, and divide. I was doing a statistical process called fitting a regression with eight variables. It'd take me about eight hours to do one. I was doing it for lots of places. I couldn't delegate it; I couldn't explain it to anybody else. It was too complicated. So I was doing this. Into my office walks a Professor Mauchly from the University of Pennsylvania, inventor of ENICA, an early computer. He and a collaborator had built an electronic computer, which was talked about.

They had been doing computing for the Navy, gunnery tables, which are very complicated computations. Essentially, he was looking for another job. He was nosing around and someone said, "Oh, Lieutenant Arrow does a lot of computing."

So he went to me and, of course, I wasn't going to do anything because I was waiting to get out. But I was curious about what this thing could do. I said, "How fast can you do this job?" He said, "Five minutes."

Well, my parents had taught me to beware of salesmen. Even if he's a professor, he's still a salesman. I called up a weather man, a meteorology friend of mine in the Navy. I figured he'd know a little more. He said, "He's telling you the truth. But he didn't tell you that it's down 80 percent of the time."

Mauchly used vacuum tubes. Do you remember vacuum tubes? You have them in your radio, and they'd all go out in the middle of your favorite program so you had a few extras. But you could see that if it's got 1,500 vacuum tubes, the chance that one is going to go out is high. But all that means is that the calculation will take 25 minutes on the average. That's a lot better than eight hours. Also, I figured that if it comes to reliability, they'll figure out a way to make it more reliable one way or another. So a new era has dawned. Now you could take the same problem, and it'll probably take a second to do. You put it in, push the key, and there's the answer. It took me eight hours. Computers used to be the size of a room, and the next thing is they can do everything, but they were—at that point in time—they were the size of a room. Of course, so long as they had vacuum tubes, they had to have the most elaborate cooling equipment to ventilate out the heat. It was something like ten or 12 years before an economist could really use those machines. We didn't have access to them, and programming had to be done. But I had a hint of the future.

Then I was discharged in January, 1946, and I go back to graduate study. I'd been given a very good fellowship for the academic year 1942–1943, which, of course, I hadn't taken up. It was now available to me, and I also had support from the GI Bill. All I had to do was write a thesis. That turned out to be a major block because I wanted to do something very, very serious. I was ambitious. I'd always been a good student and I felt I had to succeed. On the other hand, I was worried about one thing. I didn't really have any good, really original ideas. I was very concerned with the fact that here I was a bright student, I was brighter than almost—there were one or two exceptions —but, yes, I felt there were no peers among graduate students. I felt smarter than some of the professors [laughs] but not all of them. But I didn't seem to have any new ideas. Needless to say, it was very bothersome because I felt that I could do something good.

Before I went to the war, in fact, when it was clear I was going to be called up, I was waiting around. The chairman of the department urged me to do something, get the thesis out of the way. He said it doesn't have to be a "masterpiece," that was the way he put it. The word is misused. What it originally meant was when you enter the guild you have to produce a work. Let's say it's a shoemaker's guild. You make a pair of shoes to show that you are competent to be a master, a member of the guild. It didn't mean masterpiece in the modern sense. Well, I couldn't do anything routine but I admit I didn't have any particularly good ideas. The other thing I did was to read. I was very good at spotting the defects in the leading works in the field, and I figured I could start by trying to correct them. It was a grossly ambitious thing.

The faculty had changed and there were people there who were not in the economics faculty. I was now in economics. As I mentioned before, my chief statistics professor, Hotelling, always wanted independent departments. He got an offer from North Carolina. The Navy had been particularly sponsoring research during the war, the Office of Naval Research, and creating a particular statistical group–I was not part of that group–of which Hotelling was the director, although he was not a very effective administrator. Another man who played some role in my life was W. Allen Wallis, who eventually became chancellor of the University of Rochester about 20 years later. He was a statistician and the effective runner of that group. Someone else who turned out later to play a role was Albert Bowker, a student at the Massachusetts Institute of Technology (MIT). MIT was not a very big place to study statistics actually. After the war, Bowker moved to Columbia to complete his studies, and I saw a lot of him there. It happened that he'd been a research assistant to a meteorologist who was using statistical methods, and I'd had some contact with him during the war, not face-to-face, by teletype. You could sit at the typewriter and it was attached to a telephone line; you could have a conversation. We wanted to write things out because speaking wouldn't be good enough.

It was normal. It was a conversation. You typed—texting I guess is right. Texting, I guess. I don't know what texting is but my children do it. It was very helpful. Fax also existed then. We actually used it during the service. Anyway, Bowker came to work at this statistical research group and was kind of Allen Wallis' right-hand man. Wallis was the assistant director and the effective leader. I digress, but they play a role. I may come back to this.

This was during the war. It was a statistical research group. Hotelling's desire for a separate Statistics Department was reinforced by this experience. There was a woman with a PhD, which was pretty unusual for those days, Gertrude Cox. She somehow talked the University of North Carolina into creating a Department of Statistics; they could get financing from the Office of Naval Research. The Office of Naval Research continued after the war and they felt they were going to promote science. They were hoping it would be a civilian agency, but pending the civilian agency, which later was created, the National Science Foundation, in the interim, would maintain science with naval funds, not in the service of the Navy but of science in general, I mean, of course, also specifically. So Gertrude Cox had access to funds, and she created the Statistics Department at North Carolina. Hotelling wanted to use this to try to get Columbia to create a Department of Statistics and when they didn't, he left. That's when he left. They did create a department after he left, by the way, to keep another statistician, Abraham Wald, and I have mentioned him before, I think. He was a refugee. His nationality is one of those complex matters. I was told that he was Romanian. It turned out he was really born in what before the First World War was Hungary, although the land was annexed by Romania in 1919. He went to Vienna to study, which was more relevant, and so he really came from Vienna. He was clearly very brilliant. The students admired him and his lectures and probably admired him more than Hotelling actually because he was a better teacher. To keep Wald, Columbia created a department after Hotelling left, so whether this was just a device to get rid of Hotelling, we don't know.

Meanwhile my interest shifted more to economics. Even though Wald himself had written an article on economics he was in no way interested in it, unlike Hotelling. There was a new economist there, not really a mathematical economist but a very good one, Albert Hart and I sort of took up with him.

It's a little hard to say how or when my interests shifted into economics. It was a process. I kept on thinking of myself for many years as both an economist and a statistician, but I didn't do any research in statistics really. I did write one or two papers, and economics, I felt, was somehow more congenial. It's very hard to put your finger on it. My aim was to use an economic theory to create a model to which statistical methods would be applied. That was the idea. It was clear that to do statistics you need a model and then the model needed to come from economics. My aim, which was not where I went in fact, was trying to create a big statistical model based on the work of, particularly, the English economist John Hicks, to include that and make that into something into which you could fit data. Of course, the collection of data, the idea that one person could collect the necessary data, was absurd, but I didn't realize that.

So I was working in seminars, writing little papers, seminar papers, and not feeling at all satisfied with where I was going. I was reading a lot of mathematical background to deal with the economics to apply mathematics to the economics. I was studying, I was reading. In a way, I learned a lot, but I wasn't supposed to be learning. I was supposed to be doing.

There was a whole movement called econometrics. This was a coined word, essentially to do the sort of thing I was interested in. I know it sounds like I'm the only one who's thinking this. On the contrary, there was a whole bunch of people trying to take economic theory concepts and then use them as a basis. In fact, it was more European than American. There was Ragnar Frisch in Norway, Jan Tinbergen in the Netherlands. You would find this even in the nineteenth century already. The statistical method has been developed mostly for applications in biology, crops and so forth, but they were applying it to economics. Every now and then, somebody would do it and then it became a larger and larger number. There was a rich family called Cowles, who were publishers. One member of this family, Alfred R. Cowles III, was actually an investment advisor, rather, was a manager, I guess, in Chicago. He found that the Great Depression upset him a lot because he did badly. Then he had tuberculosis. In those days, tuberculosis meant you go up in the high altitudes, so I gather this makes them more comfortable. Otherwise it's absolutely useless, and there was then no cure, but that was the belief then. But it does make you more comfortable, I think that's correct. He got into contact with some people, statisticians, at—I think it was Colorado State University—and suggested we apply this to economics. As I say, he had money, and he got in touch with this movement, found there were people, and there was the great economist of the day, Irving Fisher, at Yale. Fisher had the idea of using statistical methods in economics. Somehow he got in touch with some of the leading economists of the day or they got in touch with him, I don't know. He created two institutions, one was the Econometric Society. I forget who it was who coined the word, I think it was Ragnar Frisch, meaning, "measuring economics." And Frisch and Jan Tinbergen joined. Tinbergen was a young man; Frisch was the big ticket at that point. There were other Europeans. Some of them were not all in econometrics but they lent their names, such as Joseph Schumpeter. Hotelling was involved, and Irving Fisher was the grand old man. He was a great man, with great prestige. He had been doing both theoretical and empirical work, not really econometrics, but he sort of blessed the movement, gave his name to it. He was already then about 75 or 80. Cowles created the Econometric Society with a journal, and it was very international, published in French and English. This was in 1932. Alfred Cowles also created a research group that he personally financed called the Cowles Commission for Research and Economics. That was a strange name. He ran this thing in Colorado. It was not a big scale thing, but he'd hold conferences and, for example, Wald came to one of those conferences. Another man who was active was Jacob Marshak, who had a quite varied career that was really fascinating, but I won't go into that. He had come to this country eventually about 1939, 1940. Like a lot of Europeans, he got one of the Rockefeller traveling fellowships, which were very important, sending Americans to Europe and vice versa. Well it happened that a lot of refugees came here on the Rockefeller fellowship. And they stayed. Jacob Marschak was one of them. Marschak was then at the New School for Social Research, I think it was called, in New York. It's called the New School University or something like that now. Actually, I had met him as a graduate student because he had organized a seminar on mathematical economics and econometrics, an informal group I used to go to. As a student I was one of the members, so I got in touch with him. It was also the time that some new statistical methods were developed by a Norwegian, a student of Frisch's, named Trygve Haavelmo, and I remember—while I was in this limbo state, signed up for the military but not yet gone—I heard him give this talk on these new statistical methods. I'd been thinking that somehow the existing statistical methods were not really quite appropriate for economics, but I hadn't put my finger on the issues. Haavelmo had, and he explained it very clearly. In fact, so clearly that I didn't quite realize how novel it was. It was only a little later I appreciated the novelty. In this meeting, there was a very tall Dutch economist, another one who had gotten out just before the fall of France and that sort of thing, actually had training in physics but got interested in economics. His name was Tjalling Koopmans. I remember his asking Haavelmo questions. It was quite clear to me that he was the only one in the room who understood exactly what was going on. I didn't quite—I knew it was the right approach but I couldn't quite understand. But we're all thinking along the same line. This was 1942 now. Just before I went into the service. I'm not even sure I met him or shook his hand even, at this meeting. I just heard him give questions.

When I got back, early in 1946, there was a meeting of the American Statistical Association in Ithaca at Cornell, and I got an invitation to attend a conference held by the Cowles Committee—okay, I'm sorry—the Cowles Commission. When Cowles felt better, he moved back to Chicago and he brought the Cowles Commission with him. The Cowles Commission was not affiliated with the University of Chicago, but it was—these details matter a great deal to me although they may not matter to you—but it was given space there. There was one professor there at the university who was, was more of a theorist, named Oskar Lange, a Pole. He later became very involved with the Polish Communist government. But this was the earlier stage and he was a socialist. In fact I'd seen articles of his, very anti-Stalinist, so I don't know quite what happened. I had met him because he came as a visiting professor at Columbia while I was waiting to be called up. So I had listened to his lectures for a few weeks and then I got called up. I remember going to his office and saying good-bye. He got interested in the Cowles Commission and got the university to appoint Marschak and Koopmans to the faculty. The Cowles Commission had space but no affiliation with the university. They organized a conference on these new statistical methods which Koopmans had been working on and implementing the Haavelmo program. It involved a lot of computation, and in those days, I got to tell you, a computation was done with a desk calculator, which is essentially a big adding machine but mechanized so you could multiply. In other words, if you take five times three, it would add five three times. You didn't have to do it. It would do it automatically. That's about it. You could run it by crank or a motor, but all the electric motor did was turn the thing over. The motor was a substitute for the crank. It was not electronic as we'd say. Of course, the war had been doing a lot to improve computation. We'd moved beyond the slide rule. Apart from anything else, the slide rule just doesn't do a lot of things. It doesn't add.

They held a conference and so I got introduced to all these fascinating people, and then they offered me a job. I think it was 2,000 dollars a year. The job would be in Chicago but I'd be attached to the Commission, not to the university, as a research associate. Evidently, there was a small link; most of these people that you see were refugees. Cowles didn't run the thing; he just supplied the money, and Marschak and Koopman and Wald, obviously, these people knew each other. It must've been Wald, I think, who told Allen Wallis about me, because that played a role later. Since Wald worked during the war for the statistical research group of which Wallis was the effective head, it was a networking situation. The world of econometrics, I mean statistics, was very small. It was a very small—well, statistics still isn't very big, especially theoretical statistics, you know, with few departments of statistics in the United States, even today. It's not like economics or mathematics. Any university has to have departments in these subjects.

I had this offer, but I felt I wanted to get my thesis done before I did anything. So I turned it down. I knew I wasn't going anywhere with this thesis very much. One thing that happened was while working on this thesis, forgive me for being slightly technical, but the question is, how does a firm make decisions? It chooses the decision that maximizes profit. Supposing there are a number of owners.

It suddenly struck me that the firm in Hicks is just the entity. But there were a number of people involved, and they may have different views of the future. This is the trouble. You may want one kind of investment and I may want another even though we're both trying to maximize profits, and there, I discovered, there was a paradox. So I thought, "Oh well, they choose according to majority voting, allowing for the number of shares." So one man may have 100 votes, another man has 20 votes, but allowing for that I realized this wouldn't work. This is when the logic that I'd learned from Tarski came in. My first thought is that if they choose investment project A over investment project B, and investment project B is better than investment project C, and you want to maybe say that investment project A is better than investment project C. Well, it turns out if you use majority voting, that won't work. You can have a situation where a majority prefer A to B, a majority prefer B to C and a majority prefer C to A. It's perfectly possible. At that point, this was just a big, big nuisance because I was trying to write a theory. So of course I disregarded it. I thought it was a problem, you know, I better do this in another way, but it was in the back of my mind. Then that wasn't getting very far and I was very dissatisfied and the Cowles group renewed its offer, so I decided to go out there (Chicago). I thought maybe the atmosphere would be more helpful. Marschak was the director at that point, and he was a wonderful person. I came out finally in April 1947. I came out to join the Cowles. I was a research associate and I got $3,200 a year [laughs], and that was a full year, you understand. Meanwhile, I had gotten an offer from Stanford. Before the Cowles, for an assistant professorship. I think it was explained to me then that at Stanford, because they're far away, they frequently hired without interviewing. It was a different world. I didn't have a PhD yet. That was more common then. Now it would be impossible, but then it was not uncommon. The idea was, of course, I would have to get a PhD before I got any further. Also, Stanford had a policy of giving a one-year initial appointment, always for one year. They were called acting appointments. That's what the word acting means and indeed, later I found when I got here that my colleague Moses Abramovitz, who was senior to me, came as an acting professor, acting full professor. So I got an offer. I don't remember, it paid about $3,600 a year. I don't remember, something like that, which was what would be the standard starting salary. As opposed to the $32,000 at Cowles. I knew little about Stanford and it was thought of, vaguely, as a good institution. I didn't know much about it. I really didn't realize how ignorant I was. The great institutions in economics—well, Harvard, Chicago, Yale, I would say those three, perhaps Princeton to some extent; Columbia before the war I would say was not very good. Statistics was terrific, but the economics was not very good. The war did shake up things. People left for war work and then once they were away, they didn't return. So people like Albert Hart and George Stigler came to Columbia. It was distinctly a better place. But I decided to go to Chicago, plus I thought the atmosphere—I thought—this was econometrics that I was interested in, and I felt I wasn't going to learn anything at Stanford. Cowles had people on the same track as I, and there was practically no other place where that was true. It is a very small world, this econometric world, and there was really practically no other place but Cowles. Fisher died around that time, but in any case, he was a very old man. He didn't really leave behind a similar group. There were some good people in Chicago, but there weren't at Yale. But then, Yale wasn't making me an offer. I'm Jewish. Thinking of this time period reminds me of one more thing about academia during this era: the problem of anti-Semitism. Paul Samuelson was one of the spectacular cases. He was a brilliant student at Harvard. He was given the rank of Instructor, a rank sometimes given to people without a PhD When MIT offered him an Assistant Professorship, the Harvard department made no effort to keep him. There may have been more than one reason, but anti-Semitism was clearly a major one. MIT had no reputation in economics at that point. The chair of the department, whose uncle happened to be the president of the institute, saw an opportunity. He got his uncle to increase the MIT department's budget and hired Samuelson. Chicago was different. Chicago was one of the few places where anti-Semitism was not an issue. I should also say that at Columbia it was not an issue. Columbia and Chicago. But Harvard and Yale certainly were anti-Semitic.

The other thing is that the academic career world just wasn't that big. There were not that many jobs. Graduate study was nothing like what it is today. The Economics Department at Stanford, to give you an idea, had the same undergraduate enrollments it has today, pretty much. There were about 150 students a year of the graduating class. Am I exaggerating? I don't know. It was well over 100 students of the graduating class, which is about 1,600; about ten percent are in economics. It was then, it is now. That has not changed much. Rather interesting, that in all these years it remains the same. Of course, one big difference is that in places with undergraduate business schools, economics enrollment is much lower. These are people who would like to go to business school. [Laughs] That's my interpretation anyway. I'm not the only one with that interpretation. On the other hand, there were maybe 15 to 20 graduate students then, and over 100 now.

So I go to Chicago with the idea that I'd be in a better environment, and I really didn't do that much better. I mean, the environment's terrific in the learning sense. Again, we had seminars. Marschak loved controversy. A student could contradict him, he beamed. Truly, he was a remarkable person. It was fun. All these bright, young kids. There were several from Chicago, students and faculty, people like me, a few people like me. Lawrence Klein, who later got a Nobel Prize, was working on the model of the American economy applying these statistical methods. It was generally a very bright group. I met my wife Selma Schweitzer there. That's a story, too.

That was just one of the reasons why I finally came to Stanford. She had been a student in Brooklyn College, majored in French actually, of all things, but she had to drop out because her family was very poor. She went to work as a typist in the Agriculture Department in Washington. She was assigned to work for a statistician, this fellow who—I don't if he had his PhD yet—but anyway, his name was Meyer A. Girshick. This is very important because he played a big role in Stanford. He was a Russian who came over, I don't know, at the age of about eight or ten or something. I think his father had come here before World War I and then they couldn't bring the rest of the family because of the war. He's known as Abe, in spite of the fact his first name was Meyer. Abram was his middle name, but everybody called him Abe. He got here in the early 1920s and he spoke with an accent. He studied at Columbia, though he was gone by the time I became a student, and he worked in the Agriculture Department. The Agriculture Department was always very interested in statistics. I think it arose from the biological side. He was in the Bureau of Agriculture Economics as it was called, which always had a very progressive attitude toward these new methods. Also, a progressive attitude toward women, by the way, rather interesting. They were always encouraging women to progress and some of them got PhDs. It was rather unusual. On the other hand, race was a different matter. That was not due to the people at the department; it goes back to Woodrow Wilson's administration. There was a black statistician, David Blackwell, who later went to Berkeley and we tried to get him here, who was at Howard University, got a PhD at the University of Illinois. Howard University was a black university. Abe and David were both in Washington, and they collaborated. When David came to see Abe at the Agriculture Department, he couldn't eat lunch. The cafeteria wasn't for blacks. This was with Henry Wallace as Secretary of Agriculture! I'm digressing a lot. Anyway, Abe didn't really need a typist. What he needed was somebody to do the calculating. So against Selma's considerable resistance, she gradually learned to use the calculator and, he later said, she was much better at calculating than she was at typing [laughs]. Then she started going to George Washington. Abe taught at night at George Washington University and so she started attending classes there. Then she got an undergraduate degree in statistics.

So now let me come back to Cowles. There was a woman member of the Cowles family, Sarah Frances Hutchinson Cowles, who for some reason left the scholarship for graduate study by women at the University of Chicago. It was to be given to a graduate of the Waterville (New York) Academy, which was a woman's school, but if there was no suitable candidate. Something like that, then it could be used somewhat freely. Cowles grabbed this and said, "Okay, we're going to use this to get a woman graduate student in the university to work at the Cowles Commission." They had a succession of people—none of whom I think ever got a PhD. But one of them was Lawrence Klein's wife and another was Selma Schweitzer, my wife. We met shortly thereafter. We were married in about four months. She never did get her PhD. She was studying for it, you know, but she felt it was over her head and she dropped out eventually. I don't think any of them got it. Then I think somewhere the trustees, the rest of the Cowles family, got wind of this and after a couple of years took the whole thing away. It was clearly twisting the words of the grant. We got married and found an apartment, which was very difficult in those days, but we got a rent control apartment, a nice little apartment right near the university. It was a high crime area, by the way, at that point.

The intellectual life was quite intense. The department had an informal arrangement by which they appointed one member of the Cowles research staff to the Chicago faculty. The money was short. Cowles was giving money annually. There was no endowment at that time, so Koopmans and Marschak were paid by the university. The rest of us were paid from these annual funds, so it was always a problem keeping this thing going. I was still struggling around trying to do things.

Then Abe Girshick was very much interested in these new statistical methods. He visited several times in Chicago to discuss different aspects of it and gave some advice. He then got an offer to go to a brand new organization called the RAND Corporation. I don't know the full story of how it started. The Air Force was under the army when I was in the Air Corps. Shortly thereafter it became separate. The Commanding General, General Arnold, said war is going to be totally different now, because of the nuclear war particularly. We've got to rethink everything. The Douglas Aircraft Corporation started a project, where RAND is Research and Development. Of course one of the new ideas was game theory, which was spreading. John von Neumann and Oskar Morgenstern had written a book in 1944, I guess. It's one of the few things I read when I was in the army. It's a very long book and it's got all sorts of things in it; it's rather weird but it's clearly one of the important new ideas. Abe was asked to join. They were hiring statisticians. They were hiring game mathematicians, those with new ideas, even philosophers. They were organizing it, so Abe wanted to know could I come in the summer of 1948. I could take leave from Cowles and I could probably relieve them of a little cost. RAND had become a separate corporation by this time, separated from Douglas. They had an old bank building hidden in downtown Santa Monica. Most banks in those days were open. They put up partitions, but you could hear other people's conversations. It was very exciting, but there were mostly mathematicians then, at least the ones that I associated with. Abe and Dave Blackwell and I were there and, of course, Lloyd Shapley. I was working on applied game theory, presumably applied to war and diplomacy, but they were very free. So Abe and Dave and I were working on some foundational, fundamental questions about statistics, and we wrote a paper which became quite famous. In the course of this, I remember one day at coffee. We had coffee regularly, and this philosopher, Olaf Helmer, whom I may have mentioned before, the man who translated Tarski's book, was there. Helmer said, "I don't understand something. We're trying to apply game theory to the Soviet Union and the United States, but this theory is applied to people, individuals. What do you mean by the United States? It's a collective of many people. They've got different views."

I said, "Some people have discussed this. There's a paper by Abram Bergson, and Paul Samuelson had taken it up, about how you aggregate the satisfaction state, as economists say, into a social welfare. Policy consists of maximizing that. It's all in the literature." He said, "Oh, is that so? Well why don't you write up an explanation? It would be very useful for us."

Okay, I started writing it up, but there're some problems here. I don't know how technical you want me to get here, but one of the problems is, can I compare my satisfaction to yours? It turns out if you are trying to develop economic theory that never enters. You might as well assume that I don't have a measure of satisfaction. I mean, one thing is better than another for me, another combination of things is better for you. There's no reason in economics ever to compare them.

Hotelling, for example, had taught us what's called the ordinalist point of view, namely that all I have is individual comparisons: give me two bundles of goods. I can say I like this one better than this one, and this relation is transitive. I'll say if I like bundle A better than bundle B and bundle B better than bundle C, then I like bundle A better than bundle C. I can compare any two bundles. This is like my problem with the Hicks firm, and that was discouraging because I knew that the answer was negative, that you couldn't construct it that way. So I said, "Oh, well, all right. Majority vote is just one way of doing it. There must be other methods. There are other methods like that, there are all sorts."

I don't know if you follow. Some of the local cities have adopted this rank order of voting. Theorists like me dislike the plurality measure. It's not working out so well. There must be another method. I tried other methods. Turns out they don't work well either. They may avoid that contradiction but there's something else in the problem. What exactly is wrong? I realized one of the things was, if I'm in an election, say, with two candidates, the outcome shouldn't depend on what the voters feel about a third person because only those two are running. One thing you can do is rank all the candidates. For example, if you have a three-person election and someone is chosen, suppose one of the losers drops out. Now compare that situation when one of the losers never even ran. You should get the same outcome, no matter what system you have anyway. I finally realized if you worked in very reasonable conditions, what you mean by a good system, there is no good system. There's always a way, in other words, the way people feel could be such that they would lead to a contradiction of some kind. Either the contradiction is in transitivity or the idea that if the loser drops out and you have the same information, you get a different outcome. That's it roughly, and so within a week I had this answer. I really owe it to Helmer who posed the question. I'm giving him credit for that.

Now meanwhile—this is the summer of '48—Abe had gotten an offer from Stanford, from Albert Bowker. Exactly how this happened I'm not sure I ever knew. Bowker was in contact with Stanford somehow about the idea of creating a statistics center here. He had these contacts so he figured, he could get financing and the Mathematics Department could get financing. So he's appointed to the Math Department, with the idea of creating a Statistics Department. I forgot to mention that Bowker had come to Columbia, so I had been in a lot of contact with him at Columbia after the war. He got his PhD from Columbia. Then he came to Stanford. Exactly how that was done, I don't think I ever knew. He got the idea that we needed a star because he was no star; Abe Girshick was a star, and that would create the department. Bowker knew me, thought it was a good idea if I came. The Stanford people—I told you they had made me an offer? I'm sure the reason they offered me this was that Allen Wallis, whom I mentioned before, had been appointed to Stanford before the war. I'm not sure he ever came, because the war broke out, or maybe he came. But anyway, I'm sure it was his recommendation of me that caused the first offer. In 1948, the chairman of the department was Ed Shaw. The two names of who were involved in the creation of the Modern Department were Bernard Haley and Edward Shaw. Bernard Haley was the senior, the older of the two. Shaw had been a student here and remained on, and he was considerably younger. He was the chair at this point. Haley had been the chair before that, and he was the one who made me the first offer. The department, like a lot of departments, had been shaken up by the war because people left and didn't come back. The university was in a very poor state. I think their endowment was about 100 million dollars. The story I got was that Senator Stanford, not trusting the successors to invest well, insisted they invest in railroad bonds. They did. At the time the rail industry was at the peak, and it was downhill from that point on. I think in the 1930s, they actually went to court to get this stricken. They got it. Herbert Hoover, the president of the United States, testified on their behalf [laughs]. By this time the damage had been done. You know, originally, Stanford University was free. There was no tuition until the early twenties. Did you know that? I'm not sure of the exact date, but for about 20 years, there was no tuition. Tuition was zero. By 1948, the university was not able to give the department any new positions. As a result of all this, Shaw was interested in getting me. By this time I had this idea for a thesis. I wrote it up, I mean a 20-page version of it, at RAND. I felt this was a thesis; this was the first time I felt, now I've got something. I've done something; I've got my original thought.

I was in touch with Hart who had been my advisor, whose interests had no connection to social choice, I can assure you. He had confidence in me and so I could see a thesis in hand. I left Rand, came up here and was interviewed in the summer of '48, at the beginning of the fall quarter, in September. I remember being interviewed. Now it turned out there had been a number of appointments in just a few years. There was a Canadian named Lorie Tarshis, who had studied at Cambridge at the time Keynes was developing the General Theory. There was a Hungarian, named Tibor Scitovsky. The name sounds Polish. It's a funny thing but it's a family that had moved from Poland, a very aristocratic family. One branch had moved from Poland to Hungary. They had some rights to collect tolls on a river or something like that, so they sent a member of the family to administer this. His father was a count. Also, Moe Abramovitz had come, maybe he had just come. And Paul Baran, who was quite a character in those days. He was Marxist. Before Stanford, I knew some of the names but not very well. Abramovitz and Scitovsky were names that were known to me. I'm pretty sure I never met them before they interviewed me. Shaw passed me around. He made me the offer right then and there, but for acting assistant professor. Shaw recognized that Bowker was a—well, organizer is a nice way of putting it, a better word is manipulator—so Shaw was a little suspicious of Bowker's motives; it bothered him. That was the only thing he was bugged by during my visit. I insisted that I had to have a joint appointment in statistics. Shaw assured me that my appointment would not be on a one-year basis. Shaw assured me that this was something he had to do by university rules, but I shouldn't contemplate or worry about it. So I had this offer but it took a number of months before I got a formal offer.

But, as my wife said, getting out of Chicago was the most important thing in the world. The weather was the main factor. Even compared to New York, Chicago is something. Worse. And then we were near the University of Chicago where crime was a problem. Another thing that happened was that Milton Friedman came, and he changed the whole tone of the place. He was very antagonistic to Cowles. He felt the Cowles group were Keynesians. In general he was very brilliant, very effective. Also, George Stigler came to Chicago. He had very similar views although his area of interest was different. These are very able economists, but they created a very bad atmosphere—talking down to Koopmans, for example, who was the Cowles director then. Stigler had no respect for Marschak, and both Stigler and Friedman disliked Koopmans. They felt the whole tone was wrong. The chairman of the Economics Department was a very distinguished man, Theodore Schultz, an agriculture economist. He had been chairman all through this period. He had been very friendly to Cowles, but he was being turned against the Cowles folks. So the situation became very unpleasant, very unpleasant indeed. It was a problem being a very junior person, being involved in these situations. I was assistant professor at the university. Sometime in 1948 or 1949, they gave me a half-time position. I taught some very good classes. I made some good friends there. But in some sense, although I was an assistant professor and therefore technically on the ladder, it wasn't clear Friedman and Stigler took this particular assistant professor very seriously. Koopmans was quite upset at the possibility of my leaving. I had to go to see the department's chairman, Ted Schultz. Schultz said, "Well, I'm sure you'll enjoy it at Stanford." Something like that. I don't know what I would have done had they tried to induce me to stay. Selma wanted to go in any case. Abe was there, whom I enjoyed working with. And there was a Statistics Department at Stanford. There was no Statistics Department in Chicago yet, although they were talking about it. In fact, they did create one shortly thereafter. Hanging over this, I could see already with Friedman, the antagonism was going to be a serious matter. Then when Schultz gave me the statement, there was no further question. I promptly wrote Stanford an acceptance. Two or three weeks later, I got a call to see Professor Schultz again, and he said, "Tell me, I've been hearing about this thesis of yours that you're submitting. Tell me about it."

The thesis was not at all in Schultz's line although he was a very able man, but this was just not his field, and he began suddenly talking about what we can do to keep you. It was only many years later that I found out what happened. Wallis told me this years later. It seems that Schultz met Friedman and said, "Well, Cowles had been trying to palm one of their people off on me but I got rid of him."

Friedman said, "Oh no. Arrow's different." [laughs] I had met Friedman. We had talked and argued, but not unfriendly, not personally. We just had intellectual arguments, discussing economic theories. But I'd given my word so there was nothing more to be said. That's how we wound up at Stanford.

I went back to RAND for the summer of '49, and that turned out ultimately to be very interesting. Somehow we got the idea that inventories were a problem. I don't know who raised this question. Marschak got involved in this. He organized a conference at RAND, a working group, not conference, a working group on the subject of how to control inventories better. I knew nothing about the subject. Marschak was talking about it. I said I was thinking about it and I had some ideas, and I wrote them up as a joint paper with Marschak and with a probability theorist named Theodore Harris, and this paper became quite famous.

Q. What was your experience when you first came to Stanford?

I was teaching. I don't really fully remember now. I do remember I insisted on two seminars, one in mathematical methods in microeconomics and one in mathematical methods in macroeconomics. When I got into the first one, there were three students. And then in the second one, the same three students showed up. There were three students in the first, but only one was registered because registration involved a cost. Then came the second one, the same three students, but none were registered. So I said, "I don't think I should give a course with no registered students." So they decided one of them would register [laughter]. One of the three turned out later to be my brother-in-law [laughs], Robert Summers, although my sister did not meet him through me. He was one of my graduate students.

I also taught an undergraduate course in economics and statistics, and I taught a graduate course in mathematical statistics, which was taken by people from various departments. Then I taught variations of this. I taught the graduate course in economic theory later. I'm not sure if there were more than 15 graduate students altogether, and my brother-in-law turned out to be reasonably successful and involved with some major research but I don't think any of the others really did.

My recollections were seven tenured members of the department. I mentioned Paul Baran, Tibor Scitovsky, Melvin Reder, Lorie Tarshis, Moses Abramovitz, Bernard Haley, and Edward Shaw, and this fellow named Jones. One of the things that happened was when the department became low in numbers, Haley and Shaw thought this was an opportunity to rebuild the department. They had no resources other than the fact that they had vacancies. There were no additional resources. They couldn't expand the department because the university was broke. In those days departments weren't given a sum of money, they were given positions. If a person was already in there and deserved to get a raise, he'd get a raise. But they were rationing it by positions. I don't remember how many junior positions there were, but my guess is probably five or six or seven. I don't know. I seem to count more than seven tenured positions, but anyway, whatever it was, there were seven or eight, there were probably 20 tenure-track positions. As I say, the number of undergraduates was exactly the same as today. The total number of undergraduates at Stanford was the same as today.

That has never expanded. The current president has talked about it, and suggested we should look into it but it doesn't seem to be a very live issue. Graduate student enrollment in other courses was entirely different. Engineering had a high general reputation. There were several departments that were famous. Psychology for some reason has always been famous here, right from the early stages of the university. Engineering, electrical engineering particularly, was famous. I don't know how long that was, but certainly for a number of years. The Dean was named Fred Terman. His father had been a professor of psychology, Lewis Terman, a very famous professor of psychology, and Terman was the then Dean at the School of Engineering. His successor was named Petit; he later became president, I think, of Georgia Institute of Technology. The Physics Department was rising because apparently in the late '30s or middle '30s, there was a Chair who thought Hitler was giving him an opportunity, and he hired Felix Bloch who was a Swiss, actually Swiss Jewish, but mainly his career was mostly in Germany. Bloch was one of the brilliant, young quantum physicists, and Fitzpatrick hired him. This gave a reputation, so by the time that I was there, there were young people, Willis Lamb, Robert Hofstadter and so forth. Also, there was a strong applied physics group which later separated out, but was then part of the Department of Physics. History was pretty good. Political science was terrible. It was still possible to have anti-Semitism, by the way; the Economics Department, of course, was free of it, but the Political Science Department would not hire a Jew. And History—I know less about it—but it had the same reputation. This was also true of the English Department, which was typical of English departments. On the other hand, Physics very successfully abandoned whatever feelings it had about that.

Q. You mentioned about building the economics department numbers. What other issues did the department face at that time?

Well, not internally, but there was the Keynesian issue, which was not only at Stanford. It was common. There was an organization, which I think started at Harvard, because Harvard was a pioneer in adopting Keynesian views. Alvin Hansen was a convert. He had written a rather negative review of Keynes, then he just switched over, and his influence fell on the younger people there. Chicago was very resistant to it, although there were people there who were different. But an organized group of businessmen were circulating attacks on Keynesian doctrines and their teaching, and they even identified them with Communism. Lorie Tarshis, particularly, was regarded, correctly, as an avid Keynesian. He had been a student at Cambridge University during the writing and publication of the General Theory.

I'm trying to get the sequence right. He wrote a textbook, which was the first elementary textbook which had Keynesian ideas. There was a huge volume of mail attacking him for it. The university—I must say, in its favor—did nothing about it. In '56, we wanted him to be the chairman (then called Executive Head) of the department. I was the preceding chair. I had been chair from '53 to '56. The chair was, and is, not elected by the department. The department could only make a recommendation, and the Dean and so forth could approve it, or not. So, in '56, we wanted Tarshis as chair, and I wrote a letter saying, "We think very strongly he's the right person, but I know of the adverse mail campaign." If I didn't remind them, they might feel I pulled one over on them. I told the Stanford administration, "We feel this is ridiculous, but we've got to tell you, there's a whole bunch of letters from potential donors, which is the crucial point, [laughs] saying that he was a communist." Despite this, I was behind him. Oh yes, he was the right person to be chairman. There was no real question about it. Then I got a very strange reply from the provost of the university, who was Terman by this time—he was a real right-winger. "I guess if you've never been called a communist you're not a very good economist" [laughs]. This changed my opinion of Terman [laughs]. We had, of course, a new president in '49, by the way, the same year I came. We had had some pretty weak presidents before that, at least according to the older members of the department. The president was Wallace Sterling. J. E. Wallace Sterling, yes. It is true that that he needed Terman to do things. I give Sterling more credit than a lot of people do. Terman was an administrator where Sterling was not a very good systematic man, but he could inspire you. He could get people to realize, we've got to do better, we've got to prove ourselves, we've got to appoint people better than you. Terman had no capacity that I could see to inspire anybody. He was very good at the nuts and bolts and, of course, he was terrific about making connections, particularly with the sciences and the engineering school. They would flourish, there's no question. I don't think Sterling was very good at any of that sort of stuff. Of course, Terman understood that government money was essential. But the two men worked together. It was an odd combination. The usual view is that all provosts and presidents have to be aligned, you know, work together [laughs]. Later on it was pretty clear to me that, Sterling didn't like Terman. They kind of needed each other, though. That was one of the things. It was a perfect team. [laughter] This idea that it was a perfect team, no question.

So, the professor I was recommending for department head, did go through, and Tarshis got the job. We had no problem. Where we did have a problem along these lines was Paul Baran. If you ever look at anything on the history of the university, you'll see that Baran was a Marxist. Why he was appointed in the first place I never was quite clear. That appointment occurred before I came here. There was no secret about it. There was nothing hidden about this. He was a very smart fellow, and he had worked for the Federal Reserve Bank of New York, I think. He was Russian, gone to Germany to study. He and I became really very friendly, in spite of the fact that I was an anti-communist from a pretty early stage. I had been left-wing and a socialist but it was as a high school student that I felt that the show trials in Russia were wrong. These histories won't mean a thing to you but they were a big feature among intellectuals then. When I was a high school student or a college student, Stalin started putting the old Bolsheviks on trial, people who had fought in the Revolution, people who had played a bigger role in the revolution than Stalin did. The revolutionaries of 1917 were now put on trial as traitors and conspirers or fascists and so forth. It obviously was all incredible. There was a committee in New York which actually went through the testimony and showed them they were meeting in some hotels that didn't exist, that had not yet been built, and things like that. The whole principle, the whole idea that they could be guilty, was ridiculous. So, I felt that this was a growing dictatorship. Actually, as bad as I thought it was, it was in fact much worse. After the war, lots of things came out—a lot of Russians got out and skipped. Anyway, Paul and I didn't agree but were quite friendly with one another. He was a great raconteur. One of the best storytellers I've met, unbelievably good. But for some reason, his Marxism didn't raise any issues in the university for a long time. It really only surfaced as a major issue for the alumni, that is to say, for the donors, a little later when he became a strong advocate of Castro. This was some ten or 12 years later, at the time of the Cuban revolution. There was a very strong public antagonism against Castro, and there began to be a deluge of mail to the president saying we have to fire Baran. It began when I was Chair. I don't remember now when it happened, but his salary was frozen. The university wouldn't raise his salary, and the department protested that this was an infringement of academic freedom. I didn't realize then the pressure on Sterling to fire him, and his answers. Sterling's answers were not always the greatest. They came out later because of the student riots in the late 60s. They ransacked the president's office and opened up a lot of files. It turned out Sterling's answers to the alums demanding Baran's firing sometimes were "Well, I agree with you but you know this, we can't fire him cause it's an issue of academic freedom." At other times, his letters were a strong defense of the idea that, even though we disagree with his position, that's part of the university. In any case, he never gave in to the idea. Whether he was being defensive or taking the high road, whatever it was, the idea of firing Baran never appeared as a possibility. Baran eventually died of a heart attack, though after he received a retroactive raise in salary.

Q. So, back to when you first came to Stanford, your Stanford experience. Did you like teaching?

What shall I say? I think teaching's important. I'm not a great teacher. I think I'm not that good at it. My student ratings are average. They're not bad, except for one course much later, where I did get distinctly negative things. I tried something very experimental and it was a mistake, and these were very junior students. It was too far out. That was the only time. Part of the problem is, I do like to think aloud. That's my way. I keep on thinking aloud, and I edit my thoughts as I go along. That's my way because every time I say something, I realize there's another aspect to the issue, and that's true when I write. But, of course, writing is private and doesn't impose itself on anybody else. I'm rewriting as I write. It's easier to edit. Of course, now with the computer, it's so wonderful. Oh boy, the computer fits my needs like nothing else did.

Q. I was going to ask you what your teaching style was. In a way, it's partly the way you communicate.

Yes. I always try to elicit responses from the students. Partly, it's a defensive measure. I want to know what they're thinking, [laughs] because I'm not that confident that they're understanding what I'm saying. So, I really want to hear reactions and questions because it guides me as to whether it's going across or not On the whole, that was fairly successful? On the whole. You know, you have a class with 20 students, ten do and ten don't respond well. It was always the silent ones you worry about. If I'm teaching a course, I want to teach what not only my views are but what are other people's views as well. That I think is absolutely the only right thing to do. You want to engage the range of views. If it's a controversial point, then I want to say, "Well, this is my point; this is somebody else's." I try to create a polyphony. I really do like to entertain all views. Yes, that's got its problems, and you can tell I'm a very ineffective policy advisor because I always see the objections to my policy. So I've not played a role in policy.

Q. How do you like teaching compared to doing research? My guess is you would enjoy research more.

No, I do research, but the teaching is important. A portion of my research is the result of attempting to teach it in class. I try to explain something, and then of course sometimes I see a simpler way than is in the literature. My stock in trade really is seeing diverse things as being related. In teaching, if I'm teaching this, this and this, and I say, oh there's a common element, that sometimes is sufficiently original that it's actually worth publishing. So, there's been a significant part— I wouldn't say most, but a significant part—of my research that has arisen out of attempting to teach and trying to explain the matter clearly to myself. In other words, there are some obscurities in the literature. Teaching has been very valuable from that point of view. The environment at Stanford has been very good in this regard. You know, your community is economists everywhere. It was increasingly true. I think it's much truer today than it would've been in the past because it's much easier with the communications. The econometric movement, as an example, was one that seemed to go back to the 1930s. Here's a handful of people scattered over Europe and United States, I wouldn't say the world exactly, but Europe and the United States. Now today, of course, there are econometricians everywhere. It's a success story so it loses its uniqueness. So, it doesn't matter so much where you are. It helps a little a bit always to have colleagues, at least a few. In my case, some of my research was stimulated by a development economist named Hollis Chenery. I don't know if Chenery means anything to you. The Chenery family owned Secretariat. His sister was the one that was most involved. I remember, we were looking for junior faculty. I became very influential on appointments because I actually sat down and read all the stuff. I found I was just putting in more work than my colleagues, so I'd read Chenery's dissertation. I'd read it from beginning to end. He became more of a policy person than a scholar, but he raised a number of points, and a couple of my papers are reactions to his work. I even wrote one important paper with Chenery as a co-author. I wrote a lot of collaborative papers, but they were mostly with people elsewhere.

Q. The Department of Operations Research was created in 1967 as an interdisciplinary effort, and you chaired the founding committee. Can you tell us about that experience?

Yes, it was my idea, because of the RAND connections. The ideas of Operations Research are economic ideas but applied to very, very specific problems, not to buying and selling, but to organization. The inventory paper was really an Operations Research paper. I realized after a few years, there were a whole bunch of operations researchers here scattered around different departments. I was interested in economics. I don't know if there was anybody else in economics really interested. There was a fellow in the Statistics Department, and it seemed to me we ought to have a degree. My original idea was not a department but an interdepartmental degree. Al Bowker, who, as I mentioned before, founded the Statistics Department, became very quickly an administrator here, assistant provost to Terman and so forth. He created and directed a research organization, the Applied Mathematics and Statistics Laboratories, mainly financed by the Office of Naval Research, which had mathematicians and statisticians. We were friendly over the course of these years until he died two years ago. I figured he's the person to talk to. I told him that there were about four or five operations researchers I could identify, and it seemed we could have a degree in it, not a department. He thought it was a great idea. "Okay, well, on the first committee, you'll be the chair." We organized it. Then we wanted to make an appointment, Arthur F. Veinott, Jr., a very bright PhD, and we couldn't get a department to appoint him. Bowker said maybe we should create a department so we can make our own appointment. Then on top of that it turns out that George Dantzig, who was one of the great names, one of the creators of linear programming. I would say 'the' creator, in my view, but there are people who would argue about that. He was at Berkeley, and by chance I realized he wasn't too happy. He may have been in the Electrical Engineering Department or something like that. He wasn't too happy. So I suggested we make him an offer. Dantzig was a star, and that was something, and of course, it was one of the best things I could've done. But then when we reorganized the department, I figured we need a better administrator than I am, and Jerry Lieberman—who had been a graduate student here and I'd known him—we were friendly from even when he was a graduate student. He was a man with tremendous liveliness and— what shall I say—a joy to be with at all times and great sense of ability to organize things. He did some good work, but his forte was really running things. He was a protégé of Al Bowker, and I think he's a clear thinker.

He'd been in the Statistics Department. His work was statistics. He was a PhD in statistics here. So, it was a small department. The faculty and the graduate students were very close to each other, like Lincoln Moses. He was very, very capable and had a great sense of human values involved as well as getting the money in and organizing things and a good judge. So I think he was great. At some point, he became provost, dean of research and graduate studies and provost. But by that time, he was already ill.

Q. How do you see that department today, the Department of Management Science and Engineering?

The field itself has evolved, so it probably was necessary to bring it in. There was a field of industrial engineering (IE), which was an old field and not very progressive. If the IE people were more progressive they would have to transform themselves into operations research (OR). The whole spirit is different, much more mathematical, much more precise. Then here there was a complication. There was a third group, which was something of a sect called engineering economic systems. They didn't put themselves in industrial engineering, although it would've been logical. Yet, somehow they differentiated from OR and I think it really represented a different position. It should've been in the same department from the beginning. It never should've been a separate department, in my opinion. They had very particular ideas but it's like having two economic departments, one Keynesian and one anti-Keynesian, which is wrong. They both should be working together; they're two points of view that should both be represented. I think it was a little bit that some people wanted to keep themselves aloof from the others although they were good scholars. So, eventually one of the engineering deans, I think it was Jim Gibbons, saw that EES and OR should be combined. There were these histories which didn't work so well. But when they put them in the Industrial Engineering Department, and I must say Elizabeth Pate-Cornell was a great solver of problems, she brought unity to the whole thing. The OR has evolved, too. There's an overlap. We're dealing with some problems, like how do you handle general equilibrium and things like that, so there is an overlap.

The economical ideas are permeating the whole field. The internet has introduced a whole new set of economic issues. How do you charge for advertising and all this? They've been extremely ingenious at pricing schemes. The economists tend not to want to deal with how an individual firm works. That's the way the OR or its descendants come from. So, there's all a very lively thing where they're in fact doing things which could be absorbed by economists, and there is a bit of a problem.

These in-house research groups, Microsoft, Yahoo and Google, all have economic research groups. The Microsoft research group is headed by a professor from Harvard. Somebody we had here who left—that's another story—is spending a good fraction of her time with Microsoft. Google's had some really good economists, and Yahoo too, all three of them. So, one thing, we're getting research groups outside. They maintain a very close contact. People on leave from academic life spend time at these groups. I'm not involved with this group now but I'm an emeritus member, so I go to social functions. I'm retired. I'm not involved in the Economics Department as far as that goes.

Q. In our last interview, we left off discussing your involvement and that of others with the Department of Operations Research here at Stanford. This department resulted from an interdisciplinary effort. What are your thoughts on the evolution of interdisciplinary teaching and research at Stanford?

This has a mixed record. To give you an example, when I came here, a prominent feature, in fact, in the School of Humanities and Sciences was something called Area Studies. The idea was to have integrated interdisciplinary studies of various areas, such as the Western Pacific and East Asia. After a while, there was a perception that the scholarly level wasn't really being maintained. So then, eventually, in fact, these area studies led to a Department of Anthropology, which had very good standards. Since I moved from mathematics to physics to economics and also had general intellectual interests, I was always in favor of interdisciplinary work. To involve psychologists and economics and the older members of the departments, that just means lowering your standards.

I'm afraid there was a steady conflict. On the one hand, there are clear cases where there is interaction among the disciplines. That's true in the sciences as well as in the social sciences, such as the use of biological markers in anthropology. But there are obvious conflict situations, and this is true today because we're now, again, in an era of emphasis on interdisciplinary work. It goes up and down. I've seen this all before. Essentially, the only thing I can say is when you have a solid, interdisciplinary accomplishment, solid in the scholarly sense, meeting all the demands, not with slogans but actually, then it finds its place. Sometimes there's a little in-fighting. The use of mathematics in economics, for example, was regarded with great suspicion by economics departments, certainly. Now the shoe's on the other foot and people say there's too much mathematics in economics. But that was not true when I was a student. I was sure if I just kept on doing my work, it would be recognized, and really it was. There was not a tremendous barrier in my case. Maybe people a decade earlier might have had more trouble. Bridging these gaps means a certain risk-taking on the part of the scholar. That's where the real problem comes in. For example, my late friend Amos Tversky was in the Psychology Department but there were parts of economics relevant to what he was doing. Typically psychologists keep on saying, "Oh, you economists are unrealistic in your ideas of human beings." They weren't wrong, but what they did didn't give rise to anything useful. It was clear they didn't know too well what the economists were doing; so even though their criticism may have been correct, it was easy to dismiss them. Tversky knew the relevant economics part. Nobody could dismiss what he said. He covered himself carefully. He also pointed out how experiments contradicted economic theory, and because he had formulated the economics correctly, when it contradicted, it really was contradictive. That had a very big impact and has given rise to what is called behavioral economics. Now every department's got to have a behavioral economist, even though when you do you may not be entirely cognizant of what other people are doing. But of course in any science, a good department should have contradictory tendencies. It's not a good department if it doesn't. You want to really explore everything. So this sort of work can be extremely exciting. Such interdisciplinary work is making a big change in economics, and the same thing is true in other fields. As I said, biology has had an influence on at least some branches of anthropology, and psychology, of course, has been influenced by biochemistry. The juices flow when you're reacting to something. It [the latter] served as a functional MRI in both psychology and economics, actually. It showed what goes on in your brain when you make a decision. You can effectively look into the brain. You see what parts light up, as the expression goes, which means blood flow. Sometimes a field may disappear, or more often, a new field emerges that didn't exist before. This is a rather long-winded answer, but I'm saying that "interdisciplinary" can easily be a cover for junk or slogans for things that are correct but not useful.

Q. You've talked a lot about the challenges and implications. Along the way, was there an institutional effort to bring about interdisciplinary studies within the university?

There is now. Partly, frankly, because of the funding available, though it is oh-so-questionable, for a candid view. Funding sources have a big voice. They have less influence in social sciences simply because we don't spend money on the scale of the physical sciences or the natural sciences. We have centers here that are clearly designed to appeal to funding sources. That's legitimate in a way because society wants this thing. I'm not saying it's an illegitimate idea. Most of the time I've been here the consciously interdisciplinary effort was not great but happened now and then. As I say, in biology there was a revolution because of the importance of the emphasis on chemical factors and the use of DNA. That's just an outside observation. I don't know much about that. But in economics there hasn't really been a great deal of interdisciplinary work.

Q. Your research earned you the Nobel Prize in economics in 1972.

I want to be exact. It's the Nobel Memorial Prize. I want to emphasize this because the Nobel Prizes are the ones that were created by Alfred Nobel. He did not create a prize in economics. One doesn't want to claim things that aren't true. In the 1960s the Bank of Sweden (the national bank, like the Federal Reserve Bank) decided to celebrate its 300th anniversary by endowing a prize in economics to be awarded through the Nobel Foundation. Therefore, it's known as the Bank of Sweden Prize in Memory of Alfred Nobel. Generally referred to as the Nobel Memorial Prize, but the full title is the Bank of Sweden Prize in Memory of Alfred Nobel. The Nobel Foundation did agree to sponsor this; I don't how it came about that the scientists would agree to that, but they did. The Prize was first awarded in 1968, if I remember correctly. I was awarded the Nobel Memorial Prize in Economics in 1972 with Sir John Hicks. The award was really given for two things. One was the work on social choice, which I really had done before Stanford, and the other was for work in what's called General Equilibrium Theory, which was done here.

Q. What kind of impact did winning this prize have on your work, if any?

I'd like to think none. I hope there was none [laughter].

Q. Was there a monetary prize and was it just for research?

The amount of money is much bigger today than it was when I got it, [laughter] I'll tell you that. But there is a certain amount for each prize. It was $100,000 when I got it, but that was split between two people. The Nobel Prize is occasionally given to one person, but it's frequently given to two, given to three. I think they dislike giving to more than three. The prize money is just to you; it's not for research or anything else.

Q. You mentored five students who became Nobel Laureates after you. What can you tell us about mentoring?

They were all different. For example, one of the first was John Harsanyi, a Hungarian name. He had actually published a couple of papers before he even showed up as a graduate student. I interviewed him when he applied and I asked, "Why are you coming for the doctorate? You already know all about it." He was a Hungarian refugee from communism in the very early days. He managed to cross illegally over the border to Austria, and finally wound up in Australia, where he got a Master's degree in economics. But he wanted to get to the United States. Probably, without a PhD he wouldn't—no, it doesn't matter. He had pretty much worked on his dissertation before he came here. While I gave him some advice, I find it a little hard to take much credit for anything he did. He was really very self-propelled. I enjoyed having him around. We had wonderful conversations, but he had very intelligent ideas and he developed them. He had a very successful career and eventually he got the prize, shared with Reinhard Selten and John Nash. By the way do I have Jim Mirrlees on that list? Let's see, we've got Harsanyi, Roger Myerson, A. Michael Spence, and Eric Maskin. There also was Mirrlees, in a way. I really have three that are legal and have my signatures on them. I was on leave when Harsanyi literally submitted the dissertation, so somebody else signed it. I think it was Hendrik Houthakker. But I was the one who worked with him. The other three were Eric Maskin, Roger Myerson, and Michael Spence, and those three were all at Harvard. The other one was James Mirrlees, but that's a strange story. You can argue as to what this means. His was a PhD at Cambridge, University of Cambridge. In '63–'64, I spent a year at Cambridge. That's where I interacted with him. Then he was coming up for his dissertation. Now in England, the student is much more on his own than in the United States. He submits a thesis and talks to advisors, and then they appoint examiners. The examiner may not be the person you work with at all. There's an internal examiner, somebody at Cambridge, but they always have an external examiner, not affiliated with the University. The U.S. doesn't have anything like that. Since I was visiting and since his dissertation was quite technical and not very many people were prepared in that area, they asked me if I would be the external examiner. I don't know that it's proper of me to say that I was his mentor since I really didn't see the dissertation until it was all finished. The three people I really guided were Eric Maskin, Michael Spence, and Roger Myerson. I worked with them directly; I really spent a lot of time with them.

Mentoring is an interesting process. Things are individual. I didn't get any real mentoring. When I decided I really had a dissertation topic, the Social Choice, there wasn't anybody in the field. The field didn't exist. I had been working with a professor, Albert Hart. I never signed up with him, but I was a good deal more technical than he was. He was very good, and he's a very interesting person with a lot of ideas. But when I suddenly switched to Social Choice, he was the only one I had contact with. I was pounding away at something, and I'd consult with him occasionally but he wasn't directing this. This kind of relationship is quite individual. The student can simply develop things on his own and just come in for approval, or other times he can get a lot out of it. Those three students, I actually did work with them quite a bit, especially with Spence and with Maskin, a little less so with Myerson, but I did have a lot of interaction. I've had some very nice theses here, although again, sometimes a student is in a field I don't know too much about. But I can check and can see that it's good without being able, necessarily, to contribute a great deal. Other times I have had a lot of suggestions. It depends on the student; depends on the topic. It's an individual interaction with different personalities. There's no simple formula. I did see a lot of Harsanyi, but as I said, in fact, his thesis was something that I was not particularly working on. I knew the literature well enough to know that it was original, and I decided I didn't want to stand in the way. The only thing to do is get out of the way. I do feel I'm conscientious about reading the thesis but adding anything to it is a different matter.

Q. You left Stanford for Harvard in 1968 until 1979, and you worked with these three students who later won the Nobel Prize. Do you want to share anything more about your experience at Harvard?

No, it was very good. I've no particular problems with it. I really enjoyed it. I left here, really, because I felt that Stanford could be in a position—maybe I was being grandiose—of being an absolutely first-class department, but that one of the problems was that we were too small. The department was highly expanded by 1968—the situation was much better than in 1949—but nevertheless, I felt it that it was hardly optimum. One of the department's basic problems was that there were a lot of bright young people coming up but we couldn't make offers because there weren't any vacancies. I visited MIT, where I had some very good friends, in the fall of '65, and they had a student who was very bright. So I wrote back to the department to hire him. There had been a few problems in the department because I was pushing young people, and there was a suspicion I was pushing just mathematical types. I later got to say that I recommended three people who got the Nobel Prize and the department didn't appoint them. The department was not unresponsive. I felt I did not push only mathematical types, that I was pushing policy, whatever it was. But this fellow looked like a first-class student, so I wrote back and said we've got to hire him, and the answer I got back was, we have no vacancies in the department. They just won't give us one. He's actually a professor here now, Robert Hall. He's been a president of the American Economics Association. So he did well. Even at an early stage in his career, in my mind it was a clear case. I didn't think there was much of a gamble, though you never know. People do fizzle out. So I began to reflect on the whole idea that we had chances to build here by looking for bright, young people. We were very severe. The department did not promote easily, which was good. We had very high quality standards, and so we weren't promoting. That was not a problem. The problem, however, was to attract good people, and we just needed more of them. One of the reasons why Harvard was so good was that it had some duds, but they had much bigger departments. If you just looked at stars, there were more of them. Size matters. I think the Harvard department is not less than 50 percent bigger, maybe more than that. I haven't checked, but they're very big. They have no more undergraduates than we do in terms of student demand. They have more graduate students and they get better graduate students. But part of that is chicken and egg. You have more stars, you get more top students. I got an offer [from Harvard] and I started bargaining. The bargaining was not about my salary. It was about the size of the department. I bargained here to try to get a bigger department. In the end, I couldn't get them. They gave me two new positions, and I suppose that must have been competing with Physics or Biochemistry, which is one of the great success stories of Stanford, no question. I can't argue about that. On the other hand, those were bringing in outside money. The upshot was that I already had a considerable number of friends at Harvard so it wasn't an alien environment. I mentioned earlier that in the past Harvard had some anti-Semitism. That was gone by then. Harvard, from the top down, took a different position after the war. If you're talking about students, they couldn't bring themselves to have a Jewish quota, but they did have a geographical quota. So coming from Montana was a great advantage in applying to Harvard. The president after the war, President Conant, totally changed the policies on student admission, and anti-Semitism gradually ended. By that time the issue had vanished, no question. We enjoyed life there. We had the children by this time, who were three and six, and they were wondering why I was moving them from California. But they loved the snow. Adaptation to a different climate was not an issue. The first winter, as I recall, was an unusually severe one. We bought a house and all the rest of it. We had a great time there. It's a great environment.

One thing that happened, talking about interdisciplinary background, is that this use of mathematics began to develop into something called, oh let's see, Institute for Mathematical Studies in the Social Sciences, here at Stanford. The organizer was Patrick Suppes, who is professor of philosophy. He came a year after I did, and we've been very good friends right from the beginning. We still are. Unlike myself, he's a real organizer. One thing I'm very good at it is not organizing but finding a good organizer to latch onto. Al Bowker, for example. I know it's good to have one. Pat Suppes organized this Institute for Mathematical Studies in the Social Sciences [IMSSS]. We took over an old house that had been built for the retirement of the first president of the university, Jordan [Serra House]. It was then located— do you have an idea where the co-generative plant is? It was there. It's been moved and is now somewhere near the faculty club. The time I'm speaking of now is when I am back at Stanford. In the end, I was head of the economics wing of this institute [IMSSS], and we had visitors and people on short-term at various periods. After I went to Harvard the economics wing was taken over by Mordecai Kurz, a professor here who just recently retired. He organized summer programs, so I used to come out every summer, even though I was at Harvard. He claimed that part of his motivation for creating the summer programs was to get me to come here. So I came back, I'm not sure every summer, but almost every summer. So I retained a connection here. I brought my whole family back every summer. I think there was one summer where it didn't work out for some reason, though, but every other summer I brought my family out, and they loved it. When the kids were about to enter high school, or one was and the other was close to it, the question came up what to do. Of course, I did get repeated indications from Stanford that anytime I wanted to come back I could. We talked about did we want to live in Cambridge, getting older, with the snow, [laughter] and so forth. We still maintained a great many friends here, because we were here regularly, and we made a decision to come back. We also have very good friends at Harvard and the department worked out very well. The appointment process was a bit difficult, but we had that at Stanford too, so that was not unique. They treated me very well at Harvard, made me university professor, which is a very high honor. We don't have the equivalent here. When I returned to Stanford in 1979 I was given an endowed professorship in Economics. The endowed professorship simply is a way of honoring the donor. It's really nothing to do with the faculty member. It's intended as a little bit of a signal that we honor you more than other professors, but in terms of responsibilities it's exactly the same. It's no difference whatever.

Q. SIEPR, the Stanford Institute for Economic Policy Research was founded in 1982. Were you involved in its founding?

I'm not and never really have been a big part of that. I think I'm formally a senior fellow and a member of the steering committee. That's more recent. Being a senior fellow means that you're recognized as part of the intellectual community, you may have a grant administered by the institute. I haven't chosen to move to the building. But I help review the programs and make comments, and so on. SIEPR's been a great success. They have had several very good leaders; not the sort of thing I would have ever done. Michael Boskin. John Shoven. They support research for the graduate students and junior faculty, and they hold sessions of speakers from Stanford or elsewhere for the associates, the people who donate all the money. That business community here is a particularly intellectual and intelligent community; I don't think that would work anywhere else. Silicon Valley, it fits. You've got a good group of people who can handle quite serious talks and so forth. A lot of them have academic backgrounds and would like a little academics in their life. I'm part of it, but I haven't been in any way central.

Q. What are your thoughts about the current state of economic research at Stanford as a whole?

We've got a very good faculty now. I think there are certain areas that we could cover better than we do. It's not for lack of trying, but it's a problem getting people. We're competent in competing; we get some people, we don't get others. We're not very good at economic development. We don't have a senior person in the field, really, but I consider developing countries to be an important happening. We're good at theory, we're very good at monetary economics, pretty good at macro. Foreign trade is good, which was a problem for a while. Econometrics, that's traditionally been good. I think we've got most of the fields covered quite well. I wish development was stronger. Industrial organization is very good. The one thing I miss is a topic which not every department has, and it's income distribution, the question of poverty. We don't have anybody in that field, and we've never really pushed very hard for it. It's a little off the main track, but I think we should be engaged in this topic and I feel it's a gap. The department doesn't take it too seriously.

So, there are a few gaps. On the other hand, one of the problems is the department isn't big enough. Still. It's a lot bigger than it was, but it's still not big enough. But I think I can go through every department and complain that their fields don't work out, so I don't want to make too much of this. I think we cover a lot of the fields very well.

Q. What kinds of issues do the Economics Department face today compared to when you joined Stanford?

It's much bigger. We really have good coverage of the fields. By and large I think we do a very good job. We're handling undergraduate teaching better. There was a period when it was kind of neglected—we had an awful lot of visitors teaching the undergraduates—but I think we're doing much better at that now. The visitors would come for a year or two. They'd be people who had some other affiliation. Some of them were very good teachers, but they didn't have the scholarship that would have entitled them to be on the faculty at Stanford. We tip the other way. The number of hours that a professor teaches is a good deal less than it was when I came. We were supposed to be teaching five hours a week or something like that. And now it's more like three, average over the course of the year.

That's true of the whole university. The tendency in the whole university is to give more time to research. Now the emphasis is research. That started out when they started trying to improve the quality of the department. When I first came here, the research levels weren't as high. Now, teaching, of course, is a necessary condition. Some people can't teach well. We have some troubles. But I would say that there's no question that promotion—not just in economics but throughout the whole university—depends on research. The tendency is to push the teaching hours down to give more time to research. I'm sure the research output has gone up, by the way. There's no question.

Q. During the 1980s at Stanford, you served on and chaired both the Faculty Senate and the Advisory Board of the Academic Council. What can you share about those experiences and the challenging issues that you faced?

I don't know that in either one I was particularly innovative. I faced problems as a member of the Senate, a member of the Advisory Board, but nothing especially happened during my chairmanship that was different. The Advisory Board doesn't normally have big issues. It's a question of how scrupulously you look at the individual faculty files, and we were active. I would say the Advisory Board was rejecting something like ten percent of the people who came up. These were already screened through the deans and the provost.

Obviously we spent more time on tenure cases. But initial appointments were also reviewed and renewal of assistant professors at three years. Then there are outside offers at the tenure level. I remember this one set of papers that came from. . .well, I won't tell you any details. But we looked at the person's record and it seemed pretty impressive with over 100 published papers. They were pretty short and there was a lot of repetition in the titles. We read the reference letters carefully. People don't write bad letters, even though they're supposed to be confidential. The confidentiality is a problem, as you may know, because some court cases have been through this issue. Occasionally there are people who will refuse to write letters of recommendation because they fear privacy will be broken. Actually our experience has not been that people write nasty letters and want them hidden. On the contrary, the average letter of recommendation is clearly too good. Even though it's completely confidential, people don't feel right about saying bad things. In fact, I have a feeling that they might be more frank if the process was more open. They might feel less like they were stabbing someone in the back. Anyway, you read the letters carefully. It isn't that they say anything negative, but they're not saying positive things. In this particular case, it didn't look like a good appointment. The department did not make a fuss when we turned it down. That doesn't happen often, but I'd say we turned down some. The number was surprisingly high, given that it's already pretty well reviewed. The department's recommended and the Dean has approved it. Given that, I'm a little surprised that we still were turning down something of the order of ten percent, maybe a little less I don't recall, although I may have forgotten, that there was any big issue that we came up with.

I don't really remember any issues during my chairmanship of the Faculty Senate although, candidly, I might have forgotten. The biggest issue I remember is an argument about the basic undergraduate course, whose name keeps on changing. It used to be called Western Civilization. The big complaint was that it discriminated against homosexuals, and it discriminated against women, and "Western" wasn't such a good idea. I'm kind of liberal and kind of sympathetic to these things. I happened to have dinner, however, at one of the student dorms, so I thought I'd get a conversation going and see what they thought about it. It turned out they were all enthusiastic about the course. Women, minorities, they were all very enthusiastic. I thought, well, if you've got something that people like, don't be in a hurry to change it. We had a very vigorous debate, but I think what we did was take a very successful course and it's become a mess. People make fun of it now. It's called Introduction to the Humanities. It changes the whole meaning of it. Anyway, that was something that took several sessions in the Senate.

There were one or two other issues, but, to tell you the truth, at this stage I've forgotten them. Oh, yes. There was a lot of discussion about the proposed Reagan Library. Oh, yes, indeed! The Hoover people came to the Senate with this proposal and, I must say, the librarian, Charles Palm, if I remember right now, gave a very good presentation. He was the right person. He was not antagonistic, he was low-key. Nevertheless—and it was very interesting—where did you get the first, the big complaints? From the people who lived on the side of San Juan Hill facing Junipero Serra. The Reagan Library would have been across the street from them. Half of them were Republicans, and they were opposed to this. Politics had nothing to do with the issue. They could visualize, and as a realist, they were right. It would have been enormously crowded, if it were successful at all, and of course it's not just a library, it's a museum. And that area is not a place where you want a lot of traffic. Then the Hoover people went on this false argument that it would encourage the research. That's nonsense. If a fellow wants to do research on the Reagan papers, he can go to wherever the library is, Simi Valley, or wherever it is. It seemed to me this was a false argument, and I finally got convinced that the real problem had nothing to do with politics.

In the end, I didn't speak that much on it, but I did say that you're going to have a congestion problem here if you build it. Because we had gone through this at Harvard and I was a little bit involved there. There was a proposal to put up a new Kennedy library in Cambridge, not far from the University, toward the river. The neighbors complained and there was one professor who called me in to discuss the economic impact. As soon as I looked into it I realized the number of people involved; it was a very crowded area. The problem at Stanford is the opposite. You don't want to spoil that area and you'd have to do a lot of building up of roads and so forth. I thought the whole thing was kind of preposterous. It dragged on for a while. Then they said, oh well, the donors are going to withdraw the proposal. Finally, I think we were very lucky. It was not good for the area. But there were a lot of discussion about that. It took several of our sessions. We realized that most of the time we didn't have that much to discuss. This is a bunch of academics who like to talk, although the discussion on that was pretty focused. I can't complain. It was going to be a tall building, as I recall, and it didn't fit in the landscape. The whole thing would just have ruined the place. This is not the place for it. Proximity to the university has no importance, in my opinion, for a building like that. So it's not as though we were suppressing anything. But it's true that some of the opponents were motivated by political things, and I thought that was inappropriate. There were many good reasons for opposition.

Q. In 1981, you were appointed senior fellow at the Hoover Institution on War, Reconciliation, and Peace. Can you tell us about that experience?

That was not something I regard as a very pleasant experience. The Hoover Library director in 1949 was a man named Rothwell, I think, and he was taking the Hoover Library in a rather broad and not very partisan direction. A lot of the donors, and eventually Mr. Hoover himself, withdrew support. The president of Stanford was named Sterling, who himself had been at the Hoover Library, and he was very loyal to Rothwell, but Rothwell did then retire. At that point they were looking for a successor and the way Sterling described it was, this young man Glenn Campbell, who has a PhD from Harvard, came. President Sterling assumed that he was interviewing Campbell. Campbell made it quite clear that, no, he had the job and *he* was interviewing Sterling. This is what Sterling said in the open, to the full Academic Council. That's not a confidential remark. Campbell became the director. He was a very vigorous director, and has a sort of respectability. He didn't want to be regarded as excessively partisan. I think that was the reason he asked me to be a Hoover Fellow (by courtesy). Anyway, being appointed to Hoover, that was a hard thing. However I said, "Well yes, that's fine. How about some support for my research?" And I got a grant, but it was a renewable grant, just to tell you this sort of thing. Then Campbell retired, I think after a couple years [in 1989], and the new director, who is still director, was John Raisian. One day he tells me, we have no funds. I thought this was a little ridiculous. If I'm good enough to be a senior fellow then I'm sure that what I was getting was a small part of the budget. He gave me stories about the pressure from the board, so I resigned. I refused to accept a renewed appointment. I said I was done, basically. I wasn't there very long. I was probably there for four or five years. I don't know what to say, but the obvious conjecture is that the board wanted more "reliable" people. Now they have some people who they support who are definitely not, I would say, in the usual Hoover mold, such as Larry Diamond. Seymour Martin Lipset was there for a long while. I've got to say there were a couple of people who did not stay with them, but most of them do. I think they are very partisan. Campbell wanted a policy, whatever the partisanship was. Partisanship alone, that was not enough. Campbell was also very influential in the American Enterprise Institute, which has also kept a pretty good standard of work even though they have a definite orientation. I think it really went down, became more partisan, after Campbell left. But basically Campbell was a partisan too. It's just that he did respect quality.

Q. I'd like to get your insights on the University and some of its personalities. You've talked and mentioned some before, but you have witnessed several administrations at Stanford. Did you work closely with any of the presidents?

I probably worked more closely with Sterling, actually, than with any of his successors. I was at Harvard during most of Lyman's administration, but I did overlap a little bit with Lyman. I didn't really know Casper. I was personally friendly with Kennedy, but I don't think I had any particular involvement. It was just that his problems weren't my problems. Sterling actually tried to use me for committees and things like that. I was on, for example, a study of undergraduate education, which took about a year, and that was a very serious sort of thing. That's why I was wondering why me? I never did understand why he appointed me because, after all, what reputation I had was as a scholar, but he somehow picked me out as somebody to work with, and so I spent time on it. That was an easy job because nobody had looked at undergraduate education for 20 years, or something like that, so it was a jumble. It was quite easy to make improvements. It didn't require work. It didn't require fundamental rethinking. It was just sort of straightening things out, or getting rid of all sorts of arbitrary things, and putting in others. I talked to him a bit about a number of issues. I felt closer to him in many ways than to the others, but I felt close to Kennedy.

Q. You were an academic leader in terms of your scholarship, research, and mentorship. Who in the Stanford faculty or administration do you see as leaders?

I don't know the whole university. Particularly I don't feel know-ledgeable about the Engineering School. But of the people I know or have known, I've got a high respect for a history professor, the greatest lecturer I ever heard. Gordon Craig. He is one of the most impressive. I heard his lectures, the greatest lectures I've ever heard anybody give. He's a European historian, specializing on Germany. He gave a lecture when Germany was reunified, so this was quite late in his life. He gave a lecture comparing the unification of Germany in 1871, when the German empire was founded, with the reunification of East and West Germany. The comparisons, the sense of what was similar, what was not, it really was something I would only dream of doing. I couldn't possibly perform at that level. Now, of course, I have met, over the years, a number of the physicists. Of course Felix Bloch was a really great figure when I came here, and he was a most impressive person. He was enormously intellectual; he seemed to understand what he was doing. There were some very good psychologists here that I've known over the years. Robert Sears was a difficult person; he was a dean, too. He was a very good dean, as a matter of fact. He got some people angry, but it was a clean-up job. He was an effective clean-up person. He imposed standards on some of the weak departments. The political scientist, John Ferejohn, of course, he was a very good friend of mine, a good person, very friendly. That department is so different from what it was when I started. It's really good now. But when I came, oh, it was abysmal. But soon they changed it. It was Sears who did it. Sears somehow decided. He called me up one day and said, "I'm putting the Political Science Department in receivership. They're no good. I want to appoint a committee of other professors to make the appointments. Would you serve on it?" And, of course, one of the things he spotted was the anti-Semitism in the department. I thought that there were a lot of people, especially when they drank a little bit, were somewhat anti-Semitic but Sears wasn't going to let that stand in the way of building up the department. He made some very good appointments. We got some good people in. The department was changed within five years; I didn't believe it was possible. I guess he had leverage enough to accumulate vacancies. I don't know how he did it, but within a few years it was an entirely different department. He made three major appointments right away.

There was a psychologist here who was a little difficult in some ways, personally, but a very brilliant man, Leon Festinger. He was a character. He developed the theory of what's called Cognitive Dissonance, that essentially argues that if what you're doing is out of line with what you believe, one of the two is going to change. He had some wonderful experiments and studies. In Statistics, of course, I was very close to someone who's still around, Charles Stein, whom I actually had known in the army before I ever got to Stanford. In fact, I was the one who urged his appointment because I knew how brilliant he was. He was a very sensitive personality. He really inspired a lot of good work. There was Herman Chernoff in the Statistics Department. In OR I mentioned the chairman, Jerry Lieberman, who eventually became provost and we were very, very friendly. Al Bowker, I think I mentioned him already. He was an assistant to the provost. He was the chairman, the organizer of the Statistics Department, and eventually became chancellor at Berkeley. He died only a couple years ago. We had known each other even during the war a little bit, but then as graduate students at Columbia. Of course, there was this whole bunch of brilliant scientists who came when they bought the entire Biochemistry Department of Washington University. I didn't know them all well; they weren't close. Paul Berg, and I knew Arthur Kornberg. I know his son now, too. Oh yes, there were people in the business school. I didn't know the deans very well, except, of course, Mike Spence, who was my student. He was a dean for quite a while. A. Michael Spence. I've got a funny story about him. I wrote to Stanford saying oh, he's this brilliant student. I said I've got to tell you that I have a feeling that in ten years he'll be looking for an administrative position and wants to be a dean. So they didn't appoint him. I said, "How come you're not appointing him?" I was absolutely right. He had gotten five to ten years of absolutely first class scholarship, and then he'd become a dean, exactly what happened. He actually became Dean of the Faculty in Arts and Sciences at Harvard. It was a very controversial thing. The President got rid of him there. I'm not sure why. But he became dean of the business school here eventually, and we've had a very good time. He's a very brilliant person.

I've met all sorts of people here. One of my closest friends was in the Applied Physics Department, Marvin Chodorow. He was a real intellectual, with interests in all sorts of things.

Q. It seems like you really admire scholarship, but also administration in leadership.

There are good administrators whose job it is to make scholarship first, and there are bad administrators who want things to run regularly. There's a big difference between them. I admire when they go together. Bowker really knew scholarship, and he knew his job was to promote it. He was absolutely first class. Also Lieberman. These people understood the importance of scholarship. Their job is to facilitate it. That's what I meant. That's what I'm looking for. I think Sterling in his own way, he had his limits, but I think he created the perception of what the university could be like, which I think transformed it, really. Finally, there was, David Kreps in the business school with whom I've been close. He was a great scholar and as an administrator he's also excellent. But he knows scholarship inside out.

Q. Stanford grew from being a good regional university to the great national and international university it is today. What was the role of leadership in this evolution of the university from good to great? What other internal or external factors were responsible?

History is one of those things. You know what happened. If you were to ask what would have happened had you had a different leader, who can answer? I think Sterling bears much of the responsibility for Stanford's rise. There was a perception, held by the board of trustees, that he was not a good administrator, and they kept on insisting that he appoint a provost at Stanford. You know, a lot of universities have not had provosts. That's one of those optional things. Harvard did not have one for most of the time; now it does. The idea is that provost is the inside runner, and the president is, somewhat, the outside influence. We've had some very good provosts. My understanding, what I hear, is the present provost, Etchemendy, is very good, although that's only secondhand. I have no direct knowledge, but people tell me that. One thing that showed up in Sterling's leadership was appointing the Dean of Humanities and Sciences, and he had very high standards, which led to the result that we had no dean. There was a man named John Gardner who is very highly regarded, but he left for bigger things. I think he was a foundation man or something. I think he may have been dean for the first year I was here, but I didn't know him. Sterling appointed an acting dean [in 1952] who was an architect. We had an architecture group here. We don't have it anymore. It was part of the Art Department. What was his name again? Ray Faulkner. Well, first he was an acting dean. He didn't seem to know very much. I remember we had two very good people in Economics ready to tenure, but we could only promote one, and I wanted both. The department denied that. I was chair of the department, and I was pushing for one. Most of the department wanted the other. We're meeting the dean, you see. And the dean took a position that was more or less like the majority of the department. At this point some of the older members of the department resented the idea that this nobody was telling them what to do. The result is I got both appointments. It worked out very well. I was able to browbeat this guy. Well, he had to get permission from higher up, of course he would. Being designated acting dean undermines you anyway, but I didn't think he had the ability to be the dean. But he was there about four or five years at a crucial time. Then the president makes his choice, which is some fellow who had a non-tenured position at Harvard, like an administrative position, Phillip Rhinelander, and they made him dean. That was Sterling's personal appointment. He didn't seem very impressive. Then he got, somehow, into a fight with Sterling over the budget and was holding out for a bigger budget, and he got fired as dean. It was at that point that they appointed Robert Sears [in 1961]. The problem with those two deans was not so much their bad leadership as that there was no leadership. There was nothing there. And that was fine with the Economics Department because we were just going ahead, but it was bad for, say, the Political Science

Department and that was clear. This is an indication about Sterling's administration, and the board of trustees apparently insisted, as I understand it—I was a little remote from this—that they have a provost. In 1952 they appointed [Douglas Whitaker], a rather distinguished biologist. I don't know just how good he was as administrator, actually. Didn't seem to me very strong. But anyway, within a year or two he got an offer from Chicago and went there, not as administrator, but I think as Chief of Biology. So they looked around and in 1955 they decided to appoint the very successful Dean of Engineering, Fred Terman. I think I've already indicated my feeling about that. Terman was the organizer. There's absolutely no question that he had the idea—of course he's not the only one in the United States to have it—that government research money was beginning to come on line. There was this famous report by Vannevar Bush, of MIT I think he was, to promote post war scientific accomplishments, and it sort of drifted into policy. The Office of Naval Research for wartime took the role. Finally they created the National Science Foundation, and there was also government money of other kinds. There were several things, particularly for the hard sciences. Terman really started building up and getting support for mathematics, and support for physics, and laboratories. I don't doubt that he did a very, very, very good job. In my own view, I wondered whether he didn't seem to be very inspiring at all. When I was trying to create the OR program, he was worried about space for it. Somehow, of all the important details, space! In fact, Sterling said, "Oh, he always nickels and dimes." Apparently he could work at the big level of getting the funding and, at the same time, at very, very detailed levels. It's that remark, and some other things, that led me to believe that there was not exactly a tremendous amount of harmony between the two of them [Sterling and Terman], but it was one of these things that didn't matter. The team was terrific with them. I can't believe that Terman could have inspired, or that the president wouldn't have been inspiring. Sterling, alone didn't have the drive to get things done, but the combination of Sterling and Terman did. And they started raising money. They grasped the idea, they were giving away bricks, as I recall, to raise the first big money, or 100 million dollars, big drive. Gradually they built up the university. No question financial constraints were very, very important at that time. And, probably, it wasn't until the '70s or '80s that this university really began to acquire an adequate endowment. Then they really began to build, between investments and scientific funding. And of course Terman was very good about using the land at the university for money, like the industrial properties along Page Mill Road. He saw the potential, although I'm not sure he was the only one to see that. Things were persevering at Hewlett Packard, and then actually built up. I've got to say, a combination of things, I think, transformed the university. The subsequent presidents. Of course, Lyman came in at a time with very considerable troubles with students, the Vietnam War, and all that. Amidst these happenings, Sterling feels it's time for him to quit. One of the problems you see with university presidents and other leaders, is that they stay on too long. Sterling, his time was up, and he quit. It's a new world, and I can't deal with this. If you look, university presidents everywhere had trouble in those 15 to 20 years. It was the time. I think there is a point when you've been successful that you keep on thinking, well I can always surmount these troubles. But the conditions have changed. New conditions after a certain point, ten years, 12 years, something like that. Lyman had recently come in as provost [in 1967] when I left for Harvard, so he was involved in dealing with students. Terman stepped down around '65 because he'd had enough, not that there was any problem. He may have reached retirement age, as a matter of fact. There was a mandatory retirement age, oh yes. I retired at the mandatory age. Of course it had moved up. I was retired at 70, but that was not the age when Terman retired. I think the retirement age moved from 65 at some point to 67 and up to 70. I was retired at 70.

Donald Kennedy was the immediate successor to Lyman and that was disappointing, that he let himself get into problems. I thought he'd be a great president; he was a natural leader. He did have very broad views of things. In fact, something came up earlier at Harvard I'll tell you about. Some president consulted me about appointing Kennedy to a deanship or something. He had only been a professor. I wrote and said this is one of the few people I really admire. I think you should jump at this. I think he may have turned it down, as a matter of fact. I had met him a number of times and I was very impressed with him. I recall that he was terrific in the Faculty Senate; he loved to argue. So if anybody said something, no matter how outrageous, he managed to turn it into a constructive point. No matter what the question was, he turned it into a constructive point. He was absolutely a master. I don't recall that he did anything particularly, but I may have forgotten. Before he got into the indirect cost scandals. That's a whole history, which probably you should get from someone else. Of the different government agencies that give money to Stanford, one agency picks the auditors, so that they have one auditor for all the government agencies. This fellow happened to be from the Office of Naval Research. Kennedy started to raise the, what's the word? What the university charges the research grants—overhead. They kept on raising the overhead rate. I was annoyed because overhead goes for buildings and things like that. But in social sciences it was a piddly amount to begin with. We don't use space. The only thing we use is computers and that doesn't take any space. I felt the university had buildings. They needed lab space, which is very expensive space. They have to build it, in a way. So I said, "Why should we be paying the overhead average? It was technically possible within these government rules to have separate overhead rates, but by broad categories. The government doesn't want to negotiate over every one. You could separate social science from sciences." Anyway, I was a little irritated about that. I remember there was a session of the Senate where we were, arguing this point. Kennedy was generally trying to raise it, and the people with large projects in engineering and some sciences, were more and more antagonistic to him. This auditor was, I think, a little crazy and was looking for problems. He found a lot of stories being told to him by Stanford engineering and science professors. Well one thing that turned out was that among the overhead items was a certain fraction of the cost to maintain the president's house. Because it's a cost, it's got to be distributed among the activities of the university in service. I think it was only 20 percent or 30 percent that was allocated to this overhead rate. But somebody claimed they were buying expensive sheets, $750 Irish linen sheets or something like that, and some kind of a dresser. I don't know what it was. Of course it was all very silly, because the amounts were all trivial. In fact, I happened to mention those sheets to one wealthy woman. She said, "Yeah, that's what I pay. What's wrong with that?"

It turned out that somebody—I think I can guess what the real story is—had given a yacht to Stanford, which they had not sold. It seemed to be pretty obvious to me, I mean, I'm just guessing now, but the fellow gave the yacht, valued it at some high price, and they couldn't sell it for that price, and they felt it might be a problem if they sold it for less than the claimed value, and what would Stanford do with a yacht? The only purpose is they would do is sell it, you see? Anyway, this is a guess. All I know is they gave a yacht; that I do know. Stanford had it, and the cost of running it somehow had gotten into the overhead. Although it clearly was not an overhead item. There are a couple things that happened. Then it turned out Kennedy was having an affair. The upshot was that he had to resign. And it's too bad, but as I said, I thought this squeezing of the research budget was probably not a good idea. I think he was ill-advised, but it doesn't matter who advised him, it's his responsibility. The fellow that advised him was a very honest, honorable person, but I thought it was wrong advice just the same. You see, charging the government for overhead, there's no question there's a lot of flexibility in this. For example, the library is a much bigger body of costs than any yacht or other things. Nobody complained about it, but who works in a library? The library is used by research projects, so you could make a legitimate claim within a wide range, and don't push it, you know? I suppose there was still a concern about the finances at the university. But faculty who were paying the overhead felt that they were getting less money because of the high rate, and they were annoyed. He was not well advised. So while he was punished too severely, there was some legitimacy to this whole thing.

I didn't agree either about the reform of the Western Civilization course. I thought it was again wrong. I don't know about his performance. I would have thought he'd be the greatest president. He had every attribute. As I say, he handled himself so well and he loved to talk to students. He had so many positive characteristics. I'm just a little amazed that it didn't work out so well. I haven't had much contact since.

Q. Being in Silicon Valley, do you think that Silicon Valley and the information industry in particular present unique economic issues?

Yes. The question is: how do you sell it? You're producing a product, but it's a very peculiar kind of product. If I buy a chair, what could I do with it? I could sell it, but then I don't have the chair. I bought the chair because I want a chair. If I have information, I can tell you the information, but I've still got it. This has been around for quite a while, but it's much more extreme now. Newspapers. Okay, it's true that I may want my own newspaper. I don't want a secondhand newspaper from you. It decays rapidly, the value of it. But the one thing a newspaper can do is get your attention, so people can use it to put ads in. The newspaper business for 200 years has been built partly on subscriptions, and partly on advertisements. You know there is a whole part of the newspaper business that has no subscription price at all—local newspapers such as the *Palo Alto Weekly*. And the radio is similar. You can't stop people from listening to the radio, so you can't charge them in any real sense. The British did have a license, if you have a radio you'd have to have a license fee or something. They financed the BBC that way. So the result is the only way to finance is to do something entirely different, and use the attention you grab through advertising, which is a very strange sort of thing. Of course radio is a way in which information is disseminated not only directly, but also indirectly. Television is the same thing on a bigger scale. But now you have this spread of information, and you see the problem with newspapers, which are all losing their circulation. I still prefer the newspapers, but obviously I belong to a very dwindling minority. With internet you're changing from one kind of communication channel to another, so now the question is, who charges? You've got these providers in the middle, and all of this creates an enormous number of problems, which the ordinary kind of selling of the table or chair or even food, does not ascribe to. This shows up in financial markets where people want the latest information. Now if I'm dealing with selling you something, it's a good thing if I know something you don't know, if I've got an edge. I know well that even if it's a ten-cent edge, if I sell you a million shares, it becomes a big business. So you have this extremely high speed trading and it's so fast that you can't have a human being involved, then you go to computers, which, of course, can't be altered so easily, and we have this whole question of the information flow. Now, there's no question it's a tremendous boon, but it comes with a lot of problems.

Q. Higher education has become increasingly expensive and college tuition has been rising even before the economic downturn in the last three years. Do you have any thoughts on that as an economist?

I really should, but I don't. I am very puzzled as to why it is that higher education has gone up so much more. We have inflation, but you correct for inflation. Fees today are, I don't know, maybe ten times what they were in 1945? No, tuition was 400 dollars a year. It's not ten times greater; it's 100 times more expensive. Experts say if you go through the costs of things. . . well, okay. One thing I've pointed out to you, professors teach less. So the Economics Department has many more graduate students but has the same number of undergraduates as it did in 1940. The graduate students just doubled, I don't know, tripled. We have a much bigger department and they're teaching less. So, somehow the universities have gotten fat. The buildings at Stanford when I came weren't a hell of a lot different than they were when Mrs. Stanford died. Some of them had been rebuilt because of the earthquake, but there were very few new buildings. The place is now so different. There's no relation whatsoever. It's different than it was even five years ago because there is a huge business school thing, and it's been going on steadily. Part of that is research; part of it is not research. Part of it is that the student housing is much better. I'm not an expert. I don't really know exactly how to account for it. I'm sure somebody's accounted for it. The cost of tuition, the cost of running universities has become much higher now. One thing is true, that student aid is much better. Of course it has to be. More so in the last few years. Yes, it's been a big change in the last few years. I think it was Harvard that took the initiative and everybody else copied. But the tuition has been high for a while. The tuition has been high for a long while. Then you have this problem with the state universities; they were heavily subsidized and the subsidy is going down. The appropriations per student at Berkeley, for University of California students, are half of what they were a few years ago. That's not just Berkeley, but all of them. It's made up for by increasing their tuition "fees", basically, and this is spreading. England has just had a rewriting of it. In the case of the state universities, I think part of it is other costs, particularly MediCal is squeezing the state budgets. So I think there's really a conflict between giving medical care to the poor or giving university education. You can argue that fact back and forth. It's obviously not ridiculous to worry about medical care at the expense of the universities. But the private universities, which are something like 20 percent of the students I think, roughly, have had this enormous increase in tuition. The economists are accustomed to the idea that high prices choke off demand. That certainly is not what has happened! Of course the truth is, a university education is a very good investment on the average. Students at universities over their lifetimes make that back, easily, the tuition.

Q. Now I have some questions that relate to you more personally. You retired in 1991 under what you describe as a mandatory retirement.

That mandatory time ceased two years later. Congress passed a law prohibiting discrimination on grounds of age. Universities raised a tremendous howl, so Congress said, okay, the universities have ten years to adjust to this. So it was already known that this was going to expire. It's a ridiculous thing to be teaching much beyond that. I cannot say I feel much discriminated against. As an Emeritus professor what I'm doing now is research, basically. What I am doing in terms of academic life, I still go to conferences. I go to research meetings. On the other hand, I have a colossal e-mail correspondence problem. Each letter is much easier to write, but I have to say the number of communications I write in a day is so much bigger than I used to that it makes up for it.

My main research topic, the biggest concentration has been on fundamental economic questions raised by climate change. That's not so much on climate change itself, because, for instance, this place doesn't have a big organized climate change program. It's the sort of thing you only want a few places to do. It's not the sort of thing everybody ought to be doing because it's a very elaborate process, and you need a set of specialized kinds of physicists and so forth. It raises some economic questions on how you judge what you mean by a good project because its concern is for the far distant future. So the fundamentals are something I've been working on with research assistants in a variety of ways. How do you measure it? It's been a big project we just finished on appropriate ways of measuring how sustainable the world is. We're bringing in all sorts of considerations. It's going to be published in the next year. I have been collaborating here with [Economics] Professor Goulder and with students who have gone on and who are now professors at various places. They were not necessarily my students, or they didn't necessarily write their theses on the subject.

Q. In our last interview, we left off talking about your retirement and the research you are working on now. Today we want to continue with more topics of a personal nature. How do you see yourself, Professor Arrow, as a teacher? A researcher? An economist?

I don't know. Let me put it this way, I have aims and accomplishments, and they're not too well aligned. I had the idea of a broad vision of society. I'm a social analyst. I've concentrated on economics, and, of course, it provided a tool and analytical methods I can use. I'm always aware of the limitations of analytical methods, but I've been unable to develop fully a set of insights that reflect both my real sense of what goes on in a social world and the tools to analyze them. So I want to be very careful not to make claims I can't support. Support usually means "support analytically", which restricts what I can do. An early-stage inspiration was the idea that the world is very uncertain, but that you can talk, in a meaningful way, about uncertainty so that in some sense you get a kind of second order effect. One of the things I got from my early statistical interests was the idea that there's such a thing as knowledge, and that you can reduce uncertainty by study. That's of course what the basis of any science is, but also in everyday life, too, we inquire.

This turns out to be very difficult to reduce to a model because knowledge may not be real knowledge; it may be believed knowledge. In other words, we have beliefs rather than genuine knowledge and, rationally, your beliefs should be altered by your experience. The fact is that even from a purely analytical point of view, it's very hard to formulate what you mean by knowledge. It turns out any knowledge depends on what you see, if you put it that way, but also on what you come with. It's been remarked many, many times by philosophers and scientists that, in a sense, in order to think you have to come with preconceptions.

That makes it intrinsically subjective, but then the question is where do these subjective beliefs come from? Even from the beginning of my career, in many ways the question was always the nature of knowledge. One aspect, the one that economists tend to emphasize, is the idea that knowledge is dispersed. People know different things apart from their prior beliefs. Then these different beliefs play out, and the outcome, ideally, might be better than any one person could produce, which amalgamates the knowledge of many individuals. There are a lot of problems with that process, and we see this in the form of recurrent crises. There are beliefs after all about what future securities prices will be, or what the value of homes is going to be, and these beliefs turn out to be wrong. Not just a few individuals being wrong, that's reasonable to expect, but the consensus was wrong. One of the things I was studying in graduate school, which was one of the hot topics of the day in many ways, was the business cycle. That's a term which is still used, but not as much as it used to be. This is the idea that the course of the modern economic system, capitalism, whatever you want to call it, is marked by ups and downs. There are various theories. One theory was that people are just occasionally optimistic and occasionally pessimistic. This produces waves of pessimism and optimism. This is kind of ridiculed because what kind of theory is that? In a way, it's just reposing the question. I find as I read very modern sophisticated models of the economy that say exactly the same thing. If you look closely, the basic assumption is that people have correlated beliefs, as they say. There is belief spread, and maybe beliefs are not so tied to factual considerations.

The other question is, why not? Because then it would look like somebody who could keep his vision steady would make a lot of money by not paying attention. Yet most people don't—it's not just the average person who is not very well informed but even those who you think of as very well informed. So this raises the question of how beliefs are formed. Obviously these things are tied to the fact that people are connected to each other in ways that standard economics, at least, has not emphasized. We think that people are connected just through the market, but the fact is, there's lots of evidence that people are connected in other ways. I won't go through all the details, but the simple example is about jobs. People get jobs because they know people who have jobs, and when there's a vacancy, they get recommended to the boss. More than half of all jobs are still obtained that way, not by advertising, and not by walking to the employment office and seeing if there's a job. There are similar connections in other forms of economic activity.

Several things are passed when you interact. One of them is intimate knowledge and information. There may be more than that. There may be friendship and things of that kind. My vision has been a kind of a view of the world that is not just economic but where other connections apply. From time to time, I venture out with these ideas, but I never can construct what I could call a theory. This has always bothered me because I don't like to put out things that aren't well articulated. For example, I was asked to study, as a theoretical economist, health care. This was a paper that I regard very highly, one of the best things I ever did. I think I mentioned that in fact, a fair amount of my research is the result of people asking me these kinds of questions. I studied Social Choice because somebody asked me a question. A now retired professor, Victor Fuchs, was then at the Ford Foundation, and they wanted to get studies done of social problems. They wanted studies of welfare—in the ordinary sense of the word—of medical care and of education. For each of these areas, they wanted one study by somebody who had worked in the field and one by a theorist, and I'm a theorist who had not necessarily worked with people. In my case, I was asked to work on medical care. I read up on the literature, and gradually a pattern emerged that essentially the parties know different things. The physician knows a lot that the patient doesn't, and therefore the patient can't check on the quality of medical care in the same way we buy a loaf of bread. It's not like I'll buy that loaf again. But with medical care, you can't be sure because you don't know that much. It's the same thing between the insurer and the physician or the patient. So I said that with medical care, non-economic factors, essentially ethical codes, play a role in keeping the system together. But I didn't have a theory at the time, I just had a statement. It was pretty clear to me that non-economic factors do play a major role. What is considered good practice, that's what keeps the system going. The trouble is that I've seen the limits of economic analysis. I could see one solution, but it was very different from market kinds of solutions. But I did have a theory about it. When I look at other people, they don't have theories either, or they have rather vague theories. When I try to impart this to students, of course it's a very confusing message. That's one of the reasons I don't think I've been a great teacher. I've perhaps had students who did appreciate what I was doing, although they tended to pick up the more technical parts of it. I'm a little disappointed they haven't tried to tackle the broader picture. If they're working with it, they've done very fine work, going well beyond what I did. So I'd say that would be a rather lengthy answer to your question. I see myself primarily as a scholar, as a thinker about things, trying to enlist others in this thinking. Yes, I think I would say that more so than others.

Q. *What accomplishments are you most proud of, here at Stanford and beyond?*

My life is a scholarly life, which means in some sense that my universe, or let's say the people with whom I interact, my community—It isn't really the university so much, it's people working in the same field. So even from a very early stage, when I was engaged in this high tech work, it was with econometricians, or mathematical economists, throughout the world. I've mentioned earlier that I was active in the Econometric Society. My teacher, Harold Hotelling,[12] sort of ordered me to join, [laughs] or suggested to me that I join, which I took to be a command as a student. They were then really a small, embattled minority, which has since become very respectable. I went to Europe in 1952 with my Social Science Research Council fellowship, and everywhere there were people who knew my name. The Econometric Society had a journal, and there were these French and English scholars with whom I was already in contact before we'd ever met. We felt we were part of the same group, and certainly, in terms of contact, I felt closer to them than I was to anybody at Stanford. Now that has changed a lot. I'm not, I think, a one-string violin. I was involved in my community here. Being a member of the department, I was concerned about departmental affairs; being a member of the university, I was concerned about university affairs. So I don't withdraw from all these other communities. Obviously, my immediate environment was shaped by Stanford. That was important. Of course I was trying to influence faculty appointments. I didn't do all that well. People were always suspicious. They were fearful that I was pushing for mathematical economics. There were three people who later became Nobel Prize winners whom I recommended and the department didn't appoint.

I didn't withdraw from participating in the affairs of Harvard or of Stanford. But in terms of approbation, it was more the community of theoretical economists that I was concerned with.

Q. What kind of challenges have you faced in your professional life?

I've had a pretty successful life. I cannot complain. There was the problem of recognition of the mathematical field. If I had come a few years earlier, I would have felt very different, because being mathematical was certainly not as popular then. Also, being Jewish didn't matter; it would have mattered three or four years earlier. I can't say I've had any real problems. You can point to things, this and that, but you can't go on with that sort of nonsense. I've had my honors, I think probably more than I deserve. I can't say that I've had any real challenges. I was really surprised in 1952, when all I had done was publish the Social Choice book and one or two very technical papers, that I was already known. When I visited England, even senior people, non-mathematical people, were respectful. On the whole, I can't say that my career, once it got started, was ever a problem.

Q. Were there things you would have liked to have done differently?

I don't know. There are frustrations in the sense that I don't feel I've achieved the vision that I was looking for, the big picture of knowledge and the economy. I've dabbled in one thing and another. I wish I'd done better. But now, even in retrospect, I can't say that it would have mattered if I had read that book instead of this book or spent my time in a different direction. I can't point to any obvious misstep. The challenge is still out there, and I'm still banging my head about it. I did take advantage of jumping to different things, like working at the Council of Economic Advisors and taking on the Institute of Medicine committee on anti-malarials. I've done, at least a couple of times, things out of the groove, and they were all very successful, so I really cannot point to any frustrations.

Q. In all, what have been your most memorable experiences here at Stanford?

In terms of my contributions to Stanford, the creation of the Operations Research Department was probably the most significant thing I did for the university. I feel very proud of that. I have memorable experiences but they were scholarly experiences. There are a number at Stanford, but if I were somewhere else, I would have had them too. There were some exciting things—I worked with Gerard Debreu[13] [1983 Nobel winner] on general equilibrium theory, which was very exciting. I mentioned the healthcare projects. Stanford was the locale but not necessarily the. . . . Well, your work is so much part of your whole community as an economist. In terms of contribution, I think that's probably the biggest thing.

Q. You are considered a highly abstract mathematical economist, but some people consider you a humanist, a scholar who has always tried to apply fundamental theory to social problems, such as medical care and insurance, education, race discrimination, water resources, climate change, and more. Do you see this as a dichotomy?

No. I think the abstract thought comes from these concrete cases. It's finding similar patterns in diverse things. In fact, if anything it characterizes what I'm really good at—finding mathematical structures that are common to things. I've always felt a very strong concern about the problems of mankind, if I can put it a little grandiosely, poverty and, of course, healthcare. Later on I began to get an appreciation of exhaustion of natural resources, the climate change issue which I was pre-disposed to because of my student training as a meteorologist.

These are all examples. These were problems, and it seemed to me that for most of them, even quite standard economic tools could be quite useful. I was trying to find common patterns so that what you learn in one field could be applied to another, and so forth. Of course, you've got to respect the differences. I thought healthcare had developed special codes of behavior and practice that enabled it to survive, which may not be applicable to other branches of economic activity. You have to be subtle about this sort of thing. I've been interested in human beings.

When I was very young, before I was ten or 12, I was only interested in history and astronomy or something like that. But beginning with adolescence, I became very interested in literature. I was reading novels at a very early age, and they made a big impression on me. I can still remember the excitement I felt when I read certain passages and that I still have when I read a piece of prose, or a beautiful poem, or see a work of art. An appreciation for art and music, that took a little more time. I was already doing those courses at university, by the way. Everybody had to take a course in art and a course in music. Both of them made a big impact on me. We don't do that here at Stanford but music was important in my home growing up. My mother used to play the piano and my younger sister was quite a good pianist. I never thought the fact that I would enjoy reading Dostoevsky was in any way contradictory to my mathematical interests.

Q. *When receiving the National Medal of Science in 2004, you were quoted as saying that you were glad economics is considered a branch of science as important as physics or chemistry. Can you expand on that?*

That probably was a little bit of a push for recognition of the field. I don't remember making that statement but I don't remember many things. For example, just the other day I ran across a reference to an unpublished paper that I wrote, and I have no recollection of it whatever. So my memory is not so good. I don't think economics has the—well, I'm not saying the certainty of science—but you know I had an argument with a physicist about a year ago—I ran into him at some meeting—and he was saying he was thinking of writing an op-ed piece attacking economics as being totally unscientific. "Why do you call it unscientific?" I asked. "You can't predict." I told him, "I was a meteorologist and that's applied physics after all, and there was not much predictability there either." [Laughs] I think it set him back a bit. Then I said, "What about all this universe? You say 65 percent of the universe is dark energy, and you have no idea what it is."

He's got a point that physicists have come up with astounding things. Economics, when it is convincing, most will say, "Well, yes, but it's kind of common sense." It hasn't achieved that kind of knowledge, but I think economics is intrinsically a more complex phenomenon. I was struck by that when I was studying meteorology. It didn't look any more scientific; it didn't look any more predictable. There was an awful lot of science, but from the point of view of predictability, meteorology didn't look any better than the economic forecasts.

Q. You were vocal on social issues like signing public and joint letters on healthcare costs and the budget. Do you see yourself as a public intellectual, in the sense that you bring your knowledge and expertise to address problems in society and do so in a way that can be widely shared with society?

I think I would like to be that kind of public intellectual but I have not succeeded. I don't have a public presence that is known. One thing that disappointed me—when I finished the paper on anti-malarials, I wrote an op-ed piece. I submitted it to several papers, but nobody bothered to publish it. I think one characteristic I have, at least this is my interpretation, is that I'm always seeing the other side. Even though I think we should spread the anti-malarials, I can see there are problems. Even now there are problems but I won't go into that. The United States government isn't supporting it, and it's not for selfish reasons that I can see. There's no pharmaceutical company that really cares about this issue. I think it's just a wrong policy but it's not because of special interests. My statements come out kind of cautious instead of dynamic so I think I've not had an impact as a public intellectual.

But I do sign statements. I do join in them, but signed statements opposing going to the Iraq war didn't do any good either. The outcome was much worse than anything I imagined. I thought it was going to be bad. It was worse.

Q. You are known to be knowledgeable in many diverse subjects; how do you do that?

I can't answer that question. I have a reputation for knowing all sorts of things. I don't always think in my mind, what can I say; I don't make an effort, I don't think, but there are these legends about me. I think some of this is legendary. Some of the stories I find very hard. . . . Well, one thing is this. When I was a student at college there was a professor of philosophy—Morris R. Cohen—who had exactly this reputation, that he knew everything. The story goes that his colleagues were a little tired of his knowing more about everything so they decided that they would bone up on some subject that he knew nothing about and have a conversation. They decided to talk about Chinese armor in the middle period. So they all read up and started discussing it at a weekly get-together. He said nothing. One of them then said, "Oh, Professor Cohen, we haven't heard any of your comments." "No," he said, "I'm just glad you all read my article in the *Encyclopedia Britannica*." I assume that was an apocryphal story. Cohen really did know a great deal, but the story itself was funny. In a discussion on the breeding habits of Pacific gray whales, I am supposed to have pointed out that a recent article had refuted the statements others were making. I've been assured that I said it. I cannot really remember it; doesn't even seem credible to me.

Q. My observation is that you are a great reader and that you have a good memory.

Well, I do remember an awful lot, and it's not photographic memory. I don't remember the page exactly. I read things in some order, and they come back, but I can't explain how or why it happens.

Q. Are you studying anything today that's not in economics?

Not really. I still read novels and things like that. There are a couple of books on physics I've been meaning to read, but [laughs] I've got them on my shelves.

Q. I understand you have a wide variety of interests, including music, which you mentioned. In fact in 1980, you were in the Savoyard's production of Ruddigore; do you remember anything about that experience?

Well, believe me, it was not musical. There was a scene where the ancestors appear, and the producers decided to make it interesting, to get well-known people on campus, the chaplain [Robert McAfee Brown] was dressed as a bishop. We sang but they carefully brought the chorus behind the scenes to sing along with us. I totally lack the capacity for singing on key. I can hear it. I can't correct it, but I can hear it. I know how badly I sing. It's been so throughout my life. My mother had me take piano lessons but the piano teacher, after a few months, said you're wasting your money [laughs]. So I have absolutely no musical capacities. I'm no good at acting either. But I enjoy music.

Q. What was it like to be in a family full of economists, including your wife, your sister, brother-in-law and nephew, Larry Summers?

My wife was studying economics but she became a social worker. Her career has been as a social worker. My sister, my brother-in-law— well, my brother-in-law, of course, was a student of mine. It makes very good conversation. My sister was majoring in economics before I was. I was majoring in mathematics in college. By the time I was a graduate student she was already in college and was taking major economics course already. It's a little unusual that we ended up in the same field. I don't think we had much influence on each other but who knows.

Q. Is economics often a conversation topic at the dinner table when you're with your family?

Not really. It has been, on occasion. With Larry I talk economics frequently. I used to talk to Bob, but it was one-on-one, not at the dinner table. I would talk to Bob or to Larry, one-on-one, or to my sister, but those would all be one-on-one conversations.

Notes

1 All interviews in Chapter 1 were conducted on Stanford University campus, during the fall of 2011 by Jane Hibbard, as part of the Stanford

University Oral History project. We are grateful to Stanford and to Hibbard for allowing us to edit and publish these here. Full transcripts of these interviews can be found in the Stanford University Library. Interviews for the rest of the book were conducted by Nicholas Lampros and Kristen Monroe. Transcribed interviews were shown to Kenneth Arrow for approval and verification on dates, names, etc. We followed Arrow's decisions on all such verification.

2 Arrow's parents were Lillian and Harry Arrow, of Romanian Jewish origin.

3 On September 14, 1930, the German federal elections were held. The Social Democratic Party lost seats but retained its majority, winning 143 out of the 577 seats in total. What was significant, and the event that frightened many, including Arrow's mother, was the increase in the number of seats held by the Nazi Party, which increased its seats from 12 to 107, which strengthened Nazi power and influence in Germany. Since the anti-Semitism of the Nazi party was clearly spelled out in Hitler's *Mein Kampf*, Jews throughout the world had reason to be worried.

4 An official Treaty of Non-Aggression between Germany and the USSR (Union of Soviet Socialist Republics) was signed, quite late in the day, on August 23, 1939. Because the two signatories were Joachim von Ribbentrop (for Germany) and Vyacheslav Molotov (for the USSR), the pact is frequently referred to as the Molotov–Ribbentrop Pact. Arrow was born on August 23, 1921.

5 A Polish logician, mathematician and philosopher (1901–1983), Alfred Tarski was educated at the University of Warsaw. He was a member of the Lwów–Warsaw school of logic and the Warsaw School of Mathematics. Visiting the USA at the onset of World War II, Tarski stayed and worked at Berkeley until his death. Tarski was accomplished in a wide range of fields, from metamathematics, analytic philosophy, and algebraic logic to model theory, abstract algebra, mathematical logic, and set theory. His work changed the field on twentieth century logic, especially his work on the theory of models and the concept of truth.

6 Olaf Helmer (1910–2011) was a German-trained mathematician and logician who did important work in the development of economic forecasting and prediction. Helmer worked at the RAND Corporation and co-founded the Institute for the Future.

7 Harold Hotelling was a mathematical statistician and an important economic theorist, born September 29, 1895. He taught mathematical statistics at Stanford, Columbia and the University of North Carolina at Chapel Hill until his death on December 26, 1973. Hotelling is perhaps best known for his rule or theorem, which states that the most socially

and economically profitable extraction path for a non-renewable resource is the one along which the price of the resource, as determined by the marginal net revenue from the sale of the resource, increases at the rate of interest. This rule describes the time path of natural resource extraction which maximizes the value of the resource stock, and was presented in a 1931 paper. It is widely used in research in the field of non-renewable resource economics and in public choice analyses.

8   A mathematical statistician and an influential theoretical economist, Hotelling (1895–1973) taught math at Stanford from 1927 until 1931, when he moved to Columbia University and then the University of North Carolina at Chapel Hill. Harold Hotelling is known for his leadership of the statistics profession, in particular for his vision about the importance of statistics, and he played a key role in convincing several universities to establish statistics departments. He played a key role in introducing math and statistical analysis to economics.

9   Abraham Wald was a mathematician born in Cluj, in present-day Romania (then Austria–Hungary) on October 31, 1902. His work contributed to geometry, decision theory, and econometrics. Wald is often credited with founding the field of statistical sequential analysis and, as Arrow states, taught and did research at Columbia University.

10   Wesley Clair Mitchell (born August 5, 1874) is best known for his empirical work on business cycles. He later headed the National Bureau of Economic Research in its first decades. Mitchell died October 29, 1948.

11   Arthur Frank Burns (August 27, 1904–June 26, 1987) was an economist who went back and forth between academia and government. From 1927 to the 1970s, Burns taught and researched at Rutgers University, Columbia University, and the National Bureau of Economic Research. He served as chairman of the U.S. Council of Economic Advisors (1953–1956) under Eisenhower, as Chair of the Federal Reserve (1970–1978) and as Ambassador to West Germany (1981–1985). He and Mitchell published *Measuring Business Cycles in 1946*. This work initiated the characteristic NBER methods of behavior business cycles. The method Burns began for determining recessions is still held authoritative in dating recessions. In the late 1940s, Burns asked Milton Friedman, then a professor at the University of Chicago, to join the NBER, where Friedman served as a researcher on the role of money in the business cycle. The detailed macroeconomic analysis Burns had developed influenced Friedman and Anna Schwartz in their classic work *A Monetary History of the United States, 1867–1960*.

12   Harold Hotelling is known for his leadership of the statistics profession, in particular for his vision about the importance of statistics, and he played

a key role in convincing several universities to establish statistics departments. He played a key role in introducing math and statistical analysis to economics.

13   Born in France in 1921, Gérard Debreu published a breakthrough paper in 1954 with Arrow, entitled *Existence of Equilibrium for a Competitive Economy*. This paper provided a definitive mathematical proof of the existence of a general equilibrium. Their work used topological rather than calculus-based methods. Debreu received the 1983 Bank of Sweden Prize in Economic Sciences in Memory of Alfred Nobel, for his rigorous reformulation of general equilibrium theory and for his work incorporating new analytical methods into economic theory.

2

ON ETHICS AND ECONOMICS

You asked initially if I could tell you about how I ended up doing economics and, more specifically, how I came to develop social choice theory and got interested in ethics at all.[1]

To say that I'm interested in ethics is probably just to say I'm a human being. You're brought up full of ethical concern; these things are part and parcel of life. The real issue is whether you think about ethical concerns rather than just accept them. Will you raise the level of consciousness? Of course, if you raise the level of consciousness there's some kind of dilemma. You find yourself with something that doesn't seem quite as straightforward as you thought. This is a very general observation. It doesn't speak to right and wrong, which are part and parcel of my past attitudes. This sometimes leads to counterintuitive things like trying to take advantage of immediate situations. I was, for whatever reason, concerned from a pretty early age about issues like poverty, the inequality of income, topics like racial bars, which of course were very common in the 1930s when I was coming of age; they were quite overt. Now we have a whole set of techniques in economics for detecting whether racial discrimination exists or not. You didn't need any of that in the 1930s; everybody was perfectly open about it. Everybody just said there were certain jobs, certain places to live depending on skin color. There was the

racial question, the fact that there are large inequalities of income—
a point which came up in the election politics—this took the form
for many students, to some extent myself, of being radical on social
activities of one kind or another.

On top of that, there's also what I call the practical failures, the
efficiency failures of the economy, which were manifested in 25 percent
unemployment rate, for example. These were things which, apart from
justice, made you feel that the system wasn't functioning properly. So
that's the background for me, a background that of course was not in
any way unique to me. Many students were brought up in this sort
of milieu. But a lot of this evaporated in the post-World War II
prosperity.

I also had the habit of trying to get things into logical order. That's
my talent. I like to connect things which seem to belong to different
realms. I see the parallels. I'm rather good at that. That's what I think
my talent is. As Louis Pasteur once said, "Chance favors the prepared
mind." I trained myself, and was trained by others to say, "There's
the logical consequence." One of these came up in the post-war period.
I was involved among other things in working for the RAND
Corporation[2], which was worried about the possibility of nuclear
annihilation and any other possibilities with regard to our conflict with
the Soviet Union, which I felt was personally very important. In spite
of my leftist views, in many ways I took very early the opinion that
the Soviet Union was a tyranny, and was not the beacon of justice
that many of my fellow students felt it was. Of course, many things
came to light both during and after World War II which made the
situation even worse than I had thought it was.

Of course, one of the questions that came up was: "Well, what do
we mean by the United States' interests?" The United States is an
abstraction. The country is composed of a lot of people, with different
interests, just as the Soviet Union is. The question was raised to me
by Olaf Helmer at the RAND Corporation, and I said, "There had
been an economic literature on 'When is a policy justified?'" Let's say
we're discussing imposing tariffs or some kind of taxation policy. When
is it justified? A lot of very able people had written on this question.

So my friend at RAND said, "Well, why don't you explain it?" As soon as I tried to explain it, I realized that there were some fundamental problems with the explanations that were in the literature. Rather unfortunately, from my point of view, what came out was an impossibility result. I wasn't looking for impossibility; I was looking for an answer. I tried a number of answers and none of them worked. When I thought about what I meant by saying they "didn't work," I realized I meant there were certain implicit criteria in my mind, or I think in general in people's minds, which mean finding a good way of putting people's different preferences together to form a social preference. Then I realized it couldn't be done under the rules I was working with, rules that I thought were very reasonable and that I thought were very appealing to most people. That experience led to my social choice theory, or my impossibility theorem about the impossibility of social choice. In a way, it was kind of a setback to any ethical consideration. Of course, I did have the general economist's conviction that values ultimately inhere in people. They don't come from the outside. I realized as I read more philosophical literature that this view is by no means accepted, that philosophers, particularly liberal philosophers, particularly ones that I'm most sympathetic with, are writing down what they think the good life is. Rawls for example—I'm skipping in time, of course, because Rawls published a good deal later—argued that majority voting doesn't have any particular significance.[3] Things are either good or they're not good; the fact that the majority of people agree or not is not terribly relevant.

I thought it was a bit shocking, because I had this inherent view that the aim of a society is not to have values imposed but to represent the actual values of the society. So this gave rise to the other questions: How do you represent the values? How were the values formed? These were questions that I found very difficult. I thought they were very important, but I didn't have anything to say about them. Having already shown impossibility, I wasn't in the mood to create new impossibilities, so I preferred not to say anything and I busied myself with what I thought economists could say about various things, such as what we could say about risk bearing. I regarded the task of economic policy as to remove the obstacles to the free expression of people's preferences. If the market isn't doing it, then there must be other ways of doing it. This gives rise to the whole discussion about the market failures and government expenditures. Well, this problem keeps on popping up, even in the most practical problems. It's one thing that's led me back to somewhat more fundamental discussions in the more general question of provisions for the future. When you provide for the future, especially the long-run future, markets clearly don't work. They don't work because a lot of people whose interests we're concerned with aren't even here. They can't express themselves on the markets. This is a question that's bothered me for a long time, almost from the beginning of my career. But I've always put it aside. Now I'm coming back to it. This is a concern dramatized by the climate change issue. But in many ways this question of markets and the interests of future generations exists in other forms; the climate change issue is not the only example.

There is a literature on what is called optimal savings that is in a broader sense provision of the future. You find almost everybody's written on it. It gets at some point into ethical questions. There was a classic paper in 1928 by Frank P. Ramsey, the English philosopher and logician who dabbled in economics a little bit.[4] His was a very strong statement about our responsibilities for the future. According to Ramsey, it is just taken for granted that future people count the same as present people. He had an ingenious method that sidestepped some of the issues. At least it appeared to sidestep the issues. But as you look more closely, you realize he didn't really sidestep the issues. You just didn't notice that at first. In fact, in other essays on different subjects, even he took the conventional point of view, which is that the future doesn't look like the present. It's like looking through a telescope; it's farther away so it's not as important. There's a dilemma of this kind that people are still struggling with. There's a new and important work on climate change that came out last year by the British, under the leadership of Nicholas Lord Stern[5]. This work essentially took this old English attitude that the future people count like the present people. I'm exaggerating a little bit but that's more or less it. Do you really mean that? I look in other ways at the logical implications of that of that position and say, "Do you really want to build your models on that assumption? Do these satisfy you?"

Another problem that has struck me—and which more recently has been the focus of my research—has been the problem of direct connections among people. That is, how does a consideration of one person's welfare affect another's? One way I have approached this topic in the past is the question of income distribution. I referred a few minutes ago to the individualistic basis. I don't like to have values imposed by philosophers. So then how do we explain, for example, what justifies some sort of intervention in income distribution? Well, it's got to be based on individuals. Rich individuals feel they have to give some of their income away. Of course, there is some evidence that this actually happens. I won't go in to it in a great detail here, but there is, for example, a literature on voting for schools. People without children vote for schools; they vote to tax themselves for schools. Rich people who send their children to private schools vote for public school expenditures. Things like that. So there is some evidence on this question and, in a sense, you can reduce the issue to individual preferences. I'm less and less satisfied with this; I'm more and more convinced that this isn't the whole story, that people are connected with each other in some intrinsic ways. Coming back to the time reference: if the people who are here now are really part of our community, but people who are far away in time—or in space for that matter—aren't as much part of our community, then somehow the sense of felt responsibility is less.

In the particular chapter I wrote for this first book (Monroe, 2011), I was stressing the family. Economists haven't discussed the family so much because in a sense it hasn't been regarded as problematic. It's not that people neglect the family. The family is so dominant that people just take it for granted. But of course the family is now becoming more and more problematic. Illegitimacy rates are much, much higher than they were even 30 years ago. Society is undergoing a very rapid transformation compared to what the situation was years ago. The question of responsibility to parents has changed. But I'm more concerned with the responsibility that's been socialized in a way. Social security, Medicare, things like that. There are a lot of problems with that, but having the state get involved in issues like this does mean that certain parts of the problem are being addressed in a certain way. But the relationship of parents to children, the model of the indissoluble marriage with children, this model doesn't really fit much anymore. So the question of relations with children, responsibilities for children, have become much more problematic. Of course this mixes in with ethical questions. It's also mixed in with just ordinary descriptive questions, with what does happen. We have some evidence—considerable evidence I think—that children are adversely affected by shifts in family patterns, but without any good answers as to what our responsibility is, given these shifts. The state, or the church, or some institution has always been a bit of a guardian. Perhaps its role is more than a bit. That certainly has been claimed. Certainly, it's been recognized implicitly that this role of institutions—such as the state—is a matter of public concern. It's recognized that other people, acting through the state, have the right to interfere in these personal family relationships. (So the police are called in to investigate instances of child abuse, for example.) Presumably most of the time there's no conflict between private desires and public desires, so this problem isn't acute. But I think it is becoming a significant problem in this world. There are also the responsibilities of the children through other mechanisms like education, and we have some problems in that respect also. The question is whether you can replace personal relationships with impersonal institutions. That's a major question here. So there's a whole complex set of issues for economists here that concern our ties to others. Even the description, even just predicting what the economy will do, depends in part on the ties we have to other relatives and to our response to these social ties. This is both an economic and an ethical question.

I hope that answers your question about how I got interested in ethical issues.

Q: Let me back up and ask you to comment on a few things that occurred to me as you were talking. One was that it seems as if you see economics as a

*broader discipline than it is traditionally conceptualized. The traditional view,
one that I think a lot of economists have, would consider what you are doing
as part of a broader enterprise that deals with ethics. Is that correct?*

I think so. Yes. I think I'm not alone in this move. One of the things
that is becoming increasingly recognized, just as a purely descriptive
matter as opposed to any normative consideration, is that we can't
describe the economy properly without reference to these social ties.
And these involve us in ethical ties. Well, they're partly ethical. You
feel you want to help members of your family; if you hear about a
job opportunity you convey it to those who are near and dear to you.
So the ethics of individuals has a descriptive power, an explanatory
power. For example, it's true *today* that most jobs, to this day, are filled
by personal references. There's somebody in the company who finds
a vacancy and recommends somebody. To this day more than half
of jobs are filled that way. Not by responding to advertisements or
what you might call the market. It's conditioned by the market. The
market plays a role, that's true. But there are behavioral ties, school
ties, all these relationships that enter into the hiring equation and all
of which have an ethical component. You feel, "Well, I ought to do
something for somebody I know." Indeed, in spite of our meritocratic
and impersonal criteria, most people understand that. It's not
condemned to the same extent. Obviously for some purposes you want
to avoid this kind of personalistic hiring, minimize this. Ethical ties
in the small can certainly have negative consequences for justice in
the large, because the impersonal, the faraway person, is discriminated
against. Nevertheless, we understand the nature of these ties and we
respect them in many ways. What did you ask me exactly?

Q: I was curious about your concept of economics.

I think that one thing is that even an economist who's interested solely
in predicting what the economy will do, or what would happen if
you made such and such a policy, even such an economist will have
to worry about these issues, and I think that's a matter of increasing

recognition, purely as an empirical matter. Now, of course, there was an attempt, which I certainly was a part of it, to suppress the ethical aspect of economics, to say, "Well, we're ethically neutral. Here's the fact. You want to do this? OK. This is what will happen. Do you like that outcome? That's up to you."

But the fact is that almost every economic decision has always had values built in to it. One of the difficulties is that people have different values. There's an attempt to do things that will get a broad agreement and, therefore, in order to build a consensus you may come to the same conclusion for different sets of values. You don't want to let the disagreement on values prevent your agreement on policy. But of course the opposite is also true; it can work either way. Many of the leading economists have certainly had strong ethical considerations. Milton Friedman had a very strong ethical commitment. He was pretty explicit about it. He frequently tried to argue, "Oh well, even if you don't agree with me on the values, this will be a good policy from your point of view as well as mine." But nevertheless he did have very strong views on his conceptualization of freedom. I won't go into a long discussion of his conceptualization of freedom. I don't agree with it, but nevertheless he had strong views on these matters.

Q: How would you characterize your differences with Friedman on that point?

First, I think that his concept of freedom was much too shallow. The idea that low income is a restriction on freedom—something that I think is a fairly elementary point—is something he just never recognized. His idea of somehow equating the market with freedom, well, I don't think they're unconnected but to assume it's a simple matter—as he seemed to assume—is to my mind disregarding the facts of life, and disregarding the values that are put on these ideas. Now Friedman did make some exceptions. He thought extreme poverty was a subject of government policy, but by and large I think this emphasis on freedom is misplaced because it has very little to do with the freedom of the individual, with the individual employee. It was the freedom of the employer, of a minority, that really he was pushing.

I think freedom's important. I certainly wouldn't say freedom's an unimportant matter. But the question is: What do you mean by freedom? Expanding the scope by which people can act is an important matter. And it was not just income transfers and other methods. I think Friedman let himself make rather absurd statements, like for example he opposed the licensing of physicians on the grounds that it was a restriction on freedom. So this is an illustration of how his narrow conceptualization of what freedom means led him to kind of absurd statements.

Q: There was a great deal of time, at its inception as a discipline perhaps, when economics spent a great deal of time talking about the kind of distributional issues that I think are more the ones that have occupied your time. Then there was a period when economics as a discipline tended to move away from those concerns and became more technical and narrowly focused, certainly after the Marginalist revolution. I was doing some reading before the interview and came across an article that called you one of the founders of neoclassical economics, by which I assume they mean the movement I associate with the Chicago School in the mid-twentieth century. What do you see as the essence of neoclassical economics, and how does that relate to the kinds of distributional questions that I think have occupied your professional life, versus the kinds of issues that the Chicago school, under people like Friedman and Gary Becker, have followed?

I wouldn't claim to be a founder of neoclassical economics, and neither is Friedman. The origins are much older than that. It really is a late nineteenth-century development. The creators are people like Alfred Marshall, Jevons, Walras, and Pareto. I taught the history of economic thought for a number of years here, not that I'm a scholar in that field, but I like the subject and I'm acquainted with it, and the written histories are just full of inaccuracies. It's amazing.

Q. So you'd characterize yourself not as a founder of neoclassical economics but rather as a follower of neoclassical economics as a tradition or an approach to economics?

Yes. The neoclassical tradition is carrying out what is the role of rational behavior in an interacting economy, where people are interacting with each other, but interacting through the market or market-like conditions. One of the themes has been that the market is a pretty efficient allocator. Efficiency is a somewhat technical concept but presumably people agree it's a good thing to have an efficient economy. Though the question of how the fruits of the economy are distributed may be questioned. Now, if you look at the founders of economics, many of them believed in state intervention. They weren't laissez-faire advocates. Alfred Marshall, who is maybe considered the creator—if there is one—said "I believe in laissez-faire. Let the State be up and doing." Laissez-faire applies to the state. The state should be active, too. Most of Marshall's successors have tended to be people who believe that for most things let the market operate, but you have to regulate it, you intervene with the fruits of the market. This is more or less my philosophy. You tax transfers. It suggests that certain methods of intervening are likely to be more efficient than other methods of intervening. But certainly the idea of not intervening at all is not in the standard neoclassical tradition.

There have always been groups that have taken a more extreme view, who argue that the state is the enemy of anything good. But that's not really the standard view. So actually I consider myself more mainstream in this respect than Friedman.

Q: Do you think the economics profession is moving away from the Friedmanite approach? Where is economics as a discipline going right now, at the beginning of the twenty-first century?

It's going in several directions, as it should. The economy's pretty complex, and simple economics probably would never work. It's just a lot of aspects. One topic that economics as a discipline is now considering concerns the relations among countries. One of the traditional views, of economists of almost all kinds, is that we should remove the barriers to international trade. On the whole, I think there are problems with that, but there are big gains as well. But both countries and people object to it on several grounds. One objection is that free trade is sometimes bad for the poor countries and the other view is that it's bad for the rich countries. You saw that in the primary campaign for the 2008 US presidential election. The Democratic primary campaign was one where both Clinton and Obama agreed that you should rewrite the NAFTA agreement, which is sheer nonsense in my viewpoint. So on the one hand we're told that the workers of rich countries are going to lose out in free trade; on the other hand, in some of the poor countries they say, "We've got to protect our workers from the workers in the rich countries who have all these machines." Well, it sort of cancels out and by and large the free trade argument prevails. But it's not as though it's an unqualified matter. But by and large I think the free capital movements are somewhat similar. There's a little more of a problem there and I don't want to give you a lecture on that.

Now, on the other hand, take something like securities markets or now the mortgage markets. The problem is not so much the mortgages as the securities that were built on the mortgages. It's clear that we've deregulated. Well, not so much that we've deregulated pre-existing markets but rather that we created new forms which have not previously existed and now need more regulations than they have achieved. So there's an example where the market can create instabilities in a way that I think was predictable. In fact, I must say I've thought this for a long time. The new forms of securities and contracts (mortgage-based securities and credit default swaps as leading examples) can create damages and problems for the economy well beyond those that were immediately involved in the market. It's one thing to say, "Well, you buy a bad security, that's your problem." But the trouble is we've got a financial system where people who weren't involved at all are hurting. For example, if there's a credit crunch then businesses are affected, and they lay off workers who had nothing to do with the original security at all. That's the point we really want to worry about, these indirect repercussions.

We do have, of course, a rapidly increasing inequality of income in most of the advanced countries of the world, the United States very conspicuously, and the United Kingdom, a country which used to be a bastion of equality. Less so in Northern Europe, but Italy is very bad. It seems to me that this is a disgraceful situation. What I'm astounded with is that the people who would benefit from lower taxes, who would benefit from raising taxes on the rich, are not enthusiastic about it. This finding is out of my area of professional expertise. I don't understand the politics there. There's no enthusiasm for taxing the rich. Many people think, "Oh, higher taxes, that's bad." Even though they're not paying it. Even though the taxes aren't falling on them at all.

Q: Do you understand the psychology behind the failure of the poor to demand a higher tax rate for the wealthy?

No, I don't. It's a mystery to me. There's a very conspicuous example in California about 15 years ago. We had an estate tax. There's a federal estate tax. There's also a California estate tax. It affected roughly 5 percent of all estates. Actually, I don't think it was even 5 percent of the estates that were affected. There was an initiative to abolish the estate tax, and it passed. Now, how do you explain a tax which falls on 5 percent of the people being abolished by the majority of people?

Q: I wonder if one of the explanations is that the majority of people think that they may at one point be in that category?

Well, yes. I think that's the explanation. But why should they think that? I'm sure that there's some idea—in fact it was true at that moment, housing prices were rising rapidly, a lot of people felt that they could project that their house and land would get them into the taxable area. But even if they did, it would be a very small tax. Meanwhile, there are these people with huge estates that would be taxed far more. Anyway, there is an interesting question where we see what we think of as an ethical question arises from a counterintuitive finding. It's an area where the beneficiaries, the people who we think need to be helped, don't see it that way. This creates a very interesting ethical dilemma for a democratic society if you also believe in democracy. All you can say is that the only thing we can do is just keep on explaining that inequality can be reduced by mechanisms like education, but we have some problems in that respect also. The question is whether you can replace personal relationships with impersonal institutions.

Q: This is interesting to me. I think your approach to economics is one that's very centrally grounded in philosophical assumptions about human nature, ethical concerns, and also a deep understanding of human psychology.

I hope we have that, yes. I do. One of the big tendencies in economics today is to take account of the irrationalities in individual behavior. That's not something that I'm directly involved in myself, but I applaud the fact that other people are doing such work.

Q: You mentioned that there are several directions that economics as a scholarly discipline is going now. What are those directions, the ones that you see as most interesting or potentially fruitful?

One of them is this field of behavioral economics that I just mentioned. That's capturing a lot of attention. With it is a methodological innovation: the use of experiments. I'm a little leery about experiments because the experimental situation is so far from the real world, but I've got to say that a lot of these experiments have been very illuminating. They don't have the same role that experiments in science have, but they are very indicative, and they've been very useful. So the behavioral economics movement has given economics a big additional source of information.[6]

Q: The experiments will then involve us in the whole question of, "what's the difference between behavior in an experimentally controlled situation—insofar as you ever can control it in economics or social science generally—and how people behave in the naturalistic setting?"

What it does is that it suggests hypotheses that you can then try to test in real-life situations. Frequently it turns out that when you're alerted that you still find real-life situations which you hadn't thought about before. That's one aspect. I think the emphasis on social interactions as a determinant of economic behavior is getting much more steam now than it had, although it's a recurrent theme in economics. It goes back to at least Thorstein Veblen and the *Theory of Conspicuous Consumption*.[7] The whole question of social effect is getting a much bigger play now. It's harder to get evidence on that, because the situation is too uncontrolled, but we do have a lot of evidence about behavioral effects, about effects on consumption. People consume like their neighbors. When television was new there were a spate of studies about how the use of television spread. What was clearly true was that if someone near you bought a television, then you were more likely to buy a television set. You can't test that now because everybody has a television set. There's nothing you can control, no variance in the dependent variable. But it's really the transitional things where you're likely to get some data. Of course, from a serious point of view, the questions are what we consider antisocial behavior, or even self-destructive behavior: addiction, dropping out of school, child-bearing at an early age. With all these kinds of antisocial behavior, the social effects are great. The fact that people affect each other is a serious consequence. It's very difficult to study for a lot of reasons, but there's a lot of evidence on the importance of such phenomena. But the question of whether this kind of experiential evidence can be the basis of forming public policy is less clear.

Q: Both of those movements that you mentioned, the behavioral economic experimental movement and the social interactions movement, are very closely related to social psychology, or psychology more broadly defined.

Yes. In fact I have been a little disturbed because I think the social aspects are more important than the individual irrational behavior, and the latter has been easier to study and has been driving the social aspects out. But they're both important.

Q: One of the things that I found in my own work, when I was looking at how people made moral choices, was that there seemed to be less of a rational or conscious component and more of a spontaneous behavior. We seem to act out of our sense of ourselves, particularly how we see ourselves in relation to other people at the moment of action. I wondered if you had any thoughts about that kind of behavior and how economic theory can deal with that kind of spontaneous, non-conscious behavior.

Well, the usual interpretation of economic behavior is that when we use the word rational, we don't imply that people calculate, it's just that their instinct displays some consistency. Their direct behavior is rational. But there are counters to the point that you just made. One is that your actual behavior may be overly influenced by the immediate context. You're making a decision that has future consequences, like going to school, and you make it in a very immediate context. So the things that are stimulating you at the moment, the environment, could have a disproportionate effect compared to the future consequences which you're aware of. In some sense you're aware of them, but do you give them less weight because they're not immediately present to the mind? I think that's a very important matter. There's a fundamental dilemma, I think, with studying human behavior, and that's that there's innovation. Even in your small way, every time you make a decision you're thinking creatively. Creative thinking by definition is unpredictable. Now obviously most of the time you go and engage in activities and people observe you and say, "Oh, well, this is what he or she has done in similar situations before."

But every now and then, maybe some very small element of the context has changed. You don't say, "Oh, let me rethink." You don't say anything; you rethink it without knowing you're rethinking it. Obviously on a big scale we have this problem that in the long run the economy is determined by technological innovation. By definition, innovation is unpredictable. If it were predictable it wouldn't be innovation.

Q: Let me ask you about a couple of things you mentioned that I didn't know too much about. We were speaking about the process of bringing economic ideas into the broader world, making changes in our lives based on insights derived from economics. In that context you mentioned the Pontifical Academy of Social Science. Can you tell me more about this group?

The Pontifical Academy of Social Sciences is different from the Pontifical Academy of Sciences, though the two academies share administrative staff. The Social Sciences academy is of quite recent origin. I'm not sure of the dates, but the Pontifical Academy of Social Sciences started somewhere around 1994. Earlier, Pope John Paul II decided to put out an Encyclical on social policy. It was the 100th anniversary of a famous encyclical, Rerum Novarum, by a nineteenth-century pope, Leo XIII[9], who first put out an encyclical to show that the church had social concerns, arguing that it was a concern of that church that the poor have to be protected, and unions are really a good idea, a few things of that kind. So Pope John Paul II issued his Encyclical on the 100th anniversary. I think it was called Centissimus Anno, the 100th year. Somehow he assembled a group of economists. He called upon some Catholic economists, among others, who then brought in a more general group. We had a couple of meetings which were essentially informally advising on this topic. The majority I'd say were non-Catholics, Jews. Buddhists, Protestants—well, I suppose most of us were really irreligious in fact. An outgrowth of that was the idea of creating an academy. I really don't know who proposed this within the Catholic Church.

Let me back up. The idea is that the teaching of the church represents the application of general principles in specific circumstances, and the church doesn't claim any knowledge of economics as such. If you want to translate the ideas into policies, you would need experts. That was the theory behind the Academy. A leader in all this was a French economist named Edmond Malinvaud, who is a religious Catholic but is also someone I've known. He's my type of economist: a theorist, a man of great energy. He's done a lot of administrative work. Edmond was given the lead. I mention economics here since that's why I got involved, but of course it was an academy composed of people who advise on all of the social sciences. This came into existence somewhere around 1994 or 1995, something like that. Edmond was a good friend of mine, and he wanted a certain representation so the Academy was created with a handful of non-Catholics. I was one of them; I have been ever since.

Q: So the goal, the charge of the Academy is to take the essence of the church's teachings and to try to give expert advice on how these teachings can be put into practice?

I can't say it's worked out that way but that was the theory. What happens is we more or less pick topics and we talk about them, and people will write papers drawing upon the literature and surveying it. We'll take a theme, it might be labor, the role of labor, the concept of personality, what person-hood means, what the rights of the individual are. It's kind of an erratic, shifting assemblage of knowledge. We've never really been asked, specifically, to focus on any particular topic. The idea is that we prepare what are background papers, which are not published, but printed up and made available.

Q: How do people get them then if they're not published?

They're printed, very nicely printed in fact, but they're not published. How can I describe it? There is a difference between printing and publishing. There's no commercial distribution. They're not sold. Copies are available within the church. Honestly, I don't know how they're distributed, and to whom. Now that you ask the question, I realize that I don't know what happens other than that I get a copy. How the material is distributed outside the members of the Academy, I don't know. I must say I don't have the feeling we've had any great impact.

Q: But the impact is mostly supposed to be within the church itself, not within the broader society?

Yes. That's the theory, yes. The paper is given at the Academy, and duly printed. It's certainly not published, but it is quite handsomely printed, if I may say.

Q: Presumably the idea of obligations one has to children within a Catholic hierarchy of priests where no one marries would have a limited impact anyway.

No, no, no, the hierarchy is very concerned about the family structure; I don't think that's a fair statement.

Q: I was being facetious.

There's no question about the involvement of priests. A significant fraction, maybe 20 percent of the Academy, is priests. On the other hand, the president of the Academy is a woman—after Malinvaud, the second president was a woman. I concede that the church is making a big point, to say that women are involved. She's a professor at Harvard Law School actually. In fact, she has recently served as the United States ambassador to the Vatican State.

Q: You were also one of the conveners of the Intergovernmental Panel on Climate Change, is that right?

I served on two of the panels, yes. The Intergovernmental Panel on Climate Change has governmental representation. The governments send people. What happened is that the then Chairman of the Council of Economic Advisors under President Clinton, Joseph Stiglitz, called me up to ask whether I would go, whether I would participate.[10] They had to nominate somebody to a panel; would I be the nominee? Would I accept? Of course he knew my attitudes and, in fact, he has the same attitudes I do. So I served. Then the panel breaks up into working groups, and I was on one working group, and then we finally decided that some parts of it were really a little incompatible; they didn't fit so well with other parts. So then we broke up into two groups and I was on both of them. So I participated on two of the reports and helped write them. I was what's called a "lead author," which means there were four or five lead authors.

Q: I see. Now, the basic purpose of this panel, as I understand it, was to certify that there are experts in a field and that this panel of experts would reflect what is the accepted wisdom. Is that correct?

Yes. Including expressing diversity of opinion, of course. That's correct. And in particular there's a panel on economic and social problems connected with climate change. That was the one I was involved with. I was involved in some working groups of that. I forget the terminology they use. There's the whole Intergovernmental Panel, which consists of three parts, I think, and then within the part relating to social and economic sciences there are groups within that which work on specific topics. This takes place every four or five years. This was the '95 report, something like that, 1995 or 1996.

Q: How does one go about setting up something like this? I've thought about how important it could be to establish an analogous group for scholars working on genocide and ethnic cleansing, given some of the unscholarly work that has come out on the Holocaust, work I would consider falling into the category of undocumented, unsubstantiated Holocaust denial. It would be wonderful to have a group of scholars who had widespread scholarly and political legitimacy who could act as an early warning system to alert the public, throughout the world, when a genocide is beginning to occur, perhaps increase the probability of the world responding in an appropriate fashion. So my question about how you establish this kind of network is not just an idle one. I am very curious about your insights on how scholars become more formally linked, and whether or not you need funding to do this sort of thing?

Well, this still does depend on funding, yes. The Pontifical Academy, for example, is not a very heavily financed organization, nevertheless they do have to pay my airfare to Rome, and expenses for putting you up. It's certainly not a very richly endowed thing. The Intergovernmental Panel is different. As its name implies, it is financed by the governments. They do assemble regularly. Now there's a danger to that sort of thing. It's a good thing that that research from which the reports are drawn comes from a variety of sources, because if it was all done by governmental sources you could imagine the problems. So the funding is a very tricky matter. You become beholden to the funders. The Pontifical Academy is a little different; we don't do fundamental research. The discussions there by the way are very open; that's not the issue. There's another group I'm connected with, in fact, of a similar nature, somewhat less formal, but again it depends on resources. There's an Institution in Sweden called the Beijer Institute for Ecological Economics.[11] Beijer is a wealthy family—I don't know what they manufacture, but they manufacture something—they're a rich family, let's face it. But they were induced to endow an institute for studying the intersection of ecology and economics. It was originated by an economist. It's one of these things that embodies Emerson's dictum: "Every institution is the length and shadow of one man." Which is not to suggest that I think this dictum is generally entirely true, but in this case it is. Karl-Göran Mäler was an economist by training, but right from his dissertation he was very much involved in ecological concerns. It's the Beijer Institute for Ecological Economics. As a result of these contacts I'm a little better at pronouncing Swedish names than I used to be.

Q: Is this an Academic Research Institute, do they give degrees, is it just a think tank or . . . ?

No, it's a research institute. In fact it's physically located at the Swedish Academy of Sciences. There's a complex in Stockholm. Mäler decided to start bringing in economists. In fact, I'm going to leave in about ten days for a meeting—and at least part of the time, we meet on a small island in the Stockholm Archipelago. I don't know if you know Sweden at all. There's a big archipelago about 120 miles long going out from Stockholm into the Baltic. About halfway down is a marine research station. The man who was then the director—he's since died, unfortunately—got the idea of being the host of this thing. So we meet on an island that you can walk completely around in less than two hours. It's rather primitive. It gives you an appropriate setting. The meeting is growing. Of course we're trying to be worldwide; particularly, we're trying to encourage people from developing countries to attend.

Q: Is it just academics who go?

Just academics, yes.

Q: My oldest son is currently living just outside of Warsaw, working for a company that tries to develop eco-friendly energy. It is interesting how the ecology and the economics have to intersect before we can solve some of these problems.

Yes, that's quite true. Also it turns out methodologically that we're not that different. It's all about interacting systems. Even some of the concepts—competition for resources and things like that—are common to the two groups, common to both economists and ecologists. Indeed, Darwin had his big inspiration by reading Malthus. The prefix "eco-" is not an accident. This is an example of a network, like your altruism idea. It took someone with initiative and with some financial backing. But in this case the backers are not trying to run anything, they just gave the money. Mäler's retired now, but I hope the project will continue. It's really dependent on Mäler's vigor.

Q: It's hard to institutionalize some of the enthusiasm and creativity and drive you find in certain individuals, isn't it?

Yes. I hope this particular enterprise continues all right. So far it's—well it just happened a year ago so I haven't seen the effects yet. This is an example of the kind of networking thing you were talking about. We've been issuing statements that sometimes get attention and sometimes don't. The idea is to be academically correct, and not to be propagandistic, and say what we know, or think is right, and to indicate the diversity of viewpoint.

Q: Let me ask you a question that's closely related to something you said. You've talked about ethics as usually raising dilemmas. I think in a lot of areas ethical issues aren't simply just a question of will or moral courage. Do you find that?

[A long pause] Well, yes. [Another pause] One way of looking at it is moral courage; the other way is "what's feasible?" That is, feasible given the attitudes of others. Most of these ethics, or at least the kinds of ethics I'm concerned with, are social ethics. Where a number of people have to do something for it to matter. My good behavior isn't enough to do anything. If I personally put solar cells on my roof and live off that, that's not going to really make an important difference to anybody. The impact depends on a lot of people doing it. The same thing is true about crime, about poverty, or charity, for example. It depends on collective effort in some sense. One thing I find, is say there are two policies. One I really think is only going to do a little bit of good, but I can get everybody to go along. The other is going to be very good but nobody wants to do it. There may be good reasons; there may be bad reasons. Take Darfur. Somebody's going to have to get killed to do anything in Darfur. And as soon as you start with that policy, of course it leads into the other problems. Will the interveners behave perfectly? Of course they won't. As soon as you start unleashing force, you can be sure there will be a lot of killing. You know, we had to fight Hitler, but we did an awful lot of killing. Which, in retrospect—I'm talking about aerial bombing—which, in retrospect doesn't seem justified. People are still arguing over the A-bomb. You can make arguments for things like the A-bomb. Japan was pretty evil in China in the period around World War II; their intentions toward us were hardly good. But nevertheless. Well, you can imagine the sort of things you can argue. You can really argue that the atomic bomb saved a lot of Japanese lives.

Q: *Do you have any guiding principle for yourself when you approach issues like these?*

As I've said, I have this difficulty of seeing both sides of things, of seeing different aspects to a problem. That makes it difficult in retrospect. I think there are things that are clear, or at least clear enough so you can make a very strong case. And sometimes my position has been a minority position. I don't think we should have gone into Iraq, for example. I thought that then, right away. But it was a balancing sort of thing, you know. It's just that I was totally unconvinced that Saddam Hussein had anything to do with 9/11 and I didn't see evidence that he had weapons of mass destruction. That's all. But under other circumstances and had the facts been different, who knows. I did what I could, which is to sign statements, which doesn't do any good. But in a lot of cases it is extremely difficult to know how to decide since you are balancing evils. I'm not thoroughly convinced that our policies in Kosovo are correct. That's one I really have great difficulty with. The Albanians have a right to independence; the Kosovars have a right to independence. On the other hand, there are Serbians living right there, historically. There are Serbs there, and I find that to be a very tough question, including the precedent problem. I think Bosnia was clear and Kosovo is not.

Just to give some actual cases. My view, for example, is that the inequality of income in the United States is growing at an alarming rate. This is wrong, in my opinion. Ethically wrong. I mean the differences now between what the upper 1 percent of the population gets and what everyone else gets is just growing by leaps and bounds. That's been going on for 30 years. I don't think it's the fault, by the way, of the government, but the government can take corrective actions. And now, what do you do? All right, here's something I'm pretty clear about, I know what I advocate, but it's interesting how impossible it is to get anything done.

Q: So what would you advocate?

If you say, "Yes, class warfare, right, sure, the poor have a right to squeeze the rich," that's going to fly like a lead balloon today. Furthermore, if you unleash that sort of thinking you can create problems because it will go too far. It's a very difficult matter.

Q: So then, politically, once you add that dimension, what would you advocate in terms of income distribution?

Well, the idea of increasing taxes on people who make over $250,000 a year strikes me as a minimum. And estate taxes and so forth. Having said this, I should add the following. One of my problems is that I think that my ethical views may not be right. Or, to put it another way, I have no right to impose my ethical views on others. The ethics itself should be a decision that is democratic in some sense of the word. Ethics need not necessarily represent my opinion, but should represent a widespread opinion. So even though I may think something is right I'm not sure I have the right to impose that view.

Q: That's very interesting. What are the core values? You just said things should be decided democratically. Is that a central core value to you?

Yes, I would regard it as a very core value. When I read philosophers who set down ideal states I cringe a little bit. Who are we to say?

Q: But if a society decides democratically to do the kinds of things that Hitler did, for example. . .?

That's the other side, exactly. It's true, Hitler came to power by legal methods. He didn't quite have a majority, but enough people accepted him that he legally came to power. Legally. There's a real problem there. Obviously there are situations in which it's clear to me that I don't care what the majority says. That's quite clear, I agree to that statement. Therefore, that's what my problem is. On one hand, I feel I shouldn't impose my ethics on everybody. On the other hand, I'm not necessarily willing to take the voice of the people as the voice of God. That leaves me a little bit up in the air. I don't have a consistent answer.

Q: You said you aren't religious. Do you have any core values or ethical principles that guide your own individual life that then get applied into the public domain?

Well, I certainly try to. The question of going out of your way to help people in small ways then carries over into my ideas. Even though

I'm clearly one of the people who would be hit by the kind of tax program I advocate, I still advocate it. I believe in it. I certainly am worried about any time that we talk about the use of force. I'm concerned about the people who are going to receive the force. Even though I think they may be evil, or I may not think they're evil. There are always going to be instances of what we call collateral damage. There's no way of avoiding it. Of course I would accept the principle that we have to accept some disadvantage by not torturing.

Q: You are, as far as I know, the youngest or one of the youngest people to win the Nobel Prize in economics. You wear your fame very lightly, as far as I can tell. One of the things I've noticed is that fame, money, beauty, power all can separate people, they get in the way of human relations. How did you avoid this in your life? You don't seem to be someone who's driven by the desire for fame. How did you avoid having this get in the way of your human relations with people? And second, what was the most important thing for you in your life?

I don't know exactly how to answer your first question. I've certainly always felt that I was a very good student but that didn't entitle me to be superior. I've always felt there's a lot in other people and intellectual superiority is simply one characteristic among many. I've always admired people who were very comfortable with themselves; I'm not quite so comfortable. I don't know quite what to say, other than that I feel that no one should put on airs. I'm still uncomfortable when people introduce me as a Nobel Prize winner or something like that. I can't say it's anything I'm doing; it's just the way I feel.

Q: I deal with this with my children. I've tried to explain to them that everybody gets a certain number of gifts and everybody has a certain number of weaknesses. You get that wonderful throw of the genetic dice and you should accept gracefully the things you do well and not feel bad about yourself when you can't do something well.

One problem I had—well it wasn't a problem actually, but one aspect of my youth was that I was a terrible athlete. I don't mean I was missing physically, I mean I was way down at the bottom. If you had a race, I'd come in last. I just thought, "Well, I'm good at this and I'm bad at that; that's all." I didn't get worried and I didn't take airs. I didn't feel that the other was inferior. You asked a second question.

Q: What were the things that were important in your life? A lot of people are driven by something, by the desire for fame, the desire for power, money, whatever.

[A long pause] I'm really reflecting on your question because I haven't put it that way. I think it's just a desire to understand. I just enjoy learning things. Learning, I don't mean. . . I like to systematize, not just memorize. To put them together. I have this characteristic, even when I was young, I treat everything like it was geography; in my mind I'd try to put the things on a map. When I was reading history I'd try to make up genealogical tables, of the kings of England or something. So I had this tendency to try to systematize things, to try and understand remote sounding things.

Q: I was struck though, I was thinking about the conversation we had before. It reminded a little bit of the introduction to Bertrand Russell's autobiography. Russell talks about three passions having driven his life.[12] One was the love of mathematics, but another was a concern for the unbearable suffering of people, and that had always brought him down to earth and had given a different twist to his enterprise beyond the kind of intellectual curiosity that I think you're describing. It seems to me that there's a strong theme of that concern for others in your work, too. Everything you talk about is always connected in some way to how we treat other people. Your approach to economics has a very strong ethical or humanitarian concern.

I think most people who get into economics, no matter how cold they seem, most people have a concern of that nature. I don't think it's unique to me. They do have that concern. Now they might see it in different ways—look at the long run and not the short run, that sort of thing—but I think most of them would tend to view economics that way. They're concerned. Maynard Keynes had a toast once, saying that economists are the guardians, not of civilization, but of the possibility of civilization.

Q: That's a nice toast. Let me shift the conversation a bit. I remember when you were at Irvine two years ago, you mentioned in a conversation that you have two children and that you were always home. That your wife worked and you were the one that was home in the afternoons when the boys came home.

I don't want to exaggerate it. My wife had more of the responsibility.

Q: Still, I thought that was unusual for someone in your position, certainly at that historical point in our culture.

I'm not sure of that. I really could think of others. It's a modern day and age, people do the sharing. I wasn't there all the time or anything like that but I did take turns. Particularly it was really more when my wife was going to school. She always practiced from our home. Well, that's not quite true.

Q: What does she do?

She's a psychotherapist. I was home most of the time, anyway. I'm being slightly inaccurate. I would adjust my schedule, but I'm sure she did take on more of the responsibility than I did, but I did take on a fair amount of it, anyway.

Q: One of the things that's interesting to me as a female academic, I'm always interested in how people manage to combine career and family and marriage. It seems to me that there are very few people who are able to pull it all off, and have a really good marriage, a really good family life, good relationships with their children, their parents, and a good career. Do you know many people who've done this? Do you feel you've done this and, if so, how do you think people put that together? Is it just luck? Is it serious commitment?

I'm trying to think if I know anybody where it didn't work out. One thing I learned about the scientific method is that in order to say whether something happens, find examples of where it didn't work out.

Q: Well, there must be many of those, don't you think?

I guess there must be, but I'm trying to think among my friends, and I don't really know. Now it's kind of standard, it's the norm. I mean there are problems with academic life, with two jobs, it's called the "Two Body" problem, there are problems of that kind. Maybe I'm being too cheerful but I can't really remember. Let me say, before there were two-career families, there were plenty of unhappy marriages. There was no shortage of unhappy marriages, so I'm not sure that marital relations were really all that altered by this phenomenon. There are a lot of other problems with marriage today. I may be wrong, but among my acquaintances I can't really recall many examples. I certainly know divorces and unhappy marriages, but I don't think I can think of anyone where the two careers was the big issue. It only worked in one way: it permitted the wives to live. That I think is true. It made it possible. But I don't think it was the conflict, at least in the cases I know, that it really added to the thing. I've known plenty of unhappy marriages—my parents for example—where wives didn't work.

Q: Let me rephrase the question. How do you think people manage to have good relations with their children, good careers, good marriages? How did you do it? What were the factors that made that happen?

I can't answer your question. We did what had to be done. The kids were there. We took care of them. We were with them. The main problem may have been that we were too involved with them. I don't think that's true actually, in our case; I think we were careful. But there is this force-feeding which I see among people younger than I am; it's not really my generation that does it, but a younger cohort who do this force-feeding of the kids. It's the opposite, the over-involvement with the children, not the neglect that I think had been a serious problem in previous generations. I don't think we did this; nor do I think that it's very common in our generation. I don't want to claim any credit because it seemed to me it was quite normal. I've known some children who went bad all right, but it's not clear it was due to parental neglect. You certainly had drugs among a lot of children, but I can't say it was in any way obvious to me that it was the parents' fault.

Q: Let me ask you one last question then I should let you go. Do you think about your legacy at all? I mean, Adam Smith had put on his tombstone "The author of The Wealth of Nations."[13] I assume that's not something you're going to put down on yours, but do you have a sense of what you are leaving behind? Are you pleased by that, and what would you like to still do?

All I can think of are the things I wish I had done and hadn't done.

Q: And what are those?

Well, for one thing, I should have gotten more involved in empirical work. I should have contributed to the amount of data being collected, which I never did, because I'm so good at theory and that's easy. But I didn't quite have the attention. But the other thing, which I'm trying to do something about now, is to think about the role of social relations in economics. I'm not alone in this; it's a significant movement emphasizing the role of what's called networks. That's the word that's usually used in this context. The standard case still today is that most people get jobs through references, not through some kind of market transaction. But people who have been studying this question—the question, for example, of how things like stock markets operate and how news travels—find it travels in ways that aren't reflective of the market. The economists say that people communicate through prices, and while this is a big story and I think a very important story, it isn't the only thing that's happening. There are just all sorts of examples like this. So the emphasis of the role of non-market relationships is getting increasing recognition. We don't have a good vocabulary. We economists don't have a good set of analytic tools for this and that is the problem. There's a lot of shoddy research on this. The six degrees of separation story isn't really accurate. But it's got in mind a certain truth, which is very elusive. There's something there we don't quite understand, at least the way it's there. I could go into all sorts of intellectual issues about this question of social interaction. But I think this is the part of the economic equation that we don't grasp.

The problem is that it's easy to talk about prices or easy to talk about goods since you can measure them in tons or get some idea of satisfactions. But we don't have the units of measurement for social interactions. This is something I'm increasingly interested in. The way the ethical concerns play out with regards to something like the family is a particular example of this. As you can see from my essay on the obligations of parents to children, it's there. It's a problem. It's a peak that hasn't been climbed. So what I hope is that what I do will be built on. That's what scientific progress involves. What you really hope is that you stimulate a new growth which makes yours obsolete. It's a great process.

It's been one of the great glories of humanity, I think, this idea of scientific progress. It's really only a few hundred years old, and I think it's a sharp break from our past. Like everything else it's got bad consequences, but most of them are good.

Notes

1   All interviews in Chapters 2 and 3 were conducted by Kristen Monroe and Nicholas Lampros, between the summers of 2010 and 2013.
2   The RAND Corporation is a non-profit policy think tank, so named for **R**esearch **AN**d **D**evelopment. It was first created to provide research that could be used by the US Air Force by Douglas Aircraft Company, although now it receives funding not just from the US government—its main client—but also from private individuals, pharmaceutical companies, universities, and a private endowment. It works on a wide variety of non-defense-related issues. RAND employs over 1,600 people, mostly in the US (Santa Monica is its headquarters). At least 32 winners of the Nobel

Prize, primarily in economics or physics, have been associated with RAND at some time during their careers.

3   Published originally in 1971 and revised in 1975 (for translated versions) and again in 1999, *A Theory of Justice* reflects John Rawls's attempts to solve the problem of distributive justice by utilizing a variant of the social contract. Rawls derives a theory characterized as "Justice as Fairness." Rawls begins by assuming that the most reasonable principles of justice will be those that everyone would agree constitute a fair position. Rawls then uses thought experiments, including the famous veil of ignorance example in which people are asked to design a system of justice in which they do not know where they will be located, the idea being that if one has to devise a system behind such a veil of ignorance over one's own place, one will be more likely to design a system that is fair to all. Rawls intended to determine what constitutes a fair agreement in which "everyone is impartially situated as equals," in order to determine principles of social justice.

4   Unbelievably precocious, Frank Plumpton Ramsey (1903–1930) was a British philosopher, mathematician and economist. Dead at 26, Ramsey nonetheless was a close friend of Ludwig Wittgenstein, and was instrumental in translating Wittgenstein's *Tractatus Logico-Philosophicus* into English. A friend of Keynes, Ramsey is remembered by the Decision Analysis Society, which annually awards the Frank P. Ramsey Medal for outstanding work in decision theory and its application to real decision problems.

5   Stern holds the I. G. Patel Chair at the London School of Economics and Political Science. Appointed the Chair of the Grantham Institute for Climate Change and the Environment, a research center at LSE, in 2006 Stern worked with a team at the British Treasury to produce "The Stern Review Report on the Economics of Climate Change." The Stern Review argues for immediate reductions of greenhouse gas emissions as necessary to reduce the worse risks of climate change. Several important economists praised the Stern Review, including, Sen, Solow, and Stiglitz. Other equally respected economists—including William Nordhaus and Ken Arrow—took issue with certain aspects of the Stern Review. Arrow accepted Stern's conclusions without agreeing with his analysis. This idea—that the Stern Review is "right for the wrong reasons"—seems a fairly wide-spread criticism.

6   The original founders of economics made close links between the disciplines we now call economics and psychology through their assumptions about human nature. After the Marginalist revolution in the late nineteenth century, economics moved away from this close relationship with

psychology and relied closely on the rationality assumption, assuming that people essentially acted to pursue their perceived self-interest, subject to information and opportunity costs. Beginning in the 1960s, cognitive psychologists concerned with decision theory began to question the assumptions of the economists' models and began experiments on the brain as an information-processing device. Amos Tversky and Daniel Kahneman compared their cognitive models of decision making under risk and uncertainty to economic models of rational behavior, challenging the assumptions of the traditional economic models. Prospect theory (Kahneman and Tversky 1979) used cognitive psychological techniques to explain several important ways in which human decision making diverges from neoclassical theory (Kahneman 2003). Cognitive psychologists who address economic issues using cognitive, social, and emotional factors to understand how consumers, investors, and borrowers make economic decisions and how these affect market prices, returns and allocation of resources make up what is now known as behavioral economics. The main topics in the field concern the limits of rationality (self-control and selfishness) among economic agents. In 2002, Daniel Kahneman's award from the Nobel Committee, for his work with Amos Tversky to integrate insights from psychological research into economics, especially experimental findings on how people make decisions under certainly, signaled the arrival of behavioral economics. Work on behavioral economics now deals with topics such as the verbal framing of choice, direct-acting and verbally governed contingencies, and how fairness and altruism weaken the neoclassical assumption of perfect selfishness.

There is a difference between behavioral economics (and its ability to apply psychological models to enrich economic models) and experimental economics (which uses experimental methods to study economic questions). Not all economics experiments are psychological and not all behavioral economics uses experiments; behavioral economists rely heavily on theory and on observational studies "in the field." Recent trends in behavioral economics now use fMRI (functional magnetic resonance imaging) to try to determine which areas of the brain are active during various steps of economic decision making. Some of these experiments try to simulate market situations—such as the trading at auctions or on the stock market—to isolate the effect of particular biases on behavior. Work in this area has emphasized three main themes: (1) heuristics, suggesting that people do not follow a strictly rational analytical approach in making decisions but instead follow approximate rules of thumb; (2) framing, suggesting that the way in which a problem is presented to the person making the decision will affect the outcome, hence a decision framed as 1 out of 20 chances of success is responded differently to from the same situation framed as a 95 percent failure rate; and (3) market inefficiencies, which explain observed market outcomes that are contrary to rational expectations and market efficiency, such as mis-pricing.

Behavioral economics has had a tremendous impact on economic theory by revealing the cognitive biases most of us have and how these result in strong anomalous effects in the aggregate, especially when there is a social contagion of emotions that seem to then cause collective fear or euphoria that results in economic panic, herding, or mass selling.

7   Thorstein Veblen was an American *sociologist* and *economist* at the turn of the twentieth century (July 30, 1857–August 3, 1929). Veblen worked in what is known as institutional economics. He is perhaps best known for his criticism of capitalism, as found in his best known book, *The Theory of the Leisure Class* (1899). Veblen's contribution to economic thought combined a Darwinian evolutionary perspective with the new *institutionalist* approach to economic theory. *The Theory of the Leisure Class* combined sociology with economics to argue that there is a critical distinction between the productiveness of industry (run by engineers) that manufactures goods and what Veblen held was the parasitism of business, whose existence is designed only to make profits for a leisure class. Drawing on the excesses of the Gilded Age and the Robber Barons, as well as anthropological work on potlatch, Veblen argued that the main activity of the leisure class was "conspicuous consumption," in which people try to demonstrate how much wealth they have by wasting it in elaborate rituals such as debutante balls and parties. Their major economic contribution is "waste," an activity that contributes absolutely nothing to productivity. Veblen's critique of the American economy held that it was made inefficient and corrupt by such conspicuous consumption.

8   The Pontifical Academy of Sciences originated in the Accademia dei Lincei (the Academy of Lynxes) established by Pope Clement VIII in Rome in 1603. Interestingly, the leader of the Academy was Galileo Galilei. Dissolved after the death of its founder, the Academy was recreated in 1847 by Pope Pius IX and called Accademia Pontificia dei Nuovii Lincei (the Pontifical Academy of the New Lynxes). It was re-founded in 1936 by Pope Pius XI, at which point it was given its current name. The Pontifical Academy of Sciences is not currently involved in the social sciences. There was in fact a conference on growth economics in the early 1960s but not, of course, since the creation of the Pontifical Academy of Social Sciences. Since 1936 the Pontifical Academy of Social Sciences has investigated specific scientific subjects in individual disciplines—*such as economics*—and has attempted to promote interdisciplinary co-operation.

An independent body within the Holy See, neither Academy is restricted to church censorship and both enjoy freedom of research.

9   Pope Leo XIII was born Count Vincenzo Gioacchino Rafaele Luigi Peci on March 2, 1810. The 257th Pope. from 1878 to 1903, he reigned until his death at 93. The third longest pontificate, Leo's was known for its intellectualism and the development of social teachings with Leo's Encyclical Rerum Novarum, which helped define the Church with regard to modern thinking. Leo's efforts helped reconcile the Church with the working class, which had anti-clerical and socialist sympathies. Leo opened soup kitchens for the poor, a bank to give low-interest loans to low-income people, and founded homes for homeless children and elderly women.

10   Joseph Stiglitz was awarded the Nobel Prize for economics in 2001 for his work on screening, a technique Stiglitz refers to how one economic agent obtains otherwise private information from another. Stiglitz found information asymmetry in the market. In contrast to neoclassical economics, which finds markets are always efficient except for minor and well-defined failures, Stiglitz reversed that presumption, arguing that markets are efficient only under exceptional circumstances. This means that whenever information is imperfect and markets are incomplete, even competitive market allocation will not be Pareto efficient. This means that government intervention can bring about Pareto superior outcomes, making everyone better off. This makes the optimal range of governmental interventions much larger than is recognized by the traditional "market failure" school of economics. Effectively, Stiglitz argues that markets do not work well in the presence of externalities, situations when an individual's behavior impacts on others but for which an individual neither pays nor is compensated. Further, Stiglitz suggests these externalities are widespread since there is almost always imperfect information or imperfect risks. For Stiglitz, this makes the critical debate not one between market or government but rather one about finding the correct balance between the government and the market. His most recent book—*Freefall: America, Free Markets, and the Sinking of the World Economy*, by Joseph Stiglitz and published by W.W. Norton—criticizes the Obama Administration for rearranging the deckchairs on the Titanic rather than taking the bold regulatory reforms that are needed and advocated by Arrow. Stiglitz's remarks when accepting his Nobel Prize suggest the need for a fundamental change in the prevailing paradigm within economics, one that makes central the kinds of topics Arrow outlines in our conversation.

11   The Beijer Institute is funded by the Kjell and Märta Beijer Foundation. It is an international research institute focused on ecological economics, under the auspices of the Royal Swedish Academy of Sciences.

12 In the beginning of his autobiography, Bertrand Russell writes:

> "Three passions, simple but overwhelmingly strong, have governed my life: the longing for love, the search for knowledge, and unbearable pity for the suffering of mankind. These passions, like great winds, have blown me hither and thither, in a wayward course, over a great ocean of anguish, reaching to the very verge of despair.
>
> I have sought love, first, because it brings ecstasy—ecstasy so great that I would often have sacrificed all the rest of life for a few hours of this joy. I have sought it, next, because it relieves loneliness—that terrible loneliness in which one shivering consciousness looks over the rim of the world into the cold unfathomable lifeless abyss. I have sought it finally, because in the union of love I have seen, in a mystic miniature, the prefiguring vision of the heaven that saints and poets have imagined. This is what I sought, and though it might seem too good for human life, this is what—at last—I have found.
>
> With equal passion I have sought knowledge. I have wished to understand the hearts of men. I have wished to know why the stars shine. And I have tried to apprehend the Pythagorean power by which number holds sway above the flux. A little of this, but not much, I have achieved.
>
> Love and knowledge, so far as they were possible, led upward toward the heavens. But always pity brought me back to earth. Echoes of cries of pain reverberate in my heart. Children in famine, victims tortured by oppressors, helpless old people a burden to their sons, and the whole world of loneliness, poverty, and pain make a mockery of what human life should be. I long to alleviate this evil, but I cannot, and I too suffer."

Our question thus actually misquotes Russell, substituting mathematics for his search for knowledge.

13 The tombstone reads: "Here are deposited the remains of Adam Smith. Author of the Theory of Moral Sentiments and Wealth of Nations: He was born 5th June, 1725, and died July 17, 1790."

3

THE GLOBAL ECONOMIC MELTDOWN OF 2008

By now I know that you believe economics has a lot to do with ethics, in all kinds of ways, not the least of which are the distributional aspects of economics. But economists also are frequently asked to explain current economic situations, such as what we might think of as the economic meltdown of 2008, to take just a recent illustration. How would you explain what happened so that someone who is educated and concerned, but not a professional economist, can understand it? I say that because I need someone to explain it to me!

To be frank about it, you can give all sorts of superficial explanations. The trouble is, if it's a real explanation, you should have seen what's coming. Nobody did. We have to say that we're not prepared to give an analysis.

The one thing that's been true, and it's been true through the whole history of the capitalist system, is that we have recurrent problems. There are actually two somewhat different kinds of problems. We have alternations of prosperity and depression. Every now and then, the economy seems to go down. One of the things that happens in these situations where economic activity goes down—and this manifests itself in things like unemployment, low opportunity, a little less production —is that there are people capable of working and there are plants and machinery capable of being used and they're sitting idle. This has been a recurrent feature of the economic system.

On top of that process but slightly different—although the two are related—is what is called the financial crisis. Capitalism depends on credit and the use of money. In particular, the use of credit. We borrow money to be paid back later and the terms of the pay back are of a tremendous variety. It could be a situation where the creditor can demand his money whenever he wants to. A bank depositor is a creditor of the bank. You can demand your deposit back whenever you wish. Sometimes you get the money immediately, other times it's within 24 hours. A lot of financing has created some problems. So we have credit instruments of all kinds. Sometimes the credit instrument is in the form of bonds that go for 30 or 40 years; the old railroad bonds were 100 years or more. So there are many different kinds of credit instruments, which means essentially that I give you money. You can use the money to spend or invest or whatever. You can use it to buy a house, to buy a machine if you're a business man, or just to pay your workers because you're not going to sell your product until after you have to pay them. So for all these reasons, there's a gap.

I don't want to give a lecture on monetary economics because it's complicated, but in a financial crisis, sometimes the system freezes. People somehow can't pay, and if they can't pay one person, that one person then can't pay other people, and you get a chain reaction. This has happened even in the eighteenth century, but certainly it occurred in the nineteenth century and it occurs today. Financial crises usually bring on business depressions, although business depressions sometimes occur without financial crises. That's the empirical side, not the theoretical side. Most of the time markets work, and by that I mean that there's a price and people are buying and selling at that price, and by and large a buyer can always find a seller and a seller can always find a buyer. That fails in these depression situations I was referring to because workers are trying to sell their labor and they can't find buyers. Other people are being hired and being paid a wage rate. You somehow can't get a job at that wage rate. Now, most of the time, the process works reasonably smoothly. There's a market for labor and a market for goods, and a market even for credit: if you issue a bond, there's a rate of interest at which there are people buying the amount of bonds that are being offered. On a basis of that normal course of events, you built up an elaborate theory called general equilibrium theory, that markets—you find that there is a set of prices at which suppliers and demanders will be in bounds on all markets.

Now, being an economic theorist, my interest is not so much in explaining the financial crisis itself but in explaining what the financial crisis reveals about the inadequacies of economic theory.

What's been developing over the last 50 years is one kind of insight that I'm sure practical people have but theorists didn't and that is that there are a lot of these markets that should exist in principle but don't actually exist in fact. What I mean is the following. Let's say that I'm an investor. I'm a businessman. I'm thinking about buying a new plant or buying new equipment. This equipment is justified not by present sales but by future sales. I think the investment is profitable if I look ahead and see—or predict—that there will be sales in the future. I calculate that the revenue on the sales, less the cost of materials and labor, will justify and make me feel like it's worthwhile to put down the money today. There's a lot of elaboration over what I mean by worthwhile, but let me just leave it at that for now. However, in an ideal world, I would sell my future goods today. I'd find a buyer who says, "Three years from now I'm going to buy a car from you," or "Three years from now I'm going to buy a house," or whatever. But of course those markets don't really exist. The only thing that exists with regards to the future by and large are statements that I'll borrow money from you and pay you back in the future, in money, but not in goods. It's the failure to have these future markets today that makes for problems. I may expect to be able to sell something, but when the time comes I can't. That by itself wouldn't necessarily create problems. Well, then you say, I expect one thing, you expect another, and when the time comes we live with what we have, and if I found I've overinvested, ok, I sell for a lower price than I expected to sell, and I just adjust and take my losses. The trouble is I probably borrowed money to do it, and now I can't repay that money. It isn't just that I, the manufacturer, lose because I don't have markets;

it's that the people to whom I owe money also lose. This has kind of a chain reaction.

This is further complicated and made much more important by the fact that we may be working on different information. People have different knowledge. In a way, one of the justifications of the economic system, one of the virtues of a market system is that it's a way of coping with the fact that people have limited knowledge. The fact of that limited knowledge is an essential thing. A nineteenth-century economist pointed it out. In those days, milk was delivered to the house. This was a Frenchman who made this economic discovery so he used Parisians as his example, and he said that Parisians find milk delivered at their door. They make a contract with a local supplier. They have no idea where the milk came from. They are not concerned with it. All they care about is their local knowledge. They don't know the economic system. This by the way is a very ancient bit of knowledge. Herodotus was probably one of the best informed people of his day. He traveled a great deal. He knew that the people in Athens were making things of bronze. Copper is fairly widely spread, and they imported copper from the Near East, from an area that's now Turkey. But the tin is a little more mysterious. They needed tin to make the bronze. All they knew is that tin came from Gaul, from what's now modern France. There are Greek settlers in what's now Marseilles, and they bought the tin which was rafted down the Rhone River by Gaulic merchants. They had no idea where the tin came from. Later on there began to be some vague rumors that there was some big island beyond Gaul, which they called Britain or Pritain, and it began to be surmised that that's where the tin came from, which it did in fact.

The point is that the international commerce, even in the fifth century BC, worked so well that you really didn't have to know that much. You just needed to know your bit of the puzzle. So to go back to our example, if you are a Parisian, you just needed to know the milk would be outside your door. You don't need to know where the cow came from for the system to work. So everybody has limited knowledge. That works all right when all that concerns you is that limited knowledge, if all you care about is that your milk will be delivered to your doorstep in Paris. You really don't care about what other people know.

But sometimes you do care. If I lend money to somebody, his business becomes my business. I have to know what his prospects are. The mortgage, even today, is one where the banker lends money: you want to know something about your borrower. It's not just the house the borrower owns, which is the security to be sure, but obviously you want to know what his job prospects are, what his income is—this is the sort of information when you get a mortgage you ask for. So this means that information becomes specialized. Well, when information is specialized it's hard to make deals about the future. It's hard to buy and sell credit instruments because I may know something about things that you don't.

Consider someone starting a new business venture. Consider venture capitalism, which is so common in the area that I live, in the area near Stanford, where a lot of the high-tech industry is. Well, a fellow comes with a great idea about—say—widgets. He knows a great deal about the technology of widgets. He goes to the venture capitalist, who knows a good deal less about widgets. So the venture capitalist can't really know all about widgets. But, on the other hand, the enthusiastic inventor doesn't really know about the markets. He doesn't know about his ability to borrow. So there's a mutual lack of information.

Let me say where I came across this idea first, and that's in the medical profession. I was asked to do a study of medicine, of medical health insurance, and medical practice. I was wondering what exactly the problems are. Why wasn't there a good insurance market; it was just beginning to emerge. I realized one of the problems is the insurance company—in those days it was before the HMOs, it was just insurance companies—the insurance companies were saying, "Well, we'll pay for the costs of your medical care." But they couldn't really tell what medical care was necessary. The doctor and the patient will figure, "Well, the insurance company's paying for it. If something might vaguely be of any use whatsoever, why not do it? The insurance company's paying for it." If you had to pay for it yourself you might well not do it. So the problem was that the doctor and the patient were much better informed than the insurance company. So it was very difficult, and a lot of ingenuity has gone in so we've managed to surmount part of that problem, but that remains a major problem to this day.

I could give you a long lecture on that, but I'll spare you for the moment. These concepts have become well known now; they're called moral hazard and adverse selection. These are old insurance company terms that have come into the parlance of economists. The moral hazard is the fact that the insurer is unable to really tell how much is needed. The information is in the hands of one side of the market but not the other. Adverse selection is the opposite. When you take out insurance, you know you're sick, but the insurer doesn't necessarily know that. Or you know you're more likely to get sick. This applies not only in the medical field, but in a lot of other fields as well. A lot of others, this situation really applies to financial markets of the ordinary type as well as to the medical problems. The result is that where you have risks there is a difficulty in arranging for their handling. You'd like to shift risk. The idea of insurance is that the risk is spread over a large number of people, and therefore its cost is reduced. But you can't spread these risks. There is a continual tension between the idea of creating new securities that will spread the risk widely, on the one hand, and the fact that this also means a dilution of the information so people don't know what's going on.

That, to sum up a long story, is a little bit of what happened in what you're calling the economic meltdown here. For example, take mortgages. A bank would lend you the money. That means the bank would take the risk. Of course that means the bank is limited. They don't want to take too much risk, particularly if a bank is lending in one geographic area. Maybe something will happen to that whole area. The business on which its based may take a downturn because somebody invents another product or there's foreign competition, or something like that. So the bank has to lend gingerly. Now somebody had the idea, "Why don't we take these mortgages and bundle them

up. Some will fail; some will not; most will not. And we can pool
the risk, and then sell them very widely so a lot of people are sharing
in them." Then, of course, they took these securities and built other
securities on top of them, and by the time you get through no one
really knew what the risks were.

The mystery, however, is why people were lending under those
circumstances. Why would people buy these collateral-backed
obligations, when they were effectively three or four layers deep and
couldn't really know what was going on? That's the mystery. That's
why I say there's a real problem. Because you would assume the
problem would be too little credit, not too much. People would be
afraid to take risks now because they don't know about them. But it
seems people entered into these risks very enthusiastically. You can
offer vague understandings of it—mainly the fact that markets are going
up. So one thing you do know is that these things have perhaps been
profitable in the recent past. If you have nothing else to base your
decisions on, you say, "Well, if they've been going up then they must
continue to go up, and I'm smart enough to get out before they go
down." But that's not a very good explanation really.

If you take the housing situation in this country a few years before
the crash, people were commenting on how rapidly housing prices
were rising, and it was widely stated: this can't really go on. So the
question is: why did people lend money in this situation? That's where
we stand today.

*Q: I was just thinking as you were talking. I was in Canada for the same
meetings you were in September, and one of the things people said there
was that the Canadian economic problems were much less than the United
States because the Canadian banks were more old-fashioned in their lending
policies. They tended to lend more to people they knew. They tended to do
more of the "Old Bailey's Savings and Loan routine. We know the people;
we know they're good risks so we'll lend them money." I just wondered
how much was this cultural difference something that actually occurred. Was
there a market that was so sophisticated that ordinary people didn't really
understand what these derivatives were? (I'll ask you more about that in a*

minute.) But I'm wondering how much of it was a shift in the culture that it fostered, a kind of get-rich-quick kind of thinking. There was a certain amount of greed that was driving these mortgages. People were thinking much more in the moment, as you said, "It's going to keep going and I'll get in and then get out before it crashes." How much was that a factor here?

I don't like to use greed as an explanation for these problems. Of course, as an economist, I tend to view greed as the main motive for action altogether. People have always been greedy. The capitalist system is supposed to be based on the idea that greed, tempered by competition, is the driving force of the system. Why do people invest in new projects? One of the things that capitalism is marked by—and you can find this in *The Communist Manifesto* by the way—is innovation. The capitalist period has been the most inventive period in history. We have new ideas and new products which have enriched people's lives at a rate that's unmatched. Why do people invest in new things? Because they want to make money. This is what Adam Smith said. So it's not the greed that caused the current economic problems. The question is, why was this greed so stupid? The company of Lehman Brothers was presumably greedy, but the net result was not exactly satisfying that greed.[1] It was a collapse. They didn't get rewarded the way they expected. Greedy means you want to get rich. So I don't like to use the idea of greed as an explanation for what went wrong. The question is: Why weren't they intelligently greedy?

Let me give you another example. This should have been a warning, and I must say I was disturbed at the time but I didn't follow it up and nobody else did either. In 1998, you may recall, there was a hedge fund called Long-Term Capital Management, LTCM, which had a couple of Nobel Prize winners among its members.[2] They ran into trouble. They were investing, but what was the basis of their investment? Essentially they would find there were some few different securities that somehow should be in line and were not in line. And so they'd expect that they'd adjust back. These differences are pretty small. The only way you make money from them was by investing a huge amount. And the only way you get a huge amount is by borrowing the money. They were essentially borrowing 97 cents for every dollar they invested. That, of course, turned out not to be so good. The problem is not why they did it. They're gamblers. They were doing very well on the whole. They were doing very, very well, by the way, before this.

So, OK, they finally fail. You gamble long enough, even if you're smart, you're bound to fail some time. The question really was not why they did it. That's easy to explain. The question is why the banks would lend them the money? Why were they able to borrow the money? This I found to be very puzzling. The banks knew—there was no suggestion of fraud in this—the banks knew that other banks were lending money, that essentially a 3 percent drop would mean that they would begin to have to default to some extent on their obligation to the bank. In the end, Greenspan managed to get some of the other banks together to bail them out, and take the assets over, and in the end the banks that took over the assets ended up making money. It was really a good investment if you waited long enough. Well, maybe you should say that at least it was a satisfactory investment. But the mystery was: why were they able to get credit? You expect the restraint on this to be the greed of the lenders, their intelligent self-regard. That's the puzzle as to why that failed. These markets, by the way—they're not organized markets like the stock market— you're not even allowed to participate in them unless you can show that you have wealth of several million dollars. So in the first place the idea is that you can stand the loss, and second the people who actually lent to them were extremely well informed. The lenders were the big banks. So why did Lehman Brothers, why did Bear Stearns go under? They had a big incentive not to go under, and they were also well informed. They weren't the usual investors. The picture of small investors who don't know what they're doing, that doesn't apply here. These were big investors. If anybody knew what they were doing, they should have known. Of course they didn't know what they're doing in retrospect, but the mystery is how they managed to get to this point. But I don't want to use the word greed because the problem is not greed, but that they weren't intelligently greedy.

Q: Well, if you can't rely on intelligence to restrain greed, do you then need government regulation? One of the explanations I've heard bandied about for the economic downturn is that Reagan and then Clinton got rid of so many of the important regulatory provisions like Glass-Steagall, and that then created a climate that encouraged unfettered greed. As you say, the intelligence wasn't enough to constrain the greed.[3]

There you're hitting on a major point. I've got to say the Clinton administration is probably more responsible than Reagan in this regard. The Reagan deregulation was mostly not in the financial sector. That was about deregulation of things like trucking—which probably was good, in my opinion—or airlines.

Q: Weren't there a lot of deregulation of the banking with the Savings and Loan companies?

The Savings and Loan crisis occurred with them.[4] Maybe there was deregulation of Savings and Loan, I don't remember now what there was. I honestly don't remember. I know the S and L crisis certainly occurred at that time. That was just deregulation, or just failure to enforce regulations, I'm not sure. There also was a tendency to pull back. Not so much in terms of laws, but more that the behavior of the regulatory agencies was more forbearing. For obvious reasons, for reasons of respecting pro-business activities. But some of the worst things—one of the problems is that a lot of these securities that gave rise to all of these problems are of very recent origin. They didn't exist a long time ago. Some kinds of derivatives have existed for some time.

What happened, see, is there are two kinds of regulations that have been in existence for a long while. There's regulation of banking in the first place. That's old and it's been strengthened. The Roosevelt administration put in stronger banking regulations; but more important, they put in deposit insurance. Now deposit insurance implies a certain kind of regulation, because the government regulators effectively say, "We'll insure your deposits but in return you have to show us your books, and we'll see that you're not in violation."

Otherwise banking and insurance have been a state matter rather than a federal matter.

Insurance, for example, which I happen to know best of all, is very heavily regulated. The one thing, when you take out a policy on your home or your life, you really don't worry about is the insurance company going broke. That's just not an issue, and the reason is you have very, very strong protections. The insurance companies will complain about how they think the regulations are too severe, but I think they're fine.

There are two kinds of important regulations that are relevant here. These were both created under Roosevelt. One was the stock exchange, and the other was commodities futures markets. The commodities market used to be a source of scandal, and has not been for 100 years or so, but there used to be a lot of activities. So there are two commissions. The first is the Securities Exchange Commission, which regulates stock markets essentially, and which imposes very heavy requirements. You can borrow money to finance your stocks, but not more than 50 percent. So this means if the stocks drop 10 percent, OK, you've taken a ten percent loss. That's it. You don't have to sell. The reason for these protections—what they call "margin requirements"—is that supposing, as was the case before, you have maybe a five percent margin. If stocks drop five percent, the stock is now the full value of your loan, and the broker who lent you the money says either you sell the stock and pay me back, or you put up more money. This means that when stocks start dropping people start selling in large amounts which causes the stock market to fall even more, so there is a cumulative effect. So to prevent that they switched to a 50 percent margin instead of a five percent margin, so we haven't had that kind of panic selling except for in one year, 1987, for reasons that have never been explained.

The second was the regulations of the commodity-futures markets. Say I buy wheat today for delivery in March. It's now November, and somebody else is selling the wheat. He guarantees it. Now the seller may not indeed have any wheat at all, and suppose the buyer may well be a miller, somebody who wants to produce flour, and wants to make sure what the price is. The seller may not have any wheat. He's just counting on buying the wheat by the time that he might need it. So it's a little more iffy. Now, there's no problem with commodity-futures as such, but derivatives, as they became important, were more like commodities-futures than they were like stocks. They began to be traded on the markets that sold commodities-futures. Chicago, Omaha, places like that is where there are these commodities markets. These derivatives began to be traded on those markets because they were more like commodities-futures than they were like stocks.

Q: Can you just define a derivative; tell readers simply what a derivative is?

Let me illustrate. Begin by assuming you have one thing that's valued, and then you buy something whose value depends on that price. Take the commodities-futures as one example. I buy delivery of wheat, but in March, when the wheat is supposed to be delivered, there's going to be a price for wheat, a price for the immediate delivery of wheat. So I'm essentially buying something whose price depends on something else. So I make money if, say, I agree to buy wheat for $X and it turns out the price at that point is higher than I agreed upon. Then I've made money. Either I bought it more cheaply, or I could resell it a higher price. Similarly the seller is obviously working in the opposite way. He'd be selling, and then if what's called the "spot price," the price that's actually available next March, is actually lower, he makes money. Another example, which is a very old example, but one that has emerged in importance only in the last 30 years, is options on stocks. I can buy from you the right to buy stock. Let's say, General Motors stock. Or Verizon, let's say, to take a company that's a little more viable. I can buy an option, which is a statement. You agree to sell me Verizon stock at an agreed upon price. We agree today on a price and that the transaction will take place, say, next March. I pay you some money now. And that means that at any point in time, or at a fixed point in time, I can buy from you and you agree to deliver the Verizon at the price that we have agreed upon. It may be that Verizon, for example, is worth more that time than we've agreed on, in which case I've made money, less of course what I paid you now. Then, of course, we have the opposite. I can agree to sell. Is that clear?

Q: Yes. So it's basically a financial instrument that's derived from some other asset or an event, and that's the basic underlying asset.

Yes. The other one example is the mortgage-backed security, which is a relatively recent invention, where again the payment essentially depends on whether I pay the mortgage or not. The person who was designated as chair of the Commodity Futures Trading Commission by Clinton was a lawyer named Brooksley Born.[5] She had had some practice in Securities law before her time at the Commodity Futures Trading Commission. She raised the question of whether we should be regulating these securities that were being traded on the markets under her jurisdiction. So she wanted to hold hearings on that. This was violently objected to by Alan Greenspan, by Robert Rubin, by others, and in the end Congress passed a law prohibiting the Commodity Futures Trading Commission from regulating derivatives. So that is, in a way, part of the problem.

Q: There was a big scandal over this. She was right, basically, and they were wrong.

Absolutely.

Q: Have they undone that?

Not as far as I know. They've yet to undo it. Now the government is planning regulations, but they have not come out with the details of what's planned. No doubt there'll be some kind of regulations. [Note: This statement was true at the time of the interview. A major law has since been passed increasing certain regulations.]

Q: Let me raise one of the questions that occurred to me as I was listening to you talk. I agree with you that the Clinton administration has a lot to explain here, but one of the problems is that some of the same people who are now trying to fix the system were the people who were involved in changing things via deregulation so that we had this mess in the first place. How much of this is natural since the experts who can solve a problem often almost of necessity are also the experts who would be involved in the situation in the first place? But then how do you deal with conflicts of interest, with the fact that they screwed up the first time? How can you trust them to do things right now? I don't want to put you on the spot here because I know one of them is your nephew, Larry Summers, who's been criticized a lot. I certainly don't want to make Thanksgiving dinner unpleasant for you by criticizing your nephew, but I know there is a big debate that's going on in the media and the community right now. What kinds of reforms should we be instituting? Is the Obama administration moving to institute those reforms? What do you think reforms should look like?

I'm hoping that they've learned their lessons. What can I say? I'm not privy to any of these discussions. I haven't talked to my nephew [Larry Summers] about them, or at least I have yet to do so. My own view is that we have to do something fairly drastic. Don't start saying, "Well, if we do this regulation, then they'll get around it this way, and then it'll lead to a problem with this. . ." I think we need to take a bolder view. It's like wandering around a mountain in fog. What you want to do is to stay away from the edge. You don't know where the edge is, but you want to stay far away from the edge. You may be losing some opportunities; you may miss the shortest way down. But it's important to stay away from disaster and you may just have to lose some advantages. I must admit, I wasn't in the spot to run anything—being a theorist—but I would have thought that these widespread mortgage securities were a good idea. They would enable mortgages to be issued more easily. Most people don't default. Only a small number default ordinarily. This way people who look a little shaky, but most of whom would in fact pay, get an opportunity to own houses. I think some of that did happen. But I think the answer is that we should have forgone that advantage, and this is a social advantage. We should have forgone that advantage because of the risks involved, in retrospect.

Q: What kinds of reforms would you suggest?

I would require, in the first place, that any time there's a lending operation, that there be much less leverage, to use a technical term. We should have the equivalent of margins. If a bank has mortgages and wants to resell them, it has to retain 25 percent of the obligation. They can sell off only 75 percent of the mortgages, so they're still on the hook. This is analogous to the margin requirement of stocks, so they're still on the hook for a major part of the thing. I don't know what the right figure is, 25 percent, 50 percent, but something pretty substantial. But these credit–default swaps, that's getting to a technical point which are actually enormous. It seems to me that prohibiting them would not be a bad idea; I think they serve very little in the way of a social function.

Q: We don't want to keep you too much longer. You were talking about credit-default swaps and said that these should be prohibited basically.

Someone will have to explain to me why they have any social value at all. Since the total quantity was on the order of $40 trillion. There's something absurd about it. There's a clear absurdity here.

Q: It's hard to conceptualize what that much money means, isn't it?

Well, you see it cancels out. It's obviously one of these things where A owes B and B owes C and C owes A. See what I mean? So if you could get down to it you'd see that it largely cancels out. But the trouble is that the timing is off. You can imagine a situation where A can't pay B, and B therefore can't pay C, and then C can't pay A. If they understood it then they could have cancelled the whole thing out and then nobody would have gone broke. Am I making myself clear?

Q: Yes. I think so.

The trouble there is if the markets were transparent this would be clear. When the market's at the point where you can't see simple things like this then you're probably better off not having them. Well, credit–default swaps in a sense were a kind of insurance. But they weren't subject to the ordinary rules that insurance has to protect itself. I could essentially buy a credit–default swap on General Motors defaulting, even though I own no securities in General Motors. I'm not protecting myself against anything. If you were to take ordinary insurance, you have to have an insurable interest. I cannot take an insurance policy on your house. I can't even take an insurance policy on my own house for a value greater than the value of the house. That's what's called an insurable interest. That was not true in case of the credit–default swaps. What else can I say?

Also, and what's probably more important, with insurance, as I mentioned before, you have to put up a reserve. The insurer, let's say AIG in this case. AIG's big business is being an insurer in the ordinary sense. Their insurance policies are regulated, and they have whole reserves and all that. In this case, they were also extending this credit–default swap, which is a kind of insurance. They'll say they'll pay if Company X defaults, but they weren't required to put up reserves against that. It wasn't regulated like insurance. To me this is ridiculous.

Q: So you think it should be more regulated, like insurance?

In the case of credit–default swaps I'm not even sure they should be permitted. I don't quite see what legitimate function they serve.

Q: Let me ask you one last question. It seems to me that there are a lot of distribution effects that are going on here. I have a young colleague who just came back from Southeast Asia this summer. Before he left he was doing some shopping here in Southern California in the malls and there really weren't that many people out. You could see there was an economic downturn. Then he left and went to Southeast Asia. He was in Indonesia and Malaysia, and he said it was very interesting because the malls there were packed. He said one of the things that he noticed is that they didn't seem to be as subjected to the economic downturn as the United States was. He said in the past when he'd been there, it was like when the United States gets a cold, Southeast Asia gets pneumonia. He realized that one of the things that had happened is that the Southeast Asian governments have tried very hard to build up a middle class. He wondered if some of what happened in this country was also a result of a kind of polarization in terms of more extreme income inequalities. So that over the last 30 or 40 years, we've moved toward less equitable distribution, and that is hurting the middle class. Is this one of the things that is going to hurt our economy? That you need to have a very strong middle class, economically?

Look, I think the income distribution in the United States is developing in an appalling manner, but I don't quite see any real connection between this and the current crisis. The effects are going to hit the poor, but the causes are not. The reason I'm saying that is that the rich are spending a lot of money, too. If you go to malls, at least in the part of the country where I live, they're pretty expensive. When you go to the local malls it's not really the working class you see there. I live just about across the street from one of the leading shopping centers, and believe me, most of the shops there are pretty expensive, and their clientele are the rich.

I think there's going to be a problem in our recovery, but I'm not sure it's due to the income distribution. People are going to spend less. Personal savings in the United States were about zero over the last ten years or so. Of course, some of that was because people felt better off because their houses were increasing in value, and so forth. But savings in the ordinary sense of the word, the money you get each year and how much you put aside, was close to zero. People were taking these housing prices and refinancing and spending. I think people in the first place are going to try to build up their wealth positions, so as income begins to rise, they're going to retain it, to a great extent, which mean the recovery is going to slow down. I think this is a widespread observation. Of course, in the long run, that's a good thing. People will invest more. It will be easier to finance manufacturing investment in this country. I think the inequality is very bad, and I disapprove. But I cannot trace out a link between that and the nature of the crisis we have today.

Excuse me. There is a decoupling. It's true. Not the rich and the poor, but the Asian countries for the first time are really being "decoupled," in the phrase that everybody uses. They're not responding to the crisis generated here as they would have in the past. China is not suffering from this depression. Whereas in 1997, 1996–97, I guess it was. There was a severe Asian crisis, which had very little effect on us. It's the reverse today. It's Europeans, people like the cautious Icelanders, who are in trouble. They invested in these dubious securities.

Q: Are you optimistic about the economy and about the recovery?

It's going to be very slow. I'm not optimistic. In real terms I think it's going to be a couple of years. I don't claim to be an expert on that, but I don't know that there are *any* experts. My feeling is that the recovery is going to be very slow. Of course, everyone is predicting that we're going to have two years of considerable unemployment. But I think it could have been much worse. The crisis was averted, but the recovery is going to be slow. I think that long term there may be a shift in the nature of our international situation. We've been big importers, importing much more than we're exporting. I hope this changes, but I'm not sure that it will.

Q; You're just back from China. I wonder what you thought about the situation between China and the United States. It seems like with the Obama visit, they're talking more about the importance of that relationship for us.

Well, look, the Chinese own two trillion dollars of US dollars, partly invested in government securities, and things like that. It's a very unstable situation because the Chinese are doing it for what the economists call "mercantilist" reasons. They've kept their exchange rate with the United States more or less fixed. Which means, incidentally since the dollar's been falling, that the Europeans are suffering from Chinese competition. Say, the Germans, who are big exporters, look like they're going to suffer because they have so much of their exports competing with China, and the value of the Euro is going up, compared to the dollar, which is understandable, but also compared to the Renminbi (the Chinese currency), which is artificial. But to maintain that strength, the Chinese have to keep on buying dollars. At some point, this is going to be a losing proposition. I think they're going to have to unload those dollars at some point, and I don't know what's going to happen then. But that's a number of years off; that's not an immediate problem. There's going to be international realignment that may provoke new problems. Maybe for China, not for us. But it's hard to see at the moment.

Q: What would be the one piece of advice you'd give your nephew [Larry Summers]?

Err on the side of too much regulation. Of course, that's not really the answer, because the question is what kind of regulation. My advice is going to be, essentially, do everything possible to reduce leverage, and increase margins and their equivalent. Increase capital requirements of banks. Require that credit–default swaps really be treated as insurance. Regulate the question of these derivative securities by again requiring that people keep a good part of the risk before they pass it along to others. Of course, how you draw up regulations that do all that is something that he knows much more about than I do, but I want him to think that way.

Q: We want to ask you about the 2010 mid-term elections. Obviously the economy played a significant role in the recent elections, and we wondered if you had any thoughts on what exactly was going on within the electorate. Was it a referendum on big government and a solid rejection of too much government; was it simply people who were in a lot of economic pain and want the government to do something about that?

You're asking me questions on which I only have second-hand opinions. The problem is, I don't know the "normal" person. Well, none of us do, really. We're all in our little enclaves. I have conjectures, or observations, but I certainly would not predict or claim to understand what the "average" person is thinking. One problem is that what little I've gleaned from polls and so forth seems to be a mess of contradictions. We have candidates running on the basis that government is bad and presumably, since at least some of them got elected, it is implied that voters like that position. But there have been polls going through a long list of government items, asking should we be spending more, less, or the same. The only item on which there's a really strong view that we should cut is foreign aid which, in any case, is a very small item. Whatever your opinion of foreign aid is, I think the total is around $30 billion a year. It has almost nothing to do with the larger economic issue.

So what then is meant by "government is bad"? I haven't seen any polls asking, "Do you think the government is too big?" but since a lot of people are running and getting elected on that platform, you have to assume there's some kind of accord. But there's almost no aspect of the government that appears to be too big. For example, one thing that really struck me in the debate over the last couple of years—now I'm not talking about people, I'm talking about political people, those whose voices are heard politically—is that as soon as you start talking about economizing in any way on Medicare, you get screams. For example, there was a committee that was not even appointed for the purpose of looking into economies but concluded that mammogram screenings should be reduced—they were only needed at a later age. This proposal was attacked as a vicious plot on the part of the Obama administration. One of the claims for this change was that the radiation isn't good for you. This recommendation was made by doctors, with the aim not of cutting costs, but of reducing the requirements to the minimum needed, which you'd think anybody who's seriously interested in cutting costs, cutting the budget, and reducing the size of the government would applaud. But instead it was denounced. The point is the attack came from the same people who are screaming about cutting expenditures. So you have the same people talking about the government "death panels" and reducing

Medicare costs "on the back of the elderly," inflammatory phrases of that kind, and these people are the same people who are talking about the excessive size of the government. So it's a little hard to engage this from any intellectual point of view, since I don't understand the position at all.

I haven't seen anybody say, for example, "Let's eliminate farm subsidies." It's not a huge amount of money, but it's say $50 billion or $60 billion, and the bulk of it goes to big corporations, particularly in cotton or highly industrialized livestock factory farms. So the whole purpose of allegedly preserving the family farm is not relevant. But nobody has even raised the idea of eliminating farm subsidies, although if you wake any economist up out of his sleep, no matter what his politics are, he'll say, "What about farm subsidies? Eliminate them." It's a reflex action, because there's absolutely no reason to keep them. If you want to let the market work, that's a prime place to let the market work.

So I find that it's very hard to engage in any coherent debate in this area. It's a big government; nothing in fact is going to happen. Instead, it's used as an excuse. I think I actually mentioned previously, that there's the anti-tax attitude of the public, which is widespread, and which is obviously dominating, and this goes back a long way. It's maybe become more intense of late, but it's not new. We had Proposition 13 here in California, what is it, over 30 years ago? There was also the proposition that called for the abolition of estate taxes in California. Now, any of the ordinary calculations of self-interest would say that there are a lot more people below the "rich" level at which we begin to tax estates—what is it now, $1 million or something like that in estates?—so a very small fraction of the population is affected negatively, and the other presumably gain because some other tax is reduced. Nevertheless, the same people go around cutting taxes.

The level of discourse has really changed. It used to be that you left it up to the legislature. People just sort of trusted the government. I found that in the last California election, all the candidates, Republican candidates particularly, were talking about cutting taxes, without any serious indication of the corresponding expenditure cuts.

Some of them have demonstrated on other occasions a much higher level of understanding.

Q: *It was interesting during the campaign. You would see some journalists asking people who were Tea Party candidates or people who were saying that they needed to cut government spending, well, 'Where will you cut it?' No one ever actually came up with anything.*

"We're going to eliminate the waste!" [Laughter.]

Q: *But they never actually came up with where they were going to do it.*

No, of course not. I'm saying they had these slogans. Now there are one or two consistent ones. The Pauls, father and son, do seem to seriously believe that we should cut defense spending.

Q: *Speaking of cuts to the government. Some people seem to have a very strong hostility to the Federal Reserve Board, and were furious that the Fed spent what—$600 billion—authorized the day after the election, and they say that that's going to prop up the economy and promote economic growth, but it will make long-term borrowing cheaper and effectively it's a central bank financing a national deficit on a scale that we haven't seen since WWII. I've heard some of these newly elected people say that they actually want to get rid of the Federal Reserve Board.*

There's been an element of that all along. It's much louder now, however.

Q: *Do you think they can actually do that? Economically, not politically, is it feasible to get rid of the Fed?*

No. Well, it can be done, yes. But let me put it this way. Without assuming Wall Street runs the nation, I think Wall Street's powerful enough to prevent that.

Q: So you think Wall Street would defend the Fed?

Oh yes, I'm sure they will defend the Fed. I can't take this talk seriously. But it can be enough to create a problem. The Fed may pull back its horns; they might start engaging in political behavior. There's been a slogan—not just in the United States but also in Europe and Japan—about the independence of the Central bankers. There's been an era, beginning in the 1980s where—the slogan held that the Central bankers have actually run as a signal to the world that there's going to be a firm policy. The reality is if the political establishment is seen to be influencing the Fed, then apart from any other problems there's an instability, you don't know what's going to happen. The particular fear of course is inflation. The idea is that the independence of the Central Bankers is a way of signaling to the business community that we're not going to have any inflation. And for 20 years it worked very well. You find that in Europe, you see that in England, you see that in the United States. The idea of the independence of the Fed has been made into something of a cult, which has some very positive value. But if you're starting to interfere with that, if you say that we're not going to trust the Bank, you're going to create a good deal of economic uncertainty, to say the least. I think that can be resisted.

Q: Do you think the Fed can stem off inflation given all the spending that we're seeing now?

Well, the idea is that as you begin to see inflation you start changing and restricting the policy. There's going to be a problem, but we've got a big problem. As [Federal Reserve chairman Ben] Bernanke has said, deflation is a bigger problem than inflation. We have lots of examples. We have one example of the Great Depression; we have one example much more recently of Japan. It's not as though this is theoretical, there are some good arguments that letting prices drop sharply can—will—create all sorts of negative pressures on the economy that can be very hard to get rid of. As for inflation, we have one example; in the '70s we had a good deal of inflation. I'm not going to claim to be an expert on this but a generally accepted story is that in order to ensure Nixon's re-election, the Fed took a rather easy money policy. (The Fed chair then was Arthur F. Burns, who had been a professor of mine in graduate school.) That then started an inflationary spiral that is hard to control unless you do take drastic measures. Around 1980, Paul Volker—who is actually a Democrat—Volker just clamped down. We had a very severe recession, but a very short one. In 1981, unemployment was higher than it is today, even higher than the worst it's been recently, but it lasted only a year. It was the result of really clamping down. It ended the inflation. The inflation was getting up to 20 percent per annum.

Q: Volker's reputation is getting favorable ratings these days. People think pretty highly of him.

He's been worried about the wrong investments by the strictly investment banks. The regular banks are being pretty well regulated, and they have not been the major problem this last recession. These investment banks—not the kind of bank where people go up to the window and make deposits—have been the source of the problems. That's partly because the regular banks have been heavily regulated, they have deposit insurance so nobody panics. You don't run to take your money out. The investment banks like Lehman Brothers would borrow huge amounts of money for 24 hours. So it's like a deposit, but it wasn't called a deposit. The person who put it up, the lender, could take it back, could refuse to renew the loan the next day. They were buying things that paid off only over a period of time with this 24-hour financing. So from an analytic point of view it was very similar to the old-fashioned deposit banking but without any of the regulations that protect it.

Q: Do you think that they're going to get rid of a lot of the new regulations now that the new Congress is coming in?

You know what, I think that's such a complicated matter. They may; I bet they'll be chipping away at it. From a public point of view I suspect that this is of no consequence. This is too complicated for the public to engage in, is my guess. In all of the election rhetoric, I never heard anybody talk about the regulation of banks either way, except from the left. I just saw a blog from an economist I know rather well, James Galbraith, who was attacking Obama very strongly. Actually he didn't have a good word to say about him. In the thread, one fellow compared Obama to the Nazis. He sounded exactly like the Tea Party writers.

Q: Is this John Kenneth Galbraith's son?

Yes. One of the two. The other is Peter Galbraith, the diplomat. The other one is James Galbraith, whom I know quite well. He's zealous, but he's pretty bright. It was symptomatic, the idea that [Obama has] sold out to Wall Street, that sort of thing.

Q: Do you think there was anything Obama could have done to hold off what was going to be a strong negative political reaction to what the economy was? Do you think that he could have put economic policy ahead of health care policy, had more fiscal stimulation, tried to regulate the banks, try to have a moratorium on foreclosures, things of that kind?

You've said several things which I think are very different there. There is a political argument which I have no competence to judge, that if he had concentrated on the stimulus instead of putting a lot of other things in play—this is kind of a law of conservation of Congress' time, something like that. If you do one thing you can't do another. Or a conservation of your power—if he had put his energies into stimulus, a bigger stimulus—then the economy might have been better and then after this election, he might have been able to put the Health Care reform in. That's an argument based on a political judgment which frankly I'm not qualified to make.

Q: But as an economist, if Obama had focused more on the economy, do you think it would have responded enough . . ?

Well, the first question is, could he have gotten more stimulus through, no matter what he did. The understanding I had just from reading the press was that he felt he couldn't ask for any more. There are plenty of objections to the stimulus, and a lot of fights about it. And his original proposals were cut back.

Now, the question is, if he had tried harder, and not confused the issue, would he have been able to? Certainly, looking back, it does appear, it would have better stimulated the economy and that might have created a more favorable [political] environment. It wasn't obvious to me at the time that that was the choice. Why couldn't you do both, after all?

Q: Well, that was the argument, yes. His argument was partially that health care was going to be a major economic variable that would make things much better for people.

But it's a long-term variable. In fact, look at the debt. There are some economists, including James Galbraith, who don't want to even talk about the debt as a constraint. I personally think that's wrong and think the debt is a problem. The supply of money is a problem because of future inflation, and the supply of debt is a problem because if you meet it with taxes you have higher taxes and taxes are a problem. Especially with political implications, but even ideally they're a problem. So I think this is just one of those things. But then in my view, I wouldn't worry about the debt today; we have unemployment close to ten percent. I don't think the debt is the problem we should be concerned about. If unemployment went down to five percent then I'd begin to say, "Maybe we ought to work on the debt."

Q: So do you think unemployment is the major problem we have to address right now?

If you take the short run, yes. If you said, "What's the immediate problem?" I'd say, probably unemployment is the biggest problem, yes. It's a very sluggish recovery; unemployment is a very painful thing. From a purely economic point of view it means we could have more goods than we have now, and the people who had them would be people who need them. And of course unemployment has lasting effects on the unemployed. That's been documented a lot. This is not just a product of today's events. People have studied this before, particularly in Europe, where they've had pretty high unemployment compared to the United States in the last 20 years. Your skills erode; you're just not the same, and even when prosperity comes back you've lost something permanently. From a national point of view you've lost skills; from an individual point of view you've lost economic opportunities. So there is something called the hysteresis effect, that the abilities of older workers—when I say older I mean even 35- or 40-year-old workers—take permanent damage, and they don't really recover in their lifetimes. Also, since unemployment means low demand, it means less incentive to innovate, it may have some long run consequences. Further, there is an immediate consequence which is very bad. We certainly at a minimum could be producing ten percent more goods than we're producing now, with the same investment and the same workers. That's a big loss.

On top of that, there's a sluggishness that develops in the economy. That's certainly characteristic of the Japanese economy today and for the last decade. It's sluggish. It has not recovered, even in ten years, from its collapse. They had a bubble, even bigger than our bubble. I got a postcard from an older economist, now dead, a Christmas card or something. He said things are a little bit crazy, that "land in Tokyo the size of this postcard is worth $2500." He was rather rich, and somehow I got the impression he owned some of this land. He said the land on which the imperial palace was built was worth as much as all of Manhattan. So they came down even more than we've come down in say real estate values, or stock market values. But they haven't really recovered. My point is, they haven't really recovered in ten years. Usually you say, OK, business cycles don't last that long.

Q: There's a relationship though between the unemployment and the small businesses that don't want to have a lot of government stimulus. It seems strange to me because, if the government stimulates the economy and people have jobs, even if they're just doing things like repairing infrastructure, then at least they have money to spend, which presumably they will spend at least some of at the small businesses. So I don't quite understand why some of the small business owners are so upset about the stimulus, why they think it's going to destroy them.

Well, yes, I have a great difficulty in finding a coherent point of view with regards to that. Now, what the effects of government spending are on private spending is disputed. I can't tell you that the facts of that are well established. I think the fact that they are there is clear, that they're big, but nobody knows exactly. I think one thing today is that people have lost a lot of wealth, say stock market wealth, the value of their house, something like that. The result of that is that when they get some money, they're not going to spend it. My guess today in this particular situation, is that additional money—obviously they'll spend a little of it—but additional money, a lot of it, is not going to be spent, but rather be used to try to build back their savings account, your stock holdings, to make up for the loss of, let's say for poorer people, their house, that's the big asset. Suddenly instead of having a $300,000 house they have a $50,000 house. Well, they have to build up something else. Now foreclosures are a different matter, by the way. That's very complicated. I have some sympathy; I don't know whether I have a good answer.

Q: Would you just suggest a moratorium on foreclosures?

It's complicated, I think . . . well, what about the person who at great cost to himself is paying his bills? You can see that, if I know that when I default they're not going to foreclose, then there are going to be a lot of defaults. People are just going to stop paying. And that's going to have a lot of repercussions. It's very tricky. They had this relief program, a mortgage relief program, which got nowhere apparently.

Q: The money didn't seem to get back to the homeowners did it? It seemed to stay with the banks.

No, no, nothing happened. The government provided money which was supposed to help finance the banks if they relieved the mortgage, and none of it was spent, a very small amount it was spent. It didn't go to the banks, it didn't go to anybody.

Q: Well, where is it?

It's sitting in a government account; they didn't spend it. They appropriated money and didn't spend it, that's all. I'm not fully acquainted with all of the things they tried to do, but there's no questions they've just. . . some people think that a different solution would be just to allow people to go bankrupt, so if your mortgage exceeds the value then you just go bankrupt and you don't owe it anymore. Then of course there's a settlement and the bank has claims on you, but not necessarily the full amount of the mortgage. But that's a pretty complicated solution. It means that each case has to be handled individually, which means that the courts could be completely tied up. So there's no easy way out of it. You've got this foreclosure story, I mean this mortgage collapse story, there's no easy way out of that. Unless you're going to change the whole system by which houses are financed. It's probably true that we went too far in financing houses, that we have too many people owning houses who shouldn't be owning them. The result is that today the percentage of people owning houses is the same as the number before all this started. I don't think there's any easy way out of the mortgage problem, once you get into it. We should not have gotten into it, but once you're in it . . . I should say that one of the big problems is that everything is on an individual basis; you can't make a simple law or rule that says everybody just gets a bonus. It won't work; every case is different. So therefore I think there's no simple answer on foreclosures. We can only worry about the future on that.

Q: Let me back up a little bit. If one assumes that the economic situation that Obama inherited from Bush was not good for a variety of reasons, and that it hasn't gotten better as much as the public wanted it to, and therefore they have punished the Obama administration by voting a lot of the Democrats who supported his policies out of office . . .

I should point out to you that they voted out even more of the Democrats who didn't support his policies.

Q: That's true. That's true, too. So now the situation is. . . have the politics of the economic recovery made things worse? Are we now headed for a bigger economic mess than we've had in the past two years? Or do you think that this is just a temporary economic blip and that the economic recovery is going to go on its own way?

There's a very important sense in which this election has damaged things and that is that the hope of a second stimulus, of a renewed stimulus, seems to have evaporated. I don't see how, unless the Republicans do a 180 degree switch, how there could possibly be a second stimulus.

Q: Do you think they need a second stimulus? Would you advocate for that?

Oh, I would certainly support that. I think we need more. I think [the first stimulus] just wasn't big enough. I mean it's big, everybody knows it's not a small number, but we need more. And allegedly, according to all the rumors, Bernanke believes that, too.

Q: So you wouldn't go the British route, which is where they seem to be worrying about the deficit and cutting down and getting rid of a lot of government programs that they've had in place?

I haven't followed the British situation in detail. American coverage of Britain is never that good, and I don't read the British papers. But I think it sounds awful, what they're doing. They have a bigger debt than we do, in proportion to their national income. They're worried about—well, they have close examples in Ireland and of course Greece, and Spain and Portugal—they have close examples in Europe of the devastating debt problem. The debt problem there is not something in the future as it is for us; it's in the present. But it seems to me that the British were not quite at that stage, and it seems they're damaging themselves. I know certainly the academic community, to tell you something close to me, is very, very upset. They're talking about cutting down research funds. I'm really surprised these policies haven't created a bigger backlash than they have. But no, I think the British response is very bad.

And now they're complaining, suddenly these finance ministers, like the British and German, are complaining of the American policy, of buying up outstanding debt. This recent announcement of $600 billion—what it could do is weaken the dollar, because it creates the idea that we may have inflation in the future. But if it weakens the dollar, that improves our foreign trade position. Foreign goods are more expensive, American goods are cheaper, so allegedly it should follow the foreign trade position. Of course that's exactly what the Germans and the Chinese are complaining about. Now, I suspect Bernanke is doing this quite deliberately for that reason. Of course, in the past he's taken the view that the real trouble with the American foreign trade situation is that we're running this big deficit while other countries are running big surpluses—notably the Chinese, and the Germans, too—that this can't be permanent. You can't have a permanent situation like this. In a world where every country has its own currency and currencies are allowed to trade freely, you would expect the American dollar to depreciate, that's what you would expect to happen. That's what the Market would expect. That's what Milton Friedman would expect, the American dollar would weaken, and the surplus countries would strengthen.

Now the Chinese have intervened very strongly to prevent that. What they do is just keep on acquiring dollars to prevent this from happening. So the Chinese are engaged in, I don't think there's any question, illegitimate—well, I shouldn't use that word—well, anyway, transactions designed to benefit themselves. In effect one of the consequences of this Federal Reserve move is to offset the Chinese position. Now the trouble centers on this question: is the foreign part of our economy so big as to warrant all this, because it also has domestic repercussions. I have to tell you that I'm not too optimistic that this particular kind of policy is going to be very effective. I think it's quite different from stimulus, where you re-hire people.

Q: *So you would make that your first priority? Your priority would be to re-hire people and get the unemployment rate down?*

One way to do it, by the way, a way to do it rapidly, is to finance the states. The states are laying off people.

Q: *They are. And they're pushing it back to the counties, which are then laying off people.*

Yes, they can't support them. So the fact is we're laying off school teachers, people like that, and one of the ways the government could have prevented that is by giving stimulus money to the states. That's giving people jobs in a very direct way. Another way would be, of course, infrastructure. They haven't done as much infrastructure as I would have expected. Infrastructure has one great political advantage: it's very easy to see. You have roads, you have bridges—they're visible! And also they do have the effect of putting people to work. They're producing something that's clearly going to be good. We've actually been neglecting, even in times of prosperity, we've been neglecting our infrastructure. Our roads are deteriorating, the bridges—there was a lot of comment at the time of that big accident in Minneapolis that this was far from the only bridge that should have been taken care of. Of course, it's easy to delay the reconstruction and repairs. We had this huge building program in the '60s, well the '50s really, and these things wear out—they don't last forever. So I think there's a good argument for infrastructure policy. Then there's the question of educational infrastructure, because our education system, certainly relative to other countries, is going downhill, in all these various rankings. Public universities are being squeezed, by the way. That's happening all over the country.

I think by the way, Medicaid is an important factor in all this. Because that's a state responsibility, 50 percent, anyway. Medicaid, not Medicare; Medicaid. 50 percent roughly speaking is paid by the states, and in every state it's a large number, one of the biggest single items in the budget. Nobody's opposed to it, interestingly. With all the talk about cutting government back, I haven't heard a word about that. Nobody's come out and advocated reducing Medicaid.

Q: Are you surprised that there's been less discussion of getting out of Iraq and Afghanistan than there has been? It seems to me that that's a major drain, too.

Yes, very surprised. That's been a very major drain. There's a very big argument that we can cut military spending by a huge amount. After all, if our problem is protecting ourselves against terrorists, then the last thing we need are the kind of arms we have now, the kind of arms that were developed to fight a war against the Soviet Union. The Soviet Union's not there anymore. One of the interesting things you see is that military spending—the procurement of new weapons, I should say to be precise, which is a major part of the military budget —is a political enterprise. In fact, I was talking to a colleague of mine who was Deputy Assistant Secretary of Defense under Johnson, and he said, "The ideal weapons system has parts in every state. No congressman would vote against it." So there is this political aspect. You see this, there was this fighter called the F-22, which the Department of Defense has been recommending be dropped, and they can't get it dropped. You know, these fighters now, they're $100 million apiece or something, I don't know what exactly, they're very expensive, they're heavily equipped with various equipment and so forth, quality, not quantity. I don't remember the names of all of them now, but there are several weapons systems that even the Defense Department didn't defend, and they couldn't get rid of them.

The whole thing, the fact is of course, this being a little bit outside of the current situation, is that we really haven't won a war since World War II, unless you count Grenada and Panama. But apart from that, with all of our military spending—we spend after all roughly the same as the rest of the world combined on our military expenditures—and yet we admit, the fact is we are not exactly a world power. Maybe that means we can't afford to cut it, but certainly if the immediate problem is terrorism then these weapons are absolutely useless. We fought a war in Iraq, where there were no terrorists, and we're fighting a war in Afghanistan, where there are estimates of about 1500 Al Qaeda. Those are the sort of numbers you get, and on top of that we're not even winning. It's quite clear that there's no point in this kind of spending. I think we can cut the defense budget.

Let me put it another way, if I remember the figures correctly the defense expenditures are now about double what they were in 2001. You'd think after the current war, we pull our troops home, we cut the defense budget by 50 percent, which is not a small number, and maybe even that's too big. But terrorism is not going to be fought by these kinds of methods. It hasn't been successful; we have empirical evidence to verify that. What we're doing in Afghanistan I have no idea, and we should be out of Iraq by now. But it's interesting, nobody wants to discuss it. Obama has not taken a stand. He's got this kind of middle thing where he's committed to withdrawal, but we'll see. And, of course, most people don't like the idea of not winning. But what's interesting is how this got started. The repeal of the draft, going to a voluntary army toward the end of the Nixon presidency, was to avoid what happened during the Vietnam War. I'm sure that a good part of the anti-war movement consisted of people who just didn't want to go and get drafted.

I certainly do not want to see the United States disarmed, but it doesn't seem to me that its present armaments are effective for the wars we're fighting. Actually, there is an argument for a volunteer army, which is that you really want a highly technically trained army. The draft doesn't give you people who have that kind of training.

Q: But our current army doesn't necessarily give us that either. Many of our current soldiers aren't technically sophisticated young men and women either, are they?

That's an interesting idea, but I don't know enough about the issue. I don't want to go too far into it because I don't know enough. A lot of them must be people who have been there for quite a while. Of course, the National Guard, which is the most poorly trained group, has taken a big beating. They certainly don't have the kind of highly technical training they need. I think there's a real problem. Of course, having this army is a temptation to use it, too. If we didn't have it we might have been more careful.

Q: Looking at the economy and foreign policy situation, I'm reminded of the satirical headline in The Onion the day after the 2008 election, which was "Black Man given Nation's Worst Job." One of the article's lines was "The job comes with such intense scrutiny and so certain a guarantee of failure that only one other person even bothered applying for it." Or as the saying goes, "Rule No. 1 is you play to win, Rule No. 2 is if you win, you're stuck with the prize." Now that Obama won, he has to deal with all this mess. At first he looked inspired by the challenge of it, but I don't know how he feels now. He didn't look too good the day after the 2010 election.

That press conference was kind of a disappointment; I thought it might have been an occasion to push things a little bit in a positive direction.

Q: Well, it must be hard to be in politics. Is there any last thing you'd like to leave us with? What would your wish be for your grandchildren in terms of how you would hope economists would work in the next 100 years to make things better?

I don't know how exactly to put it, but I still believe that a kind of careful, rational discourse is what we need when dealing with large problems. I don't know if it's a solution or a hope for the impossible. But I do feel when I see some of these things, I come out wondering,

"How can this possibly happen?" OK, these are things that are difficult, people have different views, and that's true. But there are some things that I do not understand. Before we actually went to Iraq, I was sure that there were no weapons of mass destruction and certainly Saddam Hussein had nothing to do with it. I knew that right away. I had no inside information. If I knew it, anybody could have known it. I find it very hard to grasp how people would get into this.

The United States isn't the only country that does these things. This [Presidential] trip to India has led to some discussion of India's problems. I don't know if you saw this Op-Ed piece, I think it was in today's paper, by an Indian writer who points out how terrible India's handling of Kashmir has been. It was an Indian novelist, and again it was something that's been perfectly obvious. India took over Kashmir quite illegally at the time of independence—quite wrongly anyway, I don't know if there was any relevant law, but it was certainly wrong that Indian troops are coming in and killing Kashmiri demonstrators; there's been military law. All that's creating a permanent problem with Pakistan. I'm no defender of Pakistan; I think India's probably much better than Pakistan, but it seems the Indian troops aren't behaving so well. It's not just that they're not behaving well, but it's creating problems for the entire world. So it's not just the United States. But that's the part we're responsible for, anyway.

Q: The idea of rational discourse is a great hope for the world, isn't it?

That's the only hope I can think of.

Notes

1   Lehman Brothers Holdings Inc. was a global financial service firm that filed for bankruptcy on September 15, 2008. Until then, it was a major player in investment banking, private banking, equity and fixed-income sales, trading, and research and was a primary dealer in US Treasury securities.

2   A hedge fund that used fixed-income arbitrage, statistical arbitrage, and pairs trading, combined with high leverage, as trading strategies, the Long-

Term Capital Management (LTCM) failed in the late 1990s. This failure led to a massive bailout by other major banks and investment houses, all of which was supervised by the Federal Reserve Board. LTCM had been founded in 1994 by John Meriwether, who had been vice-chairman and the head of the bond trading department at Salomon Brothers. The Nobel Prize winners on its Board of Directors included Robert Merton and Myron Scholes. The failure of LTCM demonstrates the potential risk in the hedge fund industry, a risk that went unheeded by most of the financial community.

3   One of the most important banking reforms, introduced to control the kind of speculation Arrow describes, was the Banking Act of 1933, which established the Federal Deposit Insurance Corporation (FDIC) to protect against the kind of runs on banks that occurred during the Great Depression, by insuring money on deposit in banks up to a certain amount per customer. This is commonly known as the Glass–Steagall Act, since its two main legislative sponsors were Carter Glass and Henry B. Steagall. Critical provisions of the Act (e.g. Regulation Q, which allowed the Federal Reserve to regulate interest rates in savings accounts) were repealed in 1980 by the passage of the Depository Institutions Deregulation and Monetary Control Act. In 1999, the Gramm-Leach-Bliley Act was passed, which further repealed the provisions of Glass-Steagall that prohibited bank holding companies from owning other financial companies. This is the deregulation critics refer to as having occurred during the Reagan and Clinton presidencies.

4   Savings and Loans are financial institutions that accept savings deposits and make car, mortgage, or other personal loans to its individual members. During the 1980s and 1990s, 747 savings and loan institutions failed, costing roughly $160.1 billion, some $124.6 billion of which was paid for directly by the US government. This Savings and Loan crisis contributed to the extreme budget deficits of the early 1990s.

5   Brooksley Born served on the Commodity Futures Trading Commission (CFTC) from April 1994 to June 1999, and as chair from August 26, 1996 until June 1, 1999. The CFTC is the federal agency charged with overseeing futures and commodity options markets. While on the CFTC, Born lobbied Congress and President Clinton to give the CFTC oversight of off-exchange markets for derivatives, not just to oversee exchange-traded derivatives. Born wanted a comprehensive regulation of derivatives, being particularly concerned about swaps, the financial instruments traded over the counter between insurance companies, banks, or other funds or companies. She argued that these trades have no transparency except to the two counterparties and the regulators of the counterparties, if there

are any. Her attempts to increase CFTC regulation were strongly, effectively and—eventually it seemed clear—mistakenly opposed by Alan Greenspan (Federal Reserve Chair) and the two Treasury secretaries under Clinton, Robert Rubin and Larry Summers. In May of 1998, Arthur Levitt, the former SEC Chairman, joined in objecting to the CFTC's request. They effectively dismissed Born's concerns out of hand, arguing that the CFTC regulation of swaps and other OTC derivative instruments would increase the legal uncertainty surrounding such instruments and would create possible turmoil in the markets and thereby contribute to reducing the value of the instruments. They also argued that Born's proposed regulatory costs would stifle innovation and move such transactions out of the US. Born lost the political fight but was vindicated when the economic/financial of 2008 affected US and world markets. It now is widely held that the rejection of Born's CFTC's proposals and the adversarial relationship Rubin, Greenspan, and Levitt had with Born also reflected an ideological difference over whether the capital markets could be trusted to regulate themselves, an issue that remains alive today.

Born did not comment publicly on these events until March 2009 when she lamented the influence of Wall Street lobbyists in the process and suggested that the market had grown so big and with such little oversight that it exacerbated the financial crisis.

Now considered one of the overlooked voices in the wilderness, Born was awarded the John F. Kennedy Profiles in Courage Award in 2009. See the October 2009 Frontline documentary, "The Warning," for further detail.

4

INFORMATION AS AN ECONOMIC COMMODITY[1]

This chapter is intended as a catalogue of questions and viewpoints, raising some serious problems with the concepts supplied by standard economic theory. I don't promise to give much in the way of interesting answers; indeed, one interpretation of what I say is that in some sense there cannot be any fully definite theory of economic behavior.

Specifically, I want to argue that the role of information in the economy is essential to our understanding of its workings. By itself, this proposition would seem to be so evident that it is not worth discussing. However, I want to argue that the process of acquiring information is more complex than is usually understood. As a result, the consequences for the economy are much different than the standard picture of economic theory. This approach may suggest some explanation of the occasionally erratic behavior of the modern economic system which has been observed throughout the last two centuries and more.

You doubtless all know that I have devoted a considerable part of my career as an economist in the elaboration of the general equilibrium approach to the understanding of the economy. One question that was much discussed when I was a beginner was the incorporation of uncertainty into general equilibrium theory. I was very proud that I developed a formalism which accomplished that.[1] The economic agents take account of the possible random events in advance and know what will happen under each possible realization. Hence, news will affect the markets, but it cannot cause a runaway reaction. I seem then to be repudiating a good part of my life's work. Actually, I was always aware of some issues, and a careful reading of my papers will show reservations and caveats. I don't intend this lecture to be a defense of myself, but I make a few remarks explaining my past thinking. What I want to stress in this lecture is that information is endogenous to the economic system. Information comes in many shapes and forms, but two important things can be said. One, it plays an essential role in directing the allocation of resources above and beyond the role of the prices of the usual commodities. Two, it is itself a commodity, being both scarce and valuable, but it has properties quite different from the usual. The special properties of information make the usual modeling of allocation through a market of limited use.

My approach will be to start with the standard approach of economic theory. I assume that consumers are rational with regard to consumption and with regard to risk-bearing. Firms maximize profits, although that term requires definition. There are markets, at least until they prove to be difficult or impossible. The markets clear at some appropriate price.

As we shall see, the program leads to some conclusions but also deep difficulties. It is these that we want to emphasize.

Given this background, I want to introduce information as an explicit economic variable, governed by the same motivations as other economic choices. But the peculiarities of information as a commodity are stressed.

To introduce the subject and show its significance, I will review the different ways in which information affects the economic system.

The Roles of Information in the Economic System

That information is important to the economy might seem to be self-evident. Ever since the work of Robert Solow, it has been evident that economic progress has been propelled for the most part by increase in knowledge, what we usually think of technological progress. This is information about the transformation of goods from one form to another. In the usual neoclassical system, these are embodied in the production possibility sets. In the simplest version, the change takes place exogenously, usually represented by an exponential factor in some part of the model. (Of course, exponential growth forever is not possible, but it could conceivably be an approximation.) Even in this simple account there are, or ought to be, complications. Technical change, after all, occurs in specific industries. It will change relative prices. If I am considering investing in that industry, I might postpone the investment to take advantage of a superior process. I might worry that a competitive product will become cheaper and so not invest today. In short, anticipating technical progress will have effects on current economic behavior.

A second and even more obvious complication is that technological change doesn't just happen. It is the result of a decision to seek it, and it is costly. There is sometimes a tendency to regard technological change as a by-product of scientific research, itself not directed to a particular technology and so exogenous. Even if this were an adequate formulation for science, which it is not, there is still a large expenditure on research and development needed to achieve viable and useful alterations in technology.

There is another issue, clearly of great importance in understanding economic history and economic development. This is the question of diffusion of knowledge. It is clear that just as production functions differ over time, they also differ among countries and even regions at a given moment of time. In fact, they differ considerably among firms in a single country. That diffusion is not instantaneous requires explanation.

There are undoubtedly many factors here, but surely one is the idea of intellectual property; new productive ideas are often owned. But this is not really compatible with the view that technological progress is exogenous. It means that a firm owns an idea because it has invested in it. There is also a second factor in the slowness of diffusion;

acquiring already existing information is itself costly. This point should be obvious to any professor watching his or her students expending considerable effort in understanding the course material.

We already see some lessons for the economics of information. (1) The information an individual has is a matter of choice, not a given. (2) Information is, in general, costly. (3) Information is not only about the natural world and its laws but also about the actions of others; the actions of others in turn depend on their information.

Most other kinds of information found in the economic system are even more clearly information about others within the economic system. The financial sector, now greatly expanded in size, is essentially an industry based on collecting information about the parts of the economy and acting on that information. The actions include purchases and sales of securities but are not confined to what are ordinarily thought of as markets. They also include two-party contracts, such as extension of credit to firms (commercial credit) and to individuals (personal loans, mortgages on real estate).

The circular nature of information in the market was given explicit recognition by Oskar Morgenstern in a paper of 1934, before his joint work with John von Neumann on game theory. He had been concerned with business cycle forecasting, as head of the Austrian Business Cycle Research Institute. He began to question whether forecasting was possible, by recognizing what we have already observed, that in effect individuals are forecasting each others' forecasts.

At about the same time, in 1936, John Maynard Keynes, in *The General Theory of Employment, Interest, and Money*, likened the capital market to an advertising campaign run by an American brewery. The advertisements contained the pictures of six models, and each participant was to choose one. The participant got a prize if his or her choice had the most votes. Clearly, the participant should choose, not the one he or she deems the prettiest, but the one which others think is the prettiest. But clearly this process leads to an infinite regress. Keynes's point is really much the same as Morgenstern's; rational forecasts are circular.

Of course, mutual dependence does not necessarily mean a failure of the system. The standard theory of general equilibrium shows that one can have a consistent outcome. I return to this question a bit later.

Rational Theory of Information Acquisition

One kind of behavior under uncertainty is the acquisition of information. Hence, a rational theory of information acquisition can be and has been deduced from the general theory of behavior under uncertainty.

Rational behavior under uncertainty is usually modeled as follows. Individuals have some choice of actions, such as investment in various risky alternatives, which yield an uncertain outcome. That is, the outcome depends on factors outside the control of the individual and about which they are uncertain. Then the hypothesis of rational action says that individuals have a utility function, $U(x)$, and they choose their actions so as to maximize, $E[U(x)]$. I am not going to examine the empirical validity of this hypothesis, but rather use it as a starting-point.

What we must consider here is the acquisition of information as one of the actions the risk-bearer might undertake. The bulk of our analysis under uncertainty has dealt with the purchase of securities with random future prices and other uncertainties of payment, the analysis of production with uncertain outcomes, or devices to maintain consumption in the presence of random shocks to income and wealth. However, it has always been somewhat true that individuals facing uncertainty try to acquire more information about the uncertainty.

The optimal choice of information has been studied especially by mathematical statisticians. A simple form is that of sampling. There is some parameter, relevant to the individual's decisions but unknown to it. This might be, for example, the mean return to be expected on a security. We can make observations which are governed by a probability distribution dependent on that parameter. Then our uncertainty about the parameter after making the observations has changed; usually, it has been reduced.

We can formalize this change in uncertainty by the use of Bayes' Theorem. Suppose our initial uncertainty about the mean return is represented by a probability distribution. Call this the *prior* distribution. Then, after drawing the sample, Bayes' Theorem yields a new distribution, called the *posterior* distribution. This is the distribution to be employed in making optimal investment decisions. It is easy to show that, in investing a given amount of money, it is always better to optimize given the posterior.

But of course sampling is in general costly. A statistical prototype is acceptance sampling. Suppose a firm orders a large number of items. Some of them may be defective. Testing any item is expensive. The firm takes a sample and tests each one. It then makes a decision to accept or reject the entire lot, taking account the posterior distribution of defects and the costs and benefits of accepting or rejecting the lot. One further decision is the size of the sample. The larger the sample, the lower the probability of a wrong decision, but also the higher the cost.

In terms of an investment portfolio, an individual may devote some of his or her initial wealth to research, then use the rest of the funds to invest on the basis of the posterior distribution. Hence, the investor has to allocate their funds among a number of alternative commodities, which include not only different securities but also information. However, there is one special way in which the demand for information differs from usual demand functions. The information is typically about the *rate* of return, not the amount. Hence, its value to the investor depends on the amount invested. We would expect that those with more wealth will buy more information, so that the rate of return on what they have invested should on the average be higher. There is some evidence that this is in fact true empirically. This proposition certainly implies that individuals in the market face different distributions of returns, since they buy different amounts of information.

There are alternative sources of information. It follows that there is a tradeoff between the quality of the information and its cost. Investors may tend to use readily available information, such as transactions on observable markets, rather than better but scarcer information. They may also tend to use information from those to whom they are close for non-economic reasons.

For all these reasons, it is clear that the market will not reflect all the information available and that the information used by different parties will be different.

The Market as Information: Theory

Let me turn to a significant strand of the economic literature, especially in the last century. This is the idea, conveyed in several different forms, that market prices are themselves information. This is an idea which has hovered between a metaphor and an expression of reality.

An early expression is Adam Smith's reference to the "invisible hand." I should say immediately that historians of thought have debated extensively about Smith's meaning. The context is a little odd, since it distinguishes between domestic and foreign investment. I have read the relevant passages very carefully, and I find the usual interpretation to be correct. Each investor seeks out the most profitable investment; the result is to increase national income. Clearly, the prices are being used as signals, but only in a metaphorical sense. Each individual takes the prices as facts and does not analyze them as a statistical sample.

In short, the "invisible hand" really merges into what we would call today, "welfare economics." It would appear that, by a happy coincidence, competitive equilibrium is efficient in some sense only made clear by gradual developments in economic analysis. One aspect of the matter is the question of computation. However defined, competitive equilibrium is a matter of solving a quite complicated set of equations. The great Italian economist, Vilfredo Pareto, analogized the market to a computer; in fact, at least in the French translation of his major work in economics, he used the word now standard in French for, "computer." Indeed, he extolled the market as able to solve systems far beyond the capacities of then-current computing, that is, in 1904.

The idea that prices might convey information in a more literal sense seems to have started with the analysis of possible socialist systems. By the end of the nineteenth century, socialist parties had significant representation in European parliaments, and the prospect that socialism might be enacted through democratic processes was a possible ace. This raised the question how a socialist system would actually operate. Pareto, though an economic liberal and anti-socialist, was interested in the question, and encouraged a younger economist, Enrico Barone, to develop a model of a socialist economy (1906). Here, the central ministry controls resources. Prices are announced, and the firms and households announce their demands and supplies at those prices. Prices are varied until supply equals demand. Although Barone's paper contained all the essence of the later discussion, it was unknown until it was rediscovered by Hayek.

The discussion became a public issue just after the end of World War I, particularly in Austria, where the prospect of a socialist take-over appeared imminent. Ludwig von Mises argued that a socialist system was impossible. Joseph Schumpeter apparently disagreed and urged a student, Kläre Tisch, to explain how a price system could serve as signaling, an analysis very similar to Barone's, which of course he knew nothing about. There followed a spate of articles, frequently not known to others, repeating, extending, and clarifying the process. Friedrich von Hayek is perhaps the most famous of these authors, but Jacob Marschak, Fred Taylor, and especially the Polish economist, Oskar Lange, must be mentioned.

The basic issue began to be seen as a problem in computing and information costs. A centralized system required the transmission of all the knowledge in individual firms to a central authority, an impossibly costly transaction. Market socialism tried to achieve an optimum by an iterative approach in which the only items of information transmitted were the supplies and demands for the successive price approximations.

A fuller formalization of the issues and an enormous clarification was the paper of Leonid Hurwicz (1960). In particular, Hurwicz emphasized what is the key requirement implicit in the market socialism discussion, what he called the "privacy-preserving" principle. Each unit was supposed to receive messages and then, on the basis of its private knowledge, send out new messages, according to certain rules. When the messages all agreed, the process stopped, and the agreement contained in the messages was carried out. The messages were from a limited set. Hurwicz demonstrated, for example, that under the usual assumptions that hold for competitive equilibrium, the price system was in some sense at least as efficient in informational terms as any other.

The Market as Information: In Practice

Let us turn to the question: To what extent can markets guide investment activity? The costs are incurred in the present, but the returns occur in the future. What are the relevant markets for investment activity? There are very few. That is, there are very few markets for the sale of future goods. There are of course securities markets, including markets for derivatives. These are commitments to pay money in the future. These do not allocate specific goods, but they do help allocate goods in some general sense across time. But an interesting question arises: Why are there any transactions? There are of course some straightforward explanations; individuals are at different points in their life cycle, so that older people sell and younger ones buy, or some people or firms have some need for resources for other purposes, foreseen or not. But clearly most transactions in existing securities are due to disagreement in expectations, which corresponds to a point already made. Let's look at some examples.

The wheat futures market is about as well-organized a market as one is likely to find. Yet, its behavior accords only in part with the basic theory of markets. Wheat is largely purchased by millers at the time of harvest for making flour. The standard account argues that risk-averting millers want to buy wheat in advance for delivery at harvest time. They do so to avoid uncertainty in the price they pay. Like most people who buy insurance, they expect to lose on the average; they are buying price certainty at price. It is then expected that the speculators who sell the futures will profit. They buy the crop as it comes to market, so they profit by the difference between the then current price and the futures price. They participate on the basis on an expected profit. A detailed study showed that the miller did indeed lose, as the standard theory would hold. But the speculators fell into two categories. One consisted of the brokers who also traded on their own account. They profited, but their incomes were not any higher than they probably could earn elsewhere, say, bank officers. The other group consisted of outsiders. They lost money on the average. The question is why did the outside speculators enter at all? Clearly the information available to them was defective.

The deviations from theory in other futures markets are much more dramatic. Consider for example the market for foreign exchange. The explanation for buying foreign exchange is that international sales are not delivered instantaneously, and it may be some time before delivery is made and payment made. The foreign exchange, for example, the ruble–dollar ratio, may change during the intervening program, and the seller may want to hedge against this uncertainty. This would imply that the demand for foreign exchange in a year should be roughly equal to world trade. In fact, the transactions are about 300 times greater. Clearly, most of the transactions are between people who have no legitimate hedging interests. Instead, these markets are used essentially for betting among people with different information and beliefs.

Still another example where behavior of a future-oriented market departs from standard economic theory is the behavior of the standard stock market. In theory, the price of a stock should be the discounted value of its dividends with adjustment for risks. This is, after all, a summary of a very long future. It should not change abruptly from day to day. Yet, a change in the aggregate stock market index of 1 percent or 2 percent in one day is considered quite normal. Again, this implies that the information sets underlying the market price is remarkably unstable.

The behavior of the securities markets and other credit transactions in the current crisis hardly suggests very good response to information. Indeed, even earlier, there was an incident which should have given warning. In 1998, a very successful hedge fund found itself in trouble.

This fund operated by investing its clients' money to arbitrage some quite small deviation from a normal relation. These deviations were so small that they yielded little profit unless borrowed money was used. The fund was in fact borrowing 97 percent of the amount it invested. When their returns fell short, they were temporarily unable to repay. The amount borrowed was so great their creditors and even the Federal Reserve Board saw this as a threat to the safety of the creditors and therefore to the financial system as a whole. It is the behavior of the lenders that is so difficult to understand. They had a lot at stake, and they were experts in understanding risks. Of course, they had had only favorable experiences with this hedge fund, and this was part of their information set.

This particular situation was ultimately resolved with little loss, except to the fund itself. The favorable outcome may have been unfortunate in building up a lack of concern to the greater speculation that followed. The latter was due to mortgage-backed securities, and again the financial sector proved unable to assemble the information to cause caution on the part of the market. The underlying facts were clear enough. The ultimate source of value was the housing market, where prices were rising rapidly. There many comments in the financial press on the possible unsustainability of this rise, so the financial sector should have at least recognized the uncertainty of the situation and curtailed its lending. Similarly, the market and the credit system seem to have been unable to anticipate the problems with Greek debt. While there was evidently some concealment on the part of the Greek government, I find it hard to believe that diligent study would not have at least raised suspicions.

General Equilibrium with Markets for Future and Uncertainty

In the final section of my chapter, I want to review briefly the general equilibrium theory for allocation over time and under uncertainty. I want to reexamine why the markets called for in the theory do not exist and what are the implications for economic behavior of their failure to exist.

Erik Lindahl seems to have been the first to note that capital theory could be regarded as ordinary value and equilibrium theory with commodities that are given dates. (So steel delivered next year is a different commodity from steel delivered today.) Equilibrium means that the market for each commodity at each date clears. Lindahl first published his ideas in a paper in Swedish in 1929, translated into English in 1939. John R. Hicks came up with a similar approach to capital theory in 1939, though it was embedded in a more sophisticated and more fundamentally based theory of firm and consumer behavior.

It turned out that a parallel construction can introduce uncertainty into general equilibrium theory. Following the general approach to probability theory as set forth by A.N. Kolmogorov, we refer to a *state of nature* as a complete description of the world (or at least the parts relevant to it). Uncertainty then is represented by a probability distribution over states of nature. We then identify commodities not only by date but also by the state of nature. A typical market transaction would be to commit to deliver a physically described commodity at a given date if a given state of nature occurs. I proposed this construction in a paper in 1952, and it was subsequently considerably deepened by Gerard Debreu (1959).

Clearly, however, this extremely rich set of markets is very far from reality. As we have already seen, only a few such markets exist. Since a market should emerge if there are any mutual gains from its creation, we have to ask why this should be. I will return to at least one explanation in a minute or so. We may also ask what the implications of this market failure are. We have already seen them. They create a need for forecasting, with all the problems already sketched. If markets for all future dates and for all risks existed, then the prices at which these transactions will take place are known, and no further information will be of any use. It is the market failure that makes information-seeking so important.

But we must observe that to have a general equilibrium which handles time and uncertainty, there are some hidden informational assumptions. Consider for example the simplest model for equilibrium over time, where there is privacy-preserving in Hurwicz's sense.

Suppose each individual has no uncertainty about his or her future income. However, some individuals wish to modify the time stream of consumption from that of income. They might want, say, to lend in period 1, and then consume more in period 2; in total, period 2 income plus repayment with interest of the loan. This sounds pretty straightforward, but how do we know, even in this simple case, that the borrower can or will desire to repay. To be sure, we can impose some penalty, that is, regard the borrower as bankrupt. But the borrower may prefer this outcome, having consumed a great deal in period 1.

Hence, even if all the relevant markets existed, it would be valuable to acquire information, in this specific information about the borrower. Banks classically have had as a main part of their business investigating the creditworthiness of those it considers lending to. It is also true that uncertainty and informational problems can prevent markets from emerging. Consider the contingent market defined earlier. For it to exist, it is necessary that all parties understand what state of nature has occurred. This is a condition on the information held by the economic agents involved.

We have come to one of the most important development in economic theory in the last 60 years, the recognition that individuals hold differing information. The term, *asymmetric information*, has been coined, and it includes such well-known phenomena as moral hazard and adverse selection. The concept is very important in understanding a number of different fields, especially those where the commodity dealt with includes a good deal of information. Medical practice and insurance and financial services are two good illustrations. The failure of the market to operate too well in these circumstances has led to a literature, usually called *mechanism design*, on creating incentives, usually within firms, to achieve some improvement.

Finally, associated with these modifications of general equilibrium theory, I must return once more to the acquisition of information.

Suppose first that each individual has a little bit of information. A price emerges, which reflects everybody's information. This price thus conveys something about everyone else's information, and therefore increases everyone's information. One can continue this process until an equilibrium is reached. This approach has been developed by a number of authors.

Suppose however the information is not initially given to the agents on the market. They may choose to acquire some, and so start the process. But, as Grossman and Stiglitz have pointed out, if the price is highly informative, then it doesn't pay any particular agent to acquire information. But if no one acquires the information, then it never enters the market price, which is therefore uninformative.

Multiple Sources of Information

We have seen the extreme importance of information in guiding the economic system in view of the absence of adequate prices for the future and for risky events. Let me just make a few simple remarks, designed to emphasize the possibility that changes in information and belief may play a major role in the rather sudden and radical alterations in economic activity to which the capitalist system has been subject since its rise to dominance.

A first remark is that information, though a commodity, has very different properties from ordinary commodities. It can be used or sold, but it still remains in existence and in the hands of its original owner. Hence, the smooth reactions we usually expect in well-running markets may fail.

Second, getting information is very subtle. Essentially, we make inferences about the inferences made by others. Even seeing that someone will buy at the price I offered to sell tells me something about his information. We are quickly led to infinite regresses. There is no necessary contradiction, but the reasoning processes may not be capable of being carried out, so we stop short.

All these characteristics suggest the possibility of excessive reaction to a minor change in information.

I know I haven't answered my questions, but I hope some of you will be stimulated to think further on the role of information in the economic system.

Note

1   This paper was written by Kenneth J. Arrow and presented first at the XIII April International Academic Conference on Economic and Social Development, National Research University, Higher School of Economics.

AFTERWORD

April, 2016

The 2016 presidential campaign season was a remarkable one; atypical, even inexplicable, in many ways. To explain the Trump and Sanders candidacies in particular, analysts raised many of the themes discussed by Arrow in our prior conversations. We thus conducted one final conversation in April 2016, presented here as an Afterword. We appreciate the publisher's help in shifting the production schedule to allow this Afterword's inclusion.

Q. I want to follow up on our earlier conversations in the context of the current (2016) presidential campaigns. In trying to make sense of this unusual political season, it occurred to me that a lot of what we spoke about in our earlier conversations has some pretty strong parallels with what is happening now. It may not be immediately obvious, but as I look at what's happening, with Trump and with Sanders, it seems that both of these candidacies are tapping into a legitimate anger and fear that people have because they feel left out of the economic recovery. The media keeps saying, "Well, these people are uneducated voters." I think that kind of terminology demeans what is a more legitimate concern, which is that there are people who tend to be without jobs, without some of the skills that are necessary to get high paying jobs, or jobs at all, and that these also tend to be people who are uneducated. But there is a legitimacy in their fear that rang a bell for me when I thought about some of the things we talked about before, especially when you spoke of the recovery from the 2008 economic meltdown, and the reforms that were made, plus the reforms that were not made. I wondered if you had any thoughts about the political fallout of the economic change, and how that relates to the economic issues we discussed.

I have thoughts. But I have no more insight than anyone else. I have no special expertise. Let me put it this way: when you think about the periods when we had much greater economic problems than we have now, none of this happened. There were no Trumps. If you take a longer perspective, you can see that there were economic downturns before. We had the great depression, after all. Now, we certainly had wild characters then, too. We had Huey Long,[1] and Father Coughlin.[2] But they were marginal. They were not serious presidential candidates. They played no serious role in the presidential campaigns. There was nothing like this Donald Trump. There were third party candidates but they got maybe a million votes at best.

We had the period when wages were not constant. Unemployment was at 20 percent. Maybe not quite that high for the entire period, but it was certainly 15 percent, not 5 percent.[3] Certainly, wages weren't going anywhere. Farmers were in great trouble. Farmers now are prosperous. So then, there was a much greater economic problem. In some sense everybody shared in the Depression. But we have had times when we were much worse off, and yet we turned to unionization. That was a unifying influence. Not like this period.

It's true that I've never seen a really good statistical analysis of what is happening now. The allegation is that the white working class feels in decline, threatened by immigration and foreign competition, but that's not an adequate explanation. It's relatively bad, yes, but what we are seeing now is not restricted to the United States. Democracy is going crazy. Look at Hungry, look at Poland. Even pillars of democracy—like the Netherlands, Denmark, Sweden—countries you never thought were in danger, and now suddenly, you have 15–20 percent of the vote going to political parties that are actually anti-democratic. A lot of that is due to immigration, and the fear of immigration. But

Hungry and Poland are making very scary compromises with democracy. Poland has had a very successful transfer from the Soviet communist regime, and yet they now have a large part of their system that is anti-democratic.

Q. But wasn't there a lot of anti-immigration sentiment and isolationism during the 1930s, here and elsewhere? I wonder if the difference you're alluding to is that FDR was perceived as doing something? The question for me about this particular election (2016) is why this particular group of voters finds Trump attractive? Sander's appeal to them is easier to understand. But I wonder if the Trump group feels that the economic, and the banking reforms of 2008 in particular, were designed to benefit Wall Street not Main Street, to use the phrase in the popular press. I wonder if some of the hostility is reflected in the electorate's distancing itself from Establishment candidates, especially candidates like Jeb Bush or Hillary Clinton, both of whom are perceived as being associated not just with "the Establishment" but also with previous presidential families.

So my question is: do you have any suggestions? If you were advising a president or a presidential candidate, what policies would you advise him or her to make, not just to protect and help the lower-middle class and the working class, but also to convey to these voters the perception that the government was concerned with them? What policies would show that the government was not just protecting the big guys, and forgetting the little fellow?

It's rather ironic. The Tea party is anti-government. Obama did pass the health bill; why didn't that kind of policy make him popular? Why people who advocate cutting taxes on the rich are popular is confusing. Especially in this context, you would think cutting taxes on the poor would be popular. But that view is not popular. So things are rather incoherent. Trump stands for cutting taxes on the rich. This is not a logical set of policies. His politics do not even meet the first test for rationality. It's crazy. You see this in other areas too, not just the economic area. How do you account for the fact that more evangelicals vote for Trump than for Cruz? Trump's lifestyle could not be more opposed to an evangelical viewpoint.

The trouble is, my view of the world assumes that people are acting rationally. This means you should take from the rich and give to the poor. But the Trump programs don't make sense from any viewpoint. Again, if you look at foreign policy, Trump has no foreign policy that I can discern. Maybe relations with Russia will get better since Trump's a great admirer of Putin. I don't understand this, but then, nobody else seems to understand Putin very well either.

So I don't feel I should put myself on the line. I'm not an expert on politics. Unlike other matters, which I do know a bit about, for example, the economy. Obama wanted extensive spending; he wanted to run a deficit now by spending money. I think we needed that. My nephew [Larry Summers][4] keeps on saying you can borrow money at practically no interest rate at all, and spend it on improving the infrastructure, and that's a good deal. Or spend it on education, which is also valuable. Sander's proposal about free public education is totally off the mark. His proposals may carry a benefit for the upper class, who undoubtedly will do better in a competition for free places than the lower classes. But what you really want to do in terms of educational reform is to level the playing field; give money to those who really need it, to the people who may have talent but not the opportunity to develop that talent. My big policy recommendation would be to pour money into education in poor districts, especially at the elementary or high school level. Higher education is a separate and different issue. But the biggest problem at the elementary and high school level of education is to get more money into lower financial districts. Get more money for poor students. The way our current taxation policy works is that local districts pay for the local education. This means rich districts have far better schools. We have to overcome that. But even aside from the redistributive aspects of education policy, total spending for education has been kept pretty low. Smaller classes are not important for good students. But small classes are very important for lower performing students, for lower income students who may be bright but who have never been exposed to certain things that upper middle class students automatically get exposed to. Travel to foreign countries, conversation at home about politics or public life, visits to art museums and symphonies, that kind of thing.

The district where I live [Stanford, California] has a very good school but the average income is over $100K per family. California is about 40th in terms of their per capita spending on education. A rich state like California! It's amazing. Part of that is because the state budget is crowded out by expenditures on prisons and health. I approve the latter but not the former. So we need higher taxes, and especially we need higher taxes on the rich to redistribute income.

Now, foreign trade is a complicated matter. There is no easy matter there. Foreign competition, in particular, is tricky. I don't think the trade agreements we've actually arrived at have been especially harmful to jobs. The main competition comes from China, with whom we have no agreements, except the World Trade Organization (WTO). NAFTA (North American Free Trade Agreement) was not a big job loser. We started out with the post-World War II world, where we were the biggest power, the most efficient country in the world. Then other countries came back, first Japan, then Germany and now China. You can't expect to have a monopoly forever. We did have it for a period. Our manufacturing was dominant, but it was inevitable that we would lose that advantage, and from the consumer point of view, it's a good thing.

Q. This relates to your ideas on educational reform. Presumably, your reason for wanting to expand education is not just for fairness, but also because it will train people to compete more effectively in the world market.

That's right. We had a period when even without good education, you would make good money. When we were focused on the kind of mass production—in automobiles, steel, rubber, things like that—people without a good deal of education could be making $40 an hour. That era has passed. Now, we must remember that not everybody is educable. There's native ability, and family structure, which is deteriorating. That's another issue nobody seems to talk about much, but I think 40 percent of births now are to single mothers. The difficult pattern in the past has been that, even controlling for income, the prospects for children of single mothers are much lower than they are for children raised in two-parent families. At least judged by the past. Who knows what the future will bring. This phenomenon is not happening only in the US. It's also evident in parts of Europe. I don't know whether history will repeat itself or not, but, historically, being in a single mother family is a disadvantage.

Q. How can society as a whole deal with this issue?

This is a good point. I'm not sure what policies will address this. It's like population. I'm not a population pessimist but I have friends who study it who are. Let me give an analogy. People talk about how the world will come crashing down because we have too many people. It certainly hasn't happened yet. People have been saying this since Malthus, but there has to be some point at which we will have problems.[5] We have various calculations. These calculations are very speculative of course, but people like Paul Ehrlich have been arguing for years that this would happen.[6] Of course he's been wrong for over 40 years now, and the population bomb has not 'gone off'. Certainly people are better fed today than when he first wrote. But this is a matter for concern, since in principle, there has to be some point at which there is a limit to the amount of land that is useful for agriculture and there is some limit to agricultural productivity. Nobody knows what that number is. We don't seem to be able to address the problems of population because limiting the number of children you have violates the elementary principles of freedom. The right to determine what number of children you have is a pretty basic right. The Chinese and Indians have tried to limit it. The Chinese have been more successful than the Indians, but the Chinese are giving up on it now.

Now in a similar way, analogously, the population question relates to whether or not you want to bring up children singly or in marriage. A lot of the children who are in non-married couples, nonetheless have two parents. There is less of this pattern in the USA than in other countries. Iceland had a higher extent of unmarried children than other countries.[7]

Q. Let me back you up a bit. I know you've talked extensively about wanting more reform, Glass-Steagall with the banking reform in particular.[8] Do you see that happening?

Well Dodd-Frank is a big step forward. It doesn't remedy all the issues. The issue is how to carry it out. There are problems. One of Dodd-Frank's steps was to designate some financial entities as too big to fail. Do we let insurance companies as well as regular banks be designated as too big to fail? The big restriction was deleveraging. You have greater capital requirements. Some of these companies have been designated as too big to fail. Met Life has succeeded; Goldman Sachs is complaining. How this will work out, I don't know. But I assume "too big to fail" means that some companies should not be allowed to go under even when they get into trouble.

Q. How would you change Dodd-Frank?

I would have required more of these dangerous securities to be regulated. Take these things like debt-based obligations, like pooling mortgages. We have these securities based on mortgages. Like in the movie, *The Big Short.* You may have noticed in the movie, there was at one point an economist. He was a real economist, a president of the AEA (American Economic Association), Richard Thaler.[9] You take these debt-based obligations and put them on a mortgage and insist they be treated so people can price them. One of the advantages in that market is that you know about the prices other people are paying. But these securities, a lot of them were sold and the prices were not easily known, or were private. The chairman of the Commodity Futures wanted to have these securities under her jurisdiction. Under the Clinton administration she tried to do this but her proposal was rejected. That was a bad rejection. It was not cured by Dodd-Frank.

You treat the prices too seriously. One of the roles of governmental regulations is to make the market work.

Q. *So, you'd like to increase governmental regulation?*

Yes. These transactions should not be private, they should be public. The same thing holds true with the default swap. They were insurance against a particular company failing. But if everybody has the information, if everybody knows the price, then they know the risk. This is what is done with the future's market, which is also a kind of insurance.

Q. *So you'd like the default swaps to be subject to the same regulations as the other future's markets?*

That's right. If the Dodd-Frank had done this, it would be better. It's a bit technical so most people don't know much about it.

Q. *So just to sum up: you would have tougher government regulations for the financial industry, and increased money for education, especially for the elementary and high school grades?*

Yes.

Q. *But you are not advocating the Sanders plan?*

He's not expanding education. He just says that people who have education should have it free. I'm sure there are some people who would benefit from that, but the real problem is one that the Sanders plan does not address, and that is that more people should have education. To make it free for those who want to go. Now, I don't think college training is going to cure everything. Some people aren't capable of it. Of those who are unemployed today, two-thirds don't have college degrees. If you increase access to education somewhat, that's not going to cure the problem but it will make us have a more equitable system and it will bring into the workforce many people of talent who otherwise might get lost.

Another advantage of greater financial regulation relates to the fact that one-third of all the profits in the country comes from the financial part of the economy. So by having so many people in that area, you take away some of the brightest people who could be doing other things, things that are actually producing goods. Instead, when that many talented people go into the financial sector, they're just dealing with regulations. We'd be better off if they were doing something more in direct production. This has not always been the case. It's more now than it was 30 years ago.

Q. Have you been consulted by any political campaigns?

Not at all! [Laughs] I've never been involved in politics. I tend to see both sides of issues, which is not the best way to be politically effective.

Q. Like Truman's joke about wanting a one-handed economist?[10]

That's right. For a period of 6 months, I was at the Council of Economic Advisors. I did draft some memoranda which had consequences, but what I did was mostly negative. I held up some proposals. The idea of the Americans building an SST, for example. I kept it from getting off the ground.[11] But my value was negative; it was to recommend *not* doing something. [Laughs] Yes, it was valuable all right but it was negative. I also helped prevent a second Panama Canal being constructed by using explosives. In that instance, I was a more collateral player since the president's science adviser was the key person who opposed it. Edward Teller had the idea of using atomic explosives to build a second Panama Canal, and he also wanted to use atomic explosives to build things in Alaska. The fear and opposition to this idea was that we might become more comfortable using atomic weapons then, too.

The President's Science adviser was violently opposed to this plan of Teller's. It would have released atomic particles in the air, with all the consequences. I examined the economics of it to ask: was there any real value in a second Panama Canal? There indeed were occasions when the ships were queuing up to use the canal. The projections were that this queue would become worse. But it turned out the oil industry was using bigger tankers, which couldn't go through the canal anyway. I discovered that, in the long run, the backup of ships waiting to use the canal would not occur. So I wrote the opinion of the Economic Council. I was on the staff of the Economic Council, not a member.

Q. I don't remember this discussion. Was it public?

Yes, it was just before your time.[12] There also were questions about the fallout of atomic use. There were tests at Bikini. You send out warnings, of course, but not everyone gets them.

Q. I see. Let me shift the subject a bit. We spoke briefly about this topic before. I just wondered, do you think much about your economic legacy, or your legacy in general?

I can't help that. In fact, I am to give a lecture at the World Bank in June (2016). They want me to reflect on what I've done. So, I've thought about what I think my legacy means. Basically, it revolves around the meaning of knowledge in economics, of the importance of information. What I said before, about the market value of debt based securities, or credit default swaps, it's a way of saying that we make the price of things itself a source of information. The big thing about prices is that they tell you what's basically going on in the rest of the economy, beyond your immediate world. You know a bit about things but not all of the economy, so prices serve an informational function. Hayek's work has emphasized this, and so the idea got picked up by opponents of Hayek, too.

There was a whole controversy at the beginning of the twentieth century, after World War I, about how you run a socialist economy. There was a real possibility of this happening then. The socialist movement was very big in Europe. When they said *socialist* they meant *government ownership*. They did not mean what Sanders means. Certainly the idea that socialism could produce an ideal version of capitalism, essentially create a price system, and that supply and demand could be guided by the government, was prominently discussed. When I was first attracted to economics this was one of the big issues. My mentor, Harold Hoteling, was definitely a socialist. He was basically a statistician but also an economist. It may not have come out in his writings but this certainly was what his position was. Oskar Lange[13] and Abba Lerner,[14] there were quite a few other economists involved in this movement. The idea was that prices were an important way of conveying information about the rest of the economy. This one intrigued me, which is why I got interested in general equilibrium theory. It seems somewhat descriptive of the capitalist society. I think the biggest thing I did was spread the idea that the knowledge question can never be equally distributed. I focused on the health industry. I wrote a paper that turned out to be influential to both the health industry and insurance. My first thought was that your pricing leads to your generalized insurance policies. I buy wheat depending on the rates, but I pay a price depending on what the future price of wheat is, depending on what the rainfall is. I later tried to apply this to health. I realized that the problem is that people have different knowledge. The physician you deal with knows a great deal more than you do, so you can't tell how sick you are. This impairs the market's ability to convey information. Prices are not all revealing.

Q. So you're setting all your work into the broader discussion about market capitalism and the value of socialism?

Yes. The impossibility theory. It's very hard to answer the question: which is the better system?

Q. You described Harold Hoteling as a market socialist. Would you describe yourself as a market socialist too?

Not now. I would have at one time.

Q. How would you describe yourself now?

A tinkerer. Making small improvements to the existing system, which is a capitalist system. I'm not prepared to make big changes. The socialist system in the USSR led not just to tyranny but also to economic starvation. Real communism led to tyranny. The trials, the show trials—these happened long before your time—were a conspicuous event in the 1930s, where the people who had been in the Bolshevik revolution got arrested and questioned—grilled, really—then they got sent to Siberia, accused of conspiring to bring down the Soviet regime.

Q. But even aside from the political excesses of communism, most people, most economists, find that the economy simply cannot function without a market. We need the market to do precisely what you say: to provide information.

Yes, but the Soviets did have a modicum of success. If the communist regime did better than capitalism would have done, we can't test. But Russia in the last decades of communism was growing pretty rapidly. Beginning in the 1930s, there were terrible things going on there. The famines, for one, but certainly after the Second World War, the Soviet economy was growing at a pretty good pace. They were even increasing their consumption levels. But then it fizzled out.

But it's not that it didn't work at all. It did. True, it was definitely falling behind the capitalist world. But to say that it wasn't functioning is a gross exaggeration. Similarly, with the satellite countries, the countries of Eastern Europe. Again they were falling behind Western Europe. I don't want to say it was a catastrophe, though eventually millions of people died of starvation, but after World War II, things were growing. Prices did play a role. Not that they abandoned prices completely. Most of these countries suffered a loss when they first switched to capitalism.

Q. I'm struck by how much of your thinking about economics relates the macro and micro together. A lot of economists separate them. You don't see them as separate.

Yes. There's no question that there are differences. I specialize in the micro, but it does not give an adequate story about why we still have unemployment. That's still a mystery. Micro does answer a lot of questions, but now there is a tendency among a lot of economists who are for slow growth, to advocate something we used to call in a depressed economy secular stagnation. This term was coined around 1938 by an American Keynesian called Alvin Hansen[15] who argued that it would be a long period where demand was going to be low and a micro point. This means the people will consume more from the macro point of view, and there would be permanently high unemployment. He wrote this up in 1938. Well, then came the War and the post-war period didn't sound at all like this description. So, now again I hear about secular stagnation. Now, it is true that there are periods where the output for a worker has apparently been growing very slowly. I say apparently because I suspect there's actually something wrong with the measurement. Now, in Silicone Valley they talk about a finite bit of output. But overall, there's a lot of tendency to project whatever is going on in the moment. From the American point of view, the post-war period of 30-year growth is a pretty good run. Around 1980 my friend Bob Solow[16] noted that we saw computers everywhere during the whole computer revolution but the statistics on productivity didn't show a great increase. In the 1990s we seemed to have a big increase. Then even before the 2008 recession the ratio of output to input was growing slowly, well before the big crash of 2008. That's the macro problem, and frankly I don't think anyone understands it. So the micro and macro don't mesh. I'm a bit on the micro side. I don't have much to say about macro issues.

Q. We've spoken a bit about your intellectual legacy. We don't speak often of the personal issues, which is fine, but I know that as people get into their 80s and 90s, they often step back and think about their lives as a whole. Forgive me if this is too personal, but I'd be curious to know: how do you make sense of your life? Are there things you want to say to anybody, students or children, about advice, about what you've learned? How do you make sense of it all, as you think about your life?

[Laughs] I'm not sure I know now to address that question! I 've always been very impressed with the accidental nature of my life. It could have been different. I look at the nature of my parents, the availability of City College as a place to go, a place with zero tuition. My life, the fact that I came into contact with someone like Hoteling, well, my life could have turned out quite differently.

Q. I remember one of the things you said to me, when we started our conversations, was your quoting Louis Pasteur about chance favoring the prepared mind.

Yes. I think that's true. That's been a very big characteristic in my life. A number of things that I've done, specifically, were the response to questions that I encountered in the literature. Two of the most important things were responses to questions; one was social choice theory and the other was my work on the health economics. In both cases a very small question led to a very big answer. Certainly, in neither case did I expect the answer I found. In social choice, I thought there was a simple answer, but I couldn't find it. Maybe there is no simple answer. The idea that there is no answer would not necessarily occur to a lot of people. That's why I say it's the prepared mind. But also, I have to laugh, of course, on the chance nature of relations, which is also an accident. Harold Hotelling was caught here by the outbreak of the war. He accepted the chance to teach at City College. I'm sure that's why I've always had a side interest in history. I might have become a historian under different circumstances. I'm willing to accept that things could be different.

Q. It's interesting that as I asked you this question, you were laughing. I can hear you laughing now. I hear a youthful exuberance in your voice, plus a kind of intellectual curiosity and honesty that translates into your being willing to go places you didn't know even existed initially. That seems to be a very critical part of who you are.

Yes, I think that is part of how I am, and always have been.

Notes

1 Huey Pierce Long Jr. (August 1893–September 1935) was the 40th Governor of Louisiana (1928–1932) and a United States Senator from 1932 until his murder in 1935. Long supported FDR in the 1932 election and was a populist who criticized both the rich and the banks. His "Share our Wealth" program proposed massive redistribution of wealth via taxes on both corporations and individuals. Like FDR, Long supported massive federal spending on public works, school, and old age pensions. Supposedly, Long hoped to challenge FDR for the presidency in 1936 with the aid of Father Coughlin. Long posed a credible threat to Roosevelt but was killed in 1935, probably by Dr Carl Weiss in what was part of a political fracas in Louisiana. Long's legacy is mixed. His supporters find him a populist and praise his expansion of education, hospitals, and massive highways that ended rural isolation in Louisiana. His detractors consider him a dictator and a demagogue.

2 Father Coughlin (1891–1979) was a charismatic and controversial Roman Catholic priest, born in Canada, but based in Michigan. Coughlin's popular radio show put him in contact with nearly thirty million listeners throughout the 1930s. Like Long, Coughlin was initially an FDR New Deal supporter; but Coughlin soon turned on FDR, and by 1934 began criticizing Roosevelt because of FDR's ties to the bankers. In 1934 Coughlin formed a National Union for Social Justice. This group advocated greater monetary reforms and protection of labor, the nationalization of railroads and major industries. While Coughlin's organization numbered in the millions, it lacked organization, and by the late 1930s, when Coughlin's anti-Semitism and support of Fascist policies became increasingly apparent, Coughlin was forced off the air. The Catholic Church insisted Coughlin cease all political activities and focus on parish duties. Coughlin submitted to these terms and stayed in his position as parish pastor until 1966, when he retired. He died in Michigan in 1979.

3 Unemployment was 3.14 percent in 1929. Its high came in 1933, when 24.75 percent of the American population were unemployed. Rates did not drop out of the 20s or teens until 1941, when it hit 9.66 percent, according to official US governmental statistics.

4 Lawrence Henry "Larry" Summers is an economist, President Emeritus and Charles W. Eliot University Professor of Harvard University, and former Secretary of the Treasury. Among his many acts while in public office, Summers was influential in the privatization of the economies of

the post-Soviet states and in the move to deregulate the U.S financial system, including the repeal of the Glass-Steagall Act.

5 An English clergyman and scholar, Thomas Robert Malthus (February 1766–December 1834) wrote *An Essay on the Principle of Population*, in which he argued that population multiplies geometrically and food arithmetically. This means that the population will eventually overtake the food supply

6 Along with his wife, Anne Ehrlich, Stanford professor Paul Ehrlich published *The Population Bomb* in 1968. The book warned that there would be mass starvation in the coming decades because of overpopulation. The book triggered fears of a "population explosion". Criticized for its alarmist tone, and predictions that turned out to be inaccurate, the book was defended by the Ehrlichs for having alerted the world of the need to pay attention to environmental issues

7 According to the Center for Disease Control's National Center of Health Statistics, 40 percent of the births in the USA are to unmarried women in 2007, compared with 34 percent in 2002. Iceland had 66 percent of the births to unmarried women, Sweden had 55 percent, 54 percent in Norway and 46 percent in Denmark in 2007, as opposed to Japan, where nearly all children born are to married couples. The Report does not look at cohabitation, so these children may be born into families with two parents, simply not to married parents. The report does note, however, that children born to a single mother are more likely to have low birth weights, pre-term births, infant mortality and limited social and financial resources.

8 The Banking Act of 1933 is commonly known as the Glass-Steagall Act, after its sponsors. It grew out of the emergency legislation passed by Franklin Roosevelt within days of taking office in March 1933, and was designed to restore confidence in the banking system. The bill attempted "to provide for the safer and more effective use of the assets of banks, to regulate interbank control, to prevent the undue diversion of funds into speculative operations, and for other purposes." Former Treasury secretary, then Senator Carter Glass (D-VA) was the main force behind the act. Rep. Henry Steagall (D-AL), then chairman of the House Banking and Currency Committee, supported the act with Glass only after Glass agreed to add an amendment to permit bank deposit insurance. The bill was signed into law on June 16, 1933. The bill has many important provisions, one of which was insisted upon by Steagall, who was concerned about small rural banks. Steagall insisted the act establish the FDIC (Federal Deposit Insurance Corporation), which insures bank deposits with a pool of money collected from banks. Essentially, then, Glass-Steagall

refs to the Depression-era bank regulation, designed to keep separate the different types of financial institutions. President Clinton signed legislation reversing it in 1999. Some analysts argue that it was the ditching of the Glass-Steagall that resulted in the 2007–8 financial crisis. (Sen. Bernie Sanders is one of these critics.) President Clinton defends his actions, however, and Hillary Clinton has so far refused to pledge to reinstate Glass-Steagall if elected president. Most analysts find the demise of Glass-Steagall was just part of a broader deregulatory climate that led to the financial crisis.

9 Richard Thaler teaches at the University of Chicago and is a past president of the American Economic Association. Influenced by Daniel Kahneman and Herbert Simon, Thaler is known for his work in behavioral economics, which argues that the classical model of economic behavior needs to be revised to allow for human cognitive biases, such as a bias toward the status quo and an aversion to loss.

10 Supposedly it was Harry Truman who joked: "Give me a one-handed economist! All my economists say, 'on one hand . . . on the other.'"

11 SST stands for supersonic transport, which was a civilian supersonic airplane designed to transport passengers at speeds faster than the speed of sound. The Tupolev Tu-144 and the Concorde were the only SSTs to conduct regular service. They ceased commercial flights in 1978 (Tupolev Tu-144) and 2003 (Concorde), largely due to noise, expensive construction and development costs, and price compared with sub-sonic airliners.

12 This discussion took place around 1963, when President Kennedy explored the feasibility of using nuclear weapons to excavate a second canal in Panama. The thinking was that a larger canal could more easily accommodate outsize transportation vehicles, such as supertankers.

13 A Polish diplomat and economist, Oskar Ryszard Lange (July 1904–October 1965) was best known for advocating the use of market pricing tools in socialist systems and for providing a model of market socialism.

14 Abraham (Abba) Ptachya Lerner (October 1903–October 1982) was born into a Jewish family in Bessarabia, but emigrated to Great Britain when only three years old, where he was raised in London's East End. Lerner entered the London School of Economics in 1929 and studied with Friedrich Hayek, and, later at Cambridge (1934–1935), with John Maynard Keynes. In 1937, Lerner came to the United States where he came to befriend Milton Friedman and Barry Goldwater. Lerner never received The Sveriges Riksbank Prize in Economic Sciences in Memory of Alfred Nobel, but is considered one of the great economists of his era.

15 Perhaps America's most influential Keynesian, Alvin Harvey Hansen (August 1887–June 1975) helped create both the Council of Economic Advisors and the Social Security system.

16 Robert Merton Solow's (August 23, 1924) work on the theory of economic growth led to the exogenous growth model. Solow received the 1961 John Bates Clark Medal, the 1987 Nobel Memorial Prize in Economic Sciences, and the 2014 Presidential Medal of Freedom.

APPENDIX

The Complete Works of Kenneth J. Arrow

Books

1. [1951] *Social Choice and Individual Values*. New York: Wiley.
2. [1958] (with S. Karlin and H. Scarf) *Studies in the Mathematical Theory of Inventory and Production*. Stanford, CA: Stanford University.
3. [1958] (with L. Hurwicz and H. Uzawa) *Studies in Linear and Non-Linear Programming*. Stanford, CA: Stanford University.
4. [1959] (with M. Hoffenberg and the assistance of H. Markowitz and R. Shephard) *A Time Series Analysis of Interindustry Demands*. Amsterdam: North-Holland.
5. [1963] *Social Choice and Individual Values*. New York: Wiley, 2nd edition.
6. [1965] *Aspects of the Theory of Risk-Bearing*. Helsinki: Yrjö Jahnssonin säätiö.
7. [1970] (with M. Kurz) *Public Investment, the Rate of Return, and Optimal Fiscal Policy*. Baltimore and London: Johns Hopkins.
8. [1971] (with F.H. Hahn) *General Competitive Analysis*. San Francisco, CA: Holden-Day; Edinburgh: Oliver & Boyd.
9. [1971] *Essays in the Theory of Risk-Bearing*. Chicago, IL: Markham; Amsterdam and London: North-Holland.
10. [1974] *The Limits of Organization*. New York: W.W. Norton.
11. [1976] (with S. Shavell and J. Yellen) *The Limits of the Market Economy* (in Japanese). Memorandum for Ministry of International Trade and Industry, Japan.

12. [1976] *The Viability and Equity of Capitalism.* E.S. Woodward lecture, Department of Economics, University of British Columbia.
13. [1977] (with L. Hurwicz) *Studies in Resource Allocation Processes.* Cambridge, London, New York, and Melbourne: Cambridge University.
14. [1983] *Collected Papers of Kenneth J. Arrow, Volume 1, Social Choice and Justice.* Cambridge, MA: The Belknap Press of Harvard University.
15. [1983] *Collected Papers of Kenneth J. Arrow, Volume 2, General Equilibrium.* Cambridge, MA: The Belknap Press of Harvard University.
16. [1984] *Collected Papers of Kenneth J. Arrow, Volume 3, Individual Choice under Certainty and Uncertainty.* Cambridge, MA: The Belknap Press of Harvard University.
17. [1984] *Collected Papers of Kenneth J. Arrow, Volume 4, The Economics of Information.* Cambridge, MA: The Belknap Press of Harvard University.
18. [1985] *Collected Papers of Kenneth J. Arrow, Volume 5, Production and Capital.* Cambridge, MA: The Belknap Press of Harvard University.
19. [1985] *Collected Papers of Kenneth J. Arrow, Volume 6, Applied Economics.* Cambridge, MA: The Belknap Press of Harvard University.
20. [1986] (with Hervé Raynaud) *Social Choice and Multicriterion Decision-Making.* Cambridge, MA: MIT.
21. [2000] *Théorie de l'information et des organisations.* Edited by T. Granger. Paris: Dunod.
22. [2014] *La Obra dde Kenneth Arrow: Una Selección.* Edited by J. María Vegara. Madrid: Instituto de Estudios Fiscals.

Books Edited

1. [1960] (with S. Karlin and P. Suppes) *Mathematical Methods in the Social Sciences, 1959: Proceedings of the First Stanford Symposium.* Stanford, CA: Stanford University.
2. [1962] (with S. Karlin and H. Scarf) *Studies in Applied Probability and Management Science.* Stanford, CA: Stanford University.
3. [1969] (with T. Scitovsky) *Readings in Welfare Economics.* American Economic Association Series of Republished Articles in Economics. Homewood, IL: Richard D. Irwin, Vol. XII.
4. [1971] *Selected Readings in Economic Theory from Econometrica.* Cambridge, MA and London: MIT.
5. [1978] (with S. J. Fitzsimmons and R. Wildenmann) *Zukunftsorientierte Planung und Forschung fur die 80er Jahre.* Koningstein/Ts., German Federal Republic: Athenaum Verlag.

6. [1981] (with C.C. Abt and S. J. Fitzsimmons) *Applied Research for Social Policy: The United States and the Federal Republic of Germany*. Cambridge, MA: Abt.

7. [1981] (with M. Intriligator) *Handbook of Mathematical Economics, Volume I*. Amsterdam, New York and London: North-Holland.

8. [1982] (with M. Intriligator) *Handbook of Mathematical Economics, Volume II*. Amsterdam, New York, and London: North-Holland.

9. [1985] (with Seppo Honkapohja) *Frontiers of Economics*. Oxford and New York: Basil Blackwell.

10. [1986] (with M. Intriligator) *Handbook of Mathematical Economics, Volume III*. Amsterdam, New York, and London: North-Holland.

11. [1988] (with M. J. Boskin) *The Economics of Public Debt*. Basingstoke and London: Macmillan in association with The International Economic Association.

12. [1988] (with P.W. Anderson and D. Pines) *The Economy as an Evolving Complex System*. Redwood City, CA: Addison-Wesley.

13. [1988] *The Balance between Industry and Agriculture in Economic Development. Volume I: Basic Issues*. Basingstoke and London: Macmillan in association with The International Economic Association.

14. [1991] *Issues in Contemporary Economics. Volume I, Markets and Welfare*. Basingstoke and London: Macmillan in association with the International Economic Association.

15. [1994] (with R. Arnott, A.B. Atkinson, and J. Drèze) *Public Economics*, by William Vickrey. Cambridge, U.K., New York, and Oakleigh, Victoria: Cambridge University.

16. [1995] (with R.H. Mnookin, L. Ross, A. Tversky, and R. Wilson) *Barriers to Conflict Resolution*. New York and London: W.W. Norton.

17. [1996] (with E. Colombatto, M. Perlman, and C. Schmidt) *The Rational Foundations of Economic Behavior*. Basingstoke and London: Macmillan in association with the International Economic Association.

18. [1996] (with R.W. Cottle, B.C. Eaves, and I. Olkin) *Education in a Research University*. Stanford, CA: Stanford University.

19. [1996–97] (with Amartya Sen and Kotaro Suzumura) *Social Choice Re-examined*. Basingstoke and London: Macmillan in association with the International Economic Association, 2 vols.

20. [1998] (with Yew-Kwang Ng and Xiaokai Yang) *Increasing Returns and Economic Progress*. Basingstoke, UK: Macmillan, and New York: St. Martin's.

21. [2000] (with S. Bowles and S. Durlauf) *Meritocracy and Economic Inequality.* Princeton, NJ: Princeton University.

22. [2001] (with G. Debreu) *Landmark Papers in General Equilibrium Theory, Social Choice, and Welfare Economics.* Cheltenham, UK, and Northampton, MA: Edward Elgar.

23. [2002] (with Amartya Sen and Kotaro Suzumura) *Handbook of Social Choice and Welfare*, Volume 1. Amsterdam: Elsevier.

24. [2010] (with Amartya Sen and Kotaro Suzumura) *Handbook of Social Choice and Welfare,* Volume 2. Amsterdam: Elsevier.

Collective Studies

1. [1971] (as member of Climatic Impact Committee of the National Research Council, National Academy of Sciences, National Academy of Engineering) *Environmental Impact of Stratospheric Flight.* Washington, DC: National Academy of Sciences.

2. [1977] (as member of Nuclear Energy Policy Study Group) S.M. Keeny, Jr., et al., *Nuclear Power Issues and Choices.* Cambridge, MA: Ballinger.

3. [1979] H.H. Landsberg, et al., *Energy: The Next Twenty Years.* Cambridge, MA: Ballinger.

4. [1981] (as Chairman of the Committee for a Planning Study for an Ongoing Study of Costs of Environment-related Health Effects, Institute of Medicine) *Costs of Environment-related Health Effects.* Washington, DC: National Academy.

5. [1991] (as member of the Oversight Review Board of the National Acid Precipitation Assessment Program) *The Experience and Legacy of NAPAP.* Washington, DC: National Acid Precipitation Assessment Program.

6. [1993] (as Co-chair) Report of the NOAA [National Oceanic and Atmospheric Administration] Panel on Contingent Valuation. *Federal Register* 58, No. 10 (January 15, 1993): 4602–4614.

7. [1995] (with B. Bolin, R. Constanza, P. Dasgupta, C. Folke, C.S. Holing, B.-O. Jansson, S. Levin, K.-G. Maler, C. Perrings, and D. Pimentel) Economic growth, carrying capacity, and the environment. *Science* 268 (April 28, 1995): 520–521.

8. [1996] (with M.L. Cropper, G.C. Eads, R.W. Hahn, L.B. Lave, R.G. Noll, P.R. Portney, M. Russell, R. Schmalensee, V.K. Smith, and R.N. Stavins) *Benefit-Cost Analysis in Environmental, Health, and Safety Regulations: A Statement of Principles.* La Vergne, TN: AEI, c/o Publisher Resources.

33. [2004] New Antimalarial drugs: biology and economics meet. *Finance and Development* 41, No. 1: 20–21.

34. [2004] A Personal Agenda for the Next Decade. *Review of International Economics*, 12(2): 2070212.

35. [2004] Kenneth J. Arrow. In D. Colander, R.P.F. Holt, and J.B. Rosser, Jr. (Eds.) *The Changing Face of Economics* Ann Arbor, MI: University of Michigan. Chapter 1, pp. 291–308.

36. [2005] (with E.L. Lehmann) Harold Hotelling, 1895–1973. *Biographical Memoirs,* National Academy of Sciences 87 (2005): 3–15.

37. [2005] No time to waste in the fight against malaria. *Financial Times* 6 January: 15.

38. [2006] Foreword. P. Gangopadhyay and M. Chaterji, *Economics of Globalisation.* Aldershot, UK: Ashgate, pp. xi–xiv.

39. [2006] Kenneth Arrow on economic thought and academic freedom. *Academe* 92 (3): 45–48 (Interview).

40. [2006] The responsibility of parents to children. In M.A. Glendon and P. Donati (Eds.) *Vanishing Youth: Solidarity with Children and Young People in an Age of Turbulence.* Vatican City: Pontifical Academy of Social Sciences, Acta 12.

41. [2008] Comment on "Historical Origins of 'Open Space'" (by Paul David). *Capitalism and Society 3*: Iss. 2, Article 6. 1–6, Available at www. bepress.com/cas/vol3/iss2/art6

42. [2009] Some developments in economic theory since 1940: an eyewitness account. *Annual Review of Economics* 1: 1–16.

43. [2009] Economists and Glory. *Occasion: Interdisciplinary Studies in the Humanities* 1, no. 1. http://occasion.stanford.edu/node/7.

44. [2010] Recollections on Cambridge economics. *Cambridge Economics* (Cambridge Faculty of Economics Newslettter) Autumn Issue No. 3, p. 5.

45. [2011] (with D.B. Bernheim, M.J. Feldstein, D.L. McFadden, J.M. Poterba, and R.M. Solow) 100 Years of the AER: The Top 20 Articles. *American Economic Review* 101: 1–8.

46. [2011] Foreword. In T. Söderqvist, A.Sundbaum, C. Folke, and K.-G. Mäler (Eds.) *Bringing Ecologists and Economists Together: The Askö Meetings and Papers.* Dordrecht, Heidelberg, London, and New York. pp. vii–viii.

47. [2015] Microeconomics and operations research: their interactions and differences. *Information Systems Frontiers* 17: 3–19.

Papers

1. [1949] On the Use of Winds in Flight Planning. *Journal of Meteorology* 6: 150–159.

2. [1949] (with D. Blackwell and M.A. Girshick) Bayes and Minimax Solutions of Sequential Decision Problems. *Econometrica* 17: 213–244.

3. [1950] Homogeneous Systems in Mathematical Economics: A Comment. *Econometrica* 18: 60–62.

4. [1950] A Difficulty in the Concept of Social Welfare. *Journal of Political Economy* 58: 328–346.

5. [1951] Alternative Proof of the Substitution Theorem for Leontief Models in the General Case. In T.C. Koopmans, (Ed.) *Activity Analysis of Production and Allocation*. New York: Wiley, Chapter IX.

6. [1951] (with T.E. Harris and J. Marschak) Optimal Inventory Policy. *Econometrica* 19: 250–272.

7. [1951] Alternative Approaches to the Theory of Choice in Risk-Taking Situations. *Econometrica* 19: 404–437.

8. [1951] Little's Critique of Welfare Economics. *American Economic Review* 41: 923–934.

9. [1951] Mathematical Models in the Social Sciences. In D. Lerner and H.D. Lasswell (Eds.), *The Policy Sciences*. Stanford, CA: Stanford University, pp. 129–154.

10. [1951] An Extension of the Basic Theorems of Classical Welfare Economics. In J. Neyman (Ed.), *Proceedings of the Second Berkeley Symposium on Mathematical Statistics and Probability*. Berkeley and Los Angeles: University of California, pp. 507–532.

11. [1952] The Determination of Many-Commodity Preference Scales by Two-Commodity Comparison. *Metroeconomica* IV: 107–115.

12. [1952] Le principe de rationalité dans les décisions collectives. *Économie Appliquée* V: 469–484.

13. [1953] Le rôle des valeurs boursières pour la répartition la meilleure des risques, *Économetrie*. Colloques Internationaux du Centre National de la Recherche Scientifique, Vol. XI, pp. 41–47.

14. [1953] (with E.W. Barankin and D. Blackwell) Admissible Points of Convex Sets, *Contributions to the Theory of Games, II*. Princeton, NJ: Princeton University, pp. 87–91.

15. [1954] (with G. Debreu) Existence of Equilibrium for a Competitive Economy. *Econometrica* 22: 265–290.

16. [1954] Import Substitution in Leontief Models. *Econometrica* 22: 481–492.

17. [1956] (with L. Hurwicz) Reduction of Constrained Maxima to Saddle-Point Problems. In J. Neyman (Ed.) *Proceedings of the Third Berkeley Symposium on Mathematical Statistics and Probability*. Berkeley and Los Angeles: University of California, Vol. V, pp. 1–20.

18. [1956] (with A.C. Enthoven) A Theorem on Expectations and the Stability of Equilibrium. *Econometrica* 24: 288–293.

19. [1957] Statistics and Economic Policy. *Econometrica* 25: 523–531.

20. [1957] (with L. Hurwicz) Gradient Methods for Constrained Maxima. *Operations Research* 5: 258–265.

21. [1957] Decision Theory and Operations Research. *Operations Research* 5: 765–774.

22. [1958] Utilities, Choices, Attitudes: A Review Note. *Econometrica* 26: 1–23.

23. [1958] Tinbergen on Economic Policy. *Journal of the American Statistical Association* 53: 89–97.

24. [1958] The Measurement of Price Changes. In Joint Economic Committee, *The Relationship of Prices to Economic Stability and Growth*. Washington, DC: U.S. Government Printing Office, pp. 77–88.

25. [1958] (with M. Nerlove) A Note on Expectations and Stability. *Econometrica* 26: 297–305.

26. [1958] (with A. Alchian and W.M. Capron) *An Economic Analysis of the Market for Scientists and Engineers*. Santa Monica, CA: The Rand Corporation, RM 2190-RC.

27. [1958] (with M. McManus) A Note on Dynamic Stability. *Econometrica* 26: 448–454.

28. [1958] (with L. Hurwicz) On the Stability of the Competitive Equilibrium. *Econometrica* 26: 522–552.

29. [1959] Toward a Theory of Price Adjustment. In M. Abramovitz and others, *The Allocation of Resources*. Stanford, CA: Stanford University, pp. 41–51.

30. [1959] (with W.M. Capron) Dynamic Shortages and Price Rises: The Engineer-Scientist Case. *Quarterly Journal of Economics* 63: 292–308.

31. [1959] Rational Choice Functions and Orderings. *Economica*, N. S. 26: 121–127.

32. [1959] (with H.D. Block and L. Hurwicz) On the Stability of the Competitive Equilibrium, II. *Econometrica* 27: 82–109.

33. [1959] Functions of a Theory of Behavior under Uncertainty. *Metroeconomica* 11: 12–20.

34. [1960] (with L. Hurwicz) Competitive Stability under Weak Gross Substitutability: The "Euclidean Distance" Approach. *International Economic Review* 1: 38–49.

35. [1960] Optimization, Decentralization, and Internal Pricing in Business Firms. In *Contributions to Scientific Research in Management.* Western Data Processing Center, Graduate School of Business Administration, University of California, Los Angeles, pp. 9–18.

36. [1960] Decision Theory and the Choice of a Level of Significance for the t-Test. In I. Olkin and others (Eds.), *Contributions to Probability and Statistics.* Stanford, CA: Stanford University, pp. 70–78.

37. [1960] The Work of Ragnar Frisch, Econometrician. *Econometrica* 28: 175–192.

38. [1960] Price-Quantity Adjustments in Multiple Markets with Rising Demands. In K.J. Arrow, S. Karlin, P. Suppes (Eds.) *Mathematical Methods in the Social Sciences, 1959.* Stanford, CA: Stanford University, pp. 3–16.

39. [1960] (with L. Hurwicz) Decentralization and Computation in Resource Allocation. In R.W. Pfouts (Ed.), *Essays in Economics and Econometrics.* Chapel Hill, NC: University of North Carolina, pp. 34–104.

40. [1960] (with L. Hurwicz) Stability of the Gradient Process in N-Person Games. *Journal of the Society for Industrial and Applied Mathematics* 8: 280–294.

41. [1960] (with L. Hurwicz) Some Remarks on the Equilibria of Economic Systems. *Econometrica* 28: 640–646.

42. [1961] Additive Logarithmic Demand Functions and the Slutsky Relations. *Review of Economic Studies* 28: 176–181.

43. [1961] (with H.B. Chenery, B. Minhas and R.M. Solow) Capital-Labor Substitution and Economic Efficiency. *Review of Economics and Statistics* 43: 225–250.

44. [1961] (with L. Hurwicz and H. Uzawa) Constraint Qualifications in Maximization Problems. *Naval Research Logistics Quarterly* 8: 175–191.

45. [1961] (with A.C. Enthoven) Quasi-Concave Programming. *Econometrica* 29: 779–800.

46. [1962] Case Studies: Comment. In National Bureau of Economic Research, *The Rate and Direction of Inventive Activity: Economic and Social Factors.* Princeton, NJ: Princeton University, pp. 335–338.

47. [1962] Economic Welfare and the Allocation of Resources for Invention. In National Bureau of Economic Research, *The Rate and Direction of Inventive Activity: Economic and Social Factors.* Princeton, NJ: Princeton University, pp. 609–625.

48. [1962] Optimal Capital Adjustment. In K.J. Arrow, S. Karlin, and H. Scarf (Eds.) *Studies in Applied Probability and Management Science*. Stanford, CA: Stanford University, pp. 1–17.

49. [1962] (with M. Nerlove) Optimal Advertising Policy under Dynamic Conditions. *Economica* N.S., 29: 129–142.

50. [1962] The Economic Implications of Learning by Doing. *Review of Economic Studies* 29: 155–173.

51. [1962] (with L. Hurwicz) Competitive Stability under Weak Gross Substitutability: Nonlinear Price Adjustment and Adaptive Expectations. *International Economic Review* 3: 233–255.

52. [1963] Conference Remarks. In M. Astrachan and A.S. Cahn (Eds.) *Proceedings of RAND'S Demand Prediction Conference, January 25–26, 1962*. Santa Monica, CA: The RAND Corporation, RM-3358-RP, pp. 125–134.

53. [1963] Utility and Expectation in Economic Behavior. In S. Koch (Ed.), *Psychology: A Study of a Science*. New York: McGraw-Hill, Vol. 6, pp. 724–752.

54. [1963] The Economic Cost to Western Europe of Restricted Availability of Oil Imports: A Linear Programming Computation. Appendix D in H. Lubell, *Middle East Oil Crises and Western Europe's Energy Supplies*. Baltimore, MD: John Hopkins, pp. 214–220.

55. [1963] Comment on Duesenberry's "The Portfolio Approach to the Demand for Money and Other Assets." *Review of Economics and Statistics* 45, Supplement, pp. 24–27.

56. [1963] Uncertainty and the Welfare Economics of Medical Care. *American Economic Review* 53: 941–973.

57. [1963–64] Control in Large Organizations. *Management Science* 10: 397–408.

58. [1964] Optimal Capital Policy, the Cost of Capital, and Myopic Decision Rules. *Annals of the Institute of Statistical Mathematics* 16: 21–30.

59. [1964] Research in Management Control: A Critical Synthesis. In C.P. Bonini, R.K. Jaedicke, and H.M. Wagner (Eds.), *Management Controls: New Directions in Basic Research*. New York: McGraw-Hill, Chapter 17, pp. 317–327.

60. [1965] Connaissance, Productivité et Pratique. *Bulletin SEDEIS*, Étude No. 909 Supplement.

61. [1965] *Statistical Requirements for Greek Economic Planning*. Center of Planning and Economic Research, Lecture Series No. 18. Athens, Greece.

62. [1965] Uncertainty and the Welfare Economics of Medical Care: Reply (The Implications of Transaction Costs and Adjustment Lags). *American Economic Review* 55: 154–158.

63. [1965] Criteria for Social Investment. *Water Resources Research* 1: 1–18.

64. [1965] The Economic Context. In S.T. Donner (Ed.) *The Future of Commercial Television, 1965–1975* (privately printed), pp. 116–139.

65. [1966] Discounting and Public Investment Criteria. In A.V. Kneese and S.C. Smith (Eds.), *Water Research*. Baltimore, MD: Johns Hopkins, pp. 13–32.

66. [1967] Values and Collective Decision-Making. In P. Laslett and W.G. Runciman (Eds.), *Philosophy, Politics and Society, Third Series*. Oxford: Basil Blackwell, Chapter 10, pp. 215–232.

67. [1967] The Place of Moral Obligation in Preference Systems. In S. Hook (Ed.) *Human Values and Economic Policy*. New York: New York University, Part II, 3, pp. 117–119.

68. [1967] Samuelson Collected. *Journal of Political Economy* 85: 506–513.

69. [1968] Economic Equilibrium. In *International Encyclopedia of The Social Sciences*. New York: The Free Press, Vol. 4, pp. 376–386.

70. [1968] The Economics of Moral Hazard: Further Comment. *American Economic Review* 58: 537–539.

71. [1968] (pseudonym of Archen Minsol; jointly with H.B. Chenery, B.S. Minhas, and R.M. Solow) Some Tests of the International Comparisons of Factor Efficiency with the CES Production Function: A Reply. *Review of Economics and Statistics* 50: 477–479.

72. [1968] Optimal Capital Policy with Irreversible Investment, in J.N. Wolfe (Ed.) *Value, Capital, and Growth*, Edinburgh: Edinburgh University, pp. 1–20.

73. [1968] Applications of Control Theory to Economic Growth, in American Mathematical Society, *Mathematics of the Decision Sciences*, Providence: American Mathematical Society, Part 2, pp. 85–119.

74. [1969] Classificatory Notes on the Production and Transmission of Technological Knowledge. *American Economic Review Papers and Proceedings* 59: 29–35.

75. [1969] The Organization of Economic Activity: Issues Pertinent to the Choice of Market Versus Nonmarket Allocation. In Joint Economic Committee, U. S. Congress, *The Analysis and Evaluation of Public Expenditures: The PPB System, Vol. 1*, pp. 47–66.

76. [1969] (with M. Kurz) Optimal Consumer Allocation Over an Infinite Horizon. *Journal of Economic Theory* 1: 68–91.

77. [1969] Tullock and an Existence Theorem. *Public Choice* VI: 105–112.
78. [1969] (with M. Kurz), Optimal Public Investment Policy and Controllability with Fixed Private Savings Ratio. *Journal of Economic Theory* 1: 141–177.
79. [1969] (with D. Levhari) Uniqueness of the Internal Rate of Return with Variable Life of Investment. *Economic Journal* 79: 560–566.
80. [1969] The Social Discount Rate. In G.G. Somers and W.D. Wood (Eds.) *Cost-Benefit Analysis of Manpower Policies*, Kingston, Ontario: Industrial Relations Centre, Queen's University.
81. [1970] Meyer A. Girshick. In *International Encyclopedia of the Social Sciences*. New York: The Free Press, Vol. 6, pp. 191–193.
82. [1970] The Effects of the Price System and Market on Urban Economic Development. In K.J. Arrow et al., *Urban Processes As Viewed by the Social Sciences*. Washington, DC: The Urban Institute, pp. 11–20.
83. [1970] (with M. Kurz) Optimal Growth with Irreversible Investment in a Ramsey Model. *Econometrica* 38: 331–344.
84. [1970] New Ideas in Pure Theory: Discussion. *American Economic Review Papers and Proceedings* 60: 462–463.
85. [1970] (with R.C. Lind) Uncertainty and the Evaluation of Public Investment Decisions. *American Economic Review* 60: 364–378.
86. [1970] Criteria, Institutions, and Function in Urban Development Decisions. In A.H. Pascal (Ed.) *Thinking About Cities*. Belmont, CA: Dickenson.
87. [1970] Induced Technical Change and Patterns of International Trade: Comment. In R. Vernon (Ed.) *The Technology Factor in International Trade*. New York: National Bureau of Economic Research, pp. 128–132.
88. [1971] The Firm in General Equilibrium Theory. In R. Marris and A. Wood (Eds.) *The Corporate Economy: Growth, Competition, and Innovative Potential*. Cambridge, MA: Harvard University, and London: Macmillan, pp.68–110.
89. [1971] A Utilitarian Approach to the Concept of Equality in Public Expenditures. *Quarterly Journal of Economics* 85: 409–415.
90. [1972] (with L. Hurwicz) An Optimality Criterion for Decision-Making Under Ignorance. In C.F. Carter and J.L. Ford (Eds.) *Uncertainty and Expectations in Economics: Essays in Honour of G.L. S. Shackle*. Oxford: Basil Blackwell, pp. 1–11.
91. [1972] (with R.C. Lind) Uncertainty and the Evaluation of Public Investment Decisions: Reply. *American Economic Review* 62: 171–172.

92. [1972] Problems of Resource Allocation in United States Medical Care. In R.M. Kurz and H. Fehr (Eds.), *The Challenge of Life*. Basel and Stuttgart: Birkhauser, pp. 392–408.

93. [1972] Models of Job Discrimination. In A.H. Pascal (Ed.) *Racial Discrimination in Economic Life*. Lexington, MA, Toronto, and London: D.C. Heath, Chapter 2, pp. 83–102.

94. [1972] Some Mathematical Models of Race in the Labor Market. In A.H. Pascal (Ed.) *Racial Discrimination in Economic Life*. Lexington, MA, Toronto and London: D.C. Heath, Chapter 6, pp. 187–204.

95. [1972] Gifts and Exchanges. *Philosophy and Public Affairs* 1: 343–362.

96. [1972] (with D. Levhari and E. Sheshinski) A Production Function for the Repairman Problem. *Review of Economic Studies* 39: 241–249.

97. [1972] Exposition of the theory of choice under uncertainty. In C.B. McGuire and R. Radner (Eds.) *Decision and Organization*. Minneapolis, MN: University of Minnesota, Chapter 2, pp. 19–56.

98. [1972] Value of and demand for information. In C.B. McGuire and R. Radner (Eds.) *Decision and Organization*. Minneapolis, MN: University of Minnesota, Chapter 6, pp. 131–140.

99. [1973] Some Ordinalist-Utilitarian Notes on Rawl's Theory of Justice. *Journal of Philosophy* 70: 245–263.

100. [1973] (with D. Starrett) Cost- and Demand- Theoretical Approaches to the Theory of Price Determination. In J.R. Hicks and W. Weber (Eds.) *Carl Menger and the Austrian School of Economics*. Oxford: Clarendon, Chapter 7, pp. 129–148.

101. [1973] Higher Education as a Filter. *Journal of Public Economics* 2: 193–216.

102. [1973] General Economic Equilibrium: Purpose, Analytic Techniques, Collective Choice. In *Les Prix Nobel en 1972*. Stockholm: The Nobel Foundation, pp. 206–231.

103. [1973] Social Responsibility and Economic Efficiency. *Public Policy* 21: 303–318.

104. [1973] Formal Theories of Social Welfare. In P.P. Wiener (Ed.) *Dictionary of the History of Ideas*. New York: Scribner, Volume IV, pp. 276–284.

105. [1973] *Information and Economic Behavior*. Stockholm (lecture): Federation of Swedish Industries.

106. [1973] The Theory of Discrimination. In O. Ashenfelter and A. Rees (Eds.) *Discrimination in Labor Markets*. Princeton, NJ: Princeton University, pp. 3–33.

107. [1973] (with F.J. Gould and S.M. Howe) A General Saddle Point Result for Constrained Optimization. *Mathematical Programming* 5: 225–234.

108. [1973] Rawls's Principle of Just Saving. *Swedish Journal of Economics* 75: 323–335.

109. [1974] The Measurement of Real Value Added. In P.A. David and M.W. Reder (Eds.) *Nations and Households in Economic Growth*. New York and London: Academic, pp. 3–19.

110. [1974] Stability Independent of Adjustment Speed. In G. Horwich and P.A. Samuelson (Eds.) *Trade, Stability, and Macroeconomics*. New York and London: Academic, pp. 181–202.

111. [1974] Capitalism, for Better or Worse. In L. Silk (Ed.) *Capitalism: The Moving Target*. New York: Quadrangle/New York Times, pp. 105–113.

112. [1974] Unbounded Utility Functions in Expected Utility Maximization: Response. *Quarterly Journal of Economics* 88: 136–138.

113. [1974] Limited Knowledge and Economic Analysis. *American Economic Review* 64: 1–10.

114. [1974] Optimal Insurance and Generalized Deductibles. *Scandinavian Actuarial Journal* 1974: 1–42.

115. [1974] (with A.C. Fisher) Environmental Preservation, Uncertainty, and Irreversibility. *Quarterly Journal of Economics* 88: 312–319.

116. [1974] On the Agenda of Organizations. In R. Marris (Ed.) *The Corporate Society*. New York and Toronto: Wiley, pp. 214–234.

117. [1974] The Combination of Time Series and Cross-Section Data in Interindustry Flow Analysis. *European Economic Review* 5: 25–32.

118. [1974] Government Decision Making and the Preciousness of Human Life. In L.R. Tancredi (Ed.) *Ethics of Health Care*. Washington, DC: National Academy of Sciences, Chapter II, pp. 33–47.

119. [1975] Vertical Integration and Communication. *The Bell Journal of Economics* 6: 173–183.

120. [1975] Thorstein Veblen as an Economic Theorist. *The American Economist* 19: 5–9.

121. [1975] On a Theorem of Arrow: Comment. *Review of Economic Studies* 62: 487.

122. [1975] Economic Development: The Present State of the Art. *Papers of the East-West Communication Institute*, No. 14.

123. [1976] Economic Dimensions of Occupational Segregation: Comment I. *Signs* 1, No. 3, Part 2: 233–237.

124. [1976] Quantity Adjustments in Resource Allocation: A Statistical Interpretation. In R.E. Grierson (Ed.) *Public and Urban Economics*, Lexington, MA, Toronto and London: Lexington Books, Chapter 1, pp. 3–11.

125. [1976] *Theoretical Issues in Health Insurance*. The University of Essex, Noel Buxton lecture for 1973.

126. [1976] Welfare Analysis of Changes in Health Coinsurance Rates. In R.N. Rossett (Ed.) *The Role of Health Insurance in the Health Services Sector*. New York: National Bureau of Economic Research, Chapter 1, pp. 2–23.

127. [1976] Evaluation of Social Experiments: Discussion. In C.G. Abt (Ed.) *The Evaluation of Social Programs*. Beverly Hills, CA, and London: Sage, pp. 49–54.

128. [1976] The Rate of Discount for Long-Term Public Investment. In H. Ashley, R.L. Rudman, and C. Whipple (Eds.) *Energy and the Environment: A Risk-Benefit Approach*. New York: Pergamon, pp. 113–140.

129. [1976] The Genesis of Dynamic Systems Generated by Metzler Matrices. In R. Henn and O. Moeschlin (Eds.) *Mathematical Economics and Game Theory: Essays in Honor of Oskar Morgenstern*. Berlin, Heidelberg, and New York: Springer-Verlag, pp. 629–644.

130. [1977] Extended Sympathy and the Possibility of Social Choice. *American Economic Review Papers and Proceedings* 67, No. 1: 219–225.

131. [1977] Current Developments in the Theory of Social Choice. *Social Research* 44: 607–622.

132. [1978] The Future and the Present in Economic Life. *Economic Inquiry* 16: 157–170.

133. [1978] Nozick's Entitlement Theory of Justice. *Philosophia* 7: 265–279.

134. [1978] Risk Allocation and Information: Some Recent Theoretical Developments. *The Geneva Papers on Risk and Insurance*, No. 8, June 1978 (Association Internationale pour l'Étude de l'Économie de l'Assurance).

135. [1978] Jacob Marschak's Contributions to the Economics of Decision and Information. *American Economic Review, Papers and Proceedings*, Vol. 68, pp. xii–xiv.

136. [1978] Jacob Marschak. In *International Encyclopedia of the Social Sciences*. New York: The Free Press, Vol. 18, Biographical Supplement, pp. 500–507.

137. [1979] (with R. Radner) Allocation of Resources in Large Teams. *Econometrica* 47: 361–385.

138. [1979] The Economics of Information. In M.L. Dertouzos and J. Moses (Eds.) *The Computer Age: A Twenty-Year View.* Cambridge, MA: MIT, pp. 306–317.

139. [1979] (with J. P. Kalt) *Petroleum Price Regulation.* Washington, DC: American Enterprise Institute for Public Policy Research.

140. [1979] The Property Rights Doctrine and Demand Revelation under Incomplete Information. In M. Boskin (Ed.) *Economics and Human Welfare.* New York and London: Academic, pp. 23–39.

141. [1979] The Trade-Off Between Growth and Equity. In H.I. Greenfield, A.M. Levenson, W. Hamovitch, and E. Rotwein (Eds.) *Theory for Economic Efficiency: Essays in Honor of Abba P. Lerner.* Cambridge, MA: MIT, pp. 1–11.

142. [1980] (with S. Chang) Optimal Pricing, Use and Exploration of Uncertain Natural Resource Stocks. In P.T. Liu (Eds.) *Dynamic Optimization and Mathematical Economics.* New York: Plenum, pp. 105–116.

143. [1980] Microdata Simulation: Current Status, Problems, Prospects. In R. Haveman and K. Hollenback (Eds.) *Microeconomic Simulation Models for Public Policy Analysis.* New York and London: Academic, Vol. 2, pp. 253–265.

144. [1980] Real and Nominal Magnitudes in Economics. *Journal of Financial and Quantitative Analysis* 25: 773–783.

145. [1981] Futures Markets: Some Theoretical Perspectives. *Journal of Futures Markets* 1: 107–113.

146. [1981] Optimal and Voluntary Income Distribution. In S. Rosefielde (Ed.) *Economic Welfare and the Economics of Soviet Socialism: Essays in Honor of Abram Bergson,* Cambridge, U.K.: Cambridge University, pp. 276–288.

147. [1981] (with L. Pesotchinsky and M. Sobel) On Partitioning a Sample with Binary-Type Questions in Lieu of Collecting Observations. *Journal of the American Statistical Association* 76: 402–409.

148. [1981] Pareto Efficiency with Costly Transfers. In J. Os (Ed.) *Studies in Economic Theory and Practice.* Amsterdam: North-Holland, Chapter 6.

149. [1981] The Social Choice Perspective. *Hofstra Law Review* 9: 1373–1380.

150. [1981] The Response of Orthodox Economics. In H.E. Daly and A.F. Umaña (Eds.) *Energy, Economics, and the Environment.* Boulder, CO: Westview, pp. 109–113.

151. [1981] On Finance and Decision Making. In R. Vernon and Y. Aharoni (Eds.) *State-Owned Enterprise in the Western Economies.* London: Croom Helm, pp. 63–69.

152. [1982] Risk Perception in Psychology and Economics. *Economic Inquiry* 20: 1–9.

153. [1982] Income Testing and Social Welfare: An Optimal Tax–Transfer Model: Discussion. In I. Garfinkel (Ed.) *Income-Tested Transfer Programs: The Case for and Against.* New York and London: Academic, pp. 319–323.

154. [1982] The Rate of Discount on Public Investments with Imperfect Capital Markets. In R.C. Lind and others, *Discounting for Time and Risk in Energy Policy.* Washington, DC: Resources for the Future, pp. 115–136.

155. [1982] Comment on Evolutionary Models in Economics and Law: Cooperative versus Conflict Strategies, by Jack Hirshleifer. In F. Zerbe (Ed.) *Research in Law and Economics*, 4: 81–87.

156. [1982] Criteria for public investment. In *The Trustee Papers: A collection of professional papers prepared for the Alaska permanent Fund Corporation Board of Trustees.* Juneau, AK: Alaska Permanent Function, pp. 9–14.

157. [1983] Contributions to Welfare Economics. In E.C. Brown and R.M. Solow (Eds.) *Paul Samuelson and Modern Economic Theory.* New York: McGraw-Hill, pp. 15–30.

158. [1983] Innovation in Large and Small Firms. In J. Ronen (Ed.) *Entrepreneurship.* Lexington, MA: Lexington Books, pp. 15–28.

159. [1983] Team Theory and Decentralized Resource Allocation: An Example. In P. Desai (Ed.) *Marxism, Central Planning, and the Soviet Economy.* Cambridge, MA, and London: MIT, Chapter 4, pp. 63–76.

160. [1983] Behavior under Uncertainty and Its Implications for Policy. In B. Stigum and F. Wentstp (Eds.) *Foundations of Utility and Risk Theory with Applications.* Dordrecht: D. Reidel, pp. 19–32.

161. [1984] Permanent and Transitory Substitution Effects in Health Insurance Experiments. *Journal of Labor Economics* 2: 259–267.

162. [1985] The Informational Structure of the Firm. *American Economic Review Papers and Proceedings* 75, 2: 303–307.

163. [1985] Maine and Texas. *American Economic Review Papers and Proceedings* 75, 2: 320–323.

164. [1985] The Economics of Agency. In J.W. Pratt and R.J. Zeckhauser (Eds.) *Principals and Agents: The Structure of Business.* Boston: Harvard Business School Press, Chapter 2, pp. 37–51.

165. [1986] Rationality of Self and Others in an Economic System. *Journal of Business* 59: S385–S399.

166. [1986] Planning and Uncertainty. In I. Adelman and J. E. Taylor (Eds.) *The Design of Alternative Development Strategies*. Rohtak, India: Jan Tinbergen Institute of Development Planning, Chapter 9.

167. [1986] Comments, in R.G. Cummings, D.S. Brookshire, and W.D. Schulze (Eds.) *Valuing Environmental Goods: An Assessment of the Contingent Valuation Method*. Totawa, NJ: Rowman and Allanheld, pp. 180–185.

168. [1987] The Demand for Information and the Distribution of Income. *Probability in the Engineering and Informational Sciences* 1: 3–13.

169. [1987] Technical Information, Returns to Scale, and the Existence of Competitive Equilibrium. In T. Groves, R. Radner, and S. Reiter (Eds.) *Information, Incentives, and Economic Mechanisms*. Minneapolis, MN: University of Minnesota, Chapter 7, pp. 243–255.

170. [1988] Ricardos Werk aus der Sicht der modernen Ökonomie. In K.J. Arrow, M. Ricardo, and H. Recktenwald, *David Ricardo: Eine moderne Würdigung*. Düsseldorf: Verlag Wirtschaft und Finanzen, pp. 43–59.

171. [1988] L'Informazione come Industria di Servizi. In G. Tamburini (Ed.) *Verso L'Economia dei Nuovi Servizi: I Settore Finanziario*. Bologna: Il Mulino, Chapter 1, pp. 29–38.

172. [1988] Presidential address: General Economic Theory and the Emergence of Theories of Economic Development. Chapter 2 in K.J. Arrow (Ed.) *The Balance between Industry and Agriculture in Economic Development*, Volume 1: Basic Issues. Basingstoke and London: Macmillan for the International Economic Association, pp. 22–32.

173. [1988] Overview of the Conference. In S. Borner (Ed.) *International Finance and Trade in a Polycentric World*. London: Macmillan in association with the International Economic Association, pp. 392–396.

174. [1989] Joan Robinson and Modern Economic Theory: An Interview. In G. Feiwel (Ed.) *Joan Robinson and Modern Economic Theory*. New York: New York University, Chapter 3, pp. 147–185.

175. [1989] Von Neumann and the Existence Theorem for General Equilibrium. In M. Dore, S. Chakravarty, and R. Goodwin (Eds.) *John von Neumann and Modern Economics*. Oxford: Clarendon, Chapter 2, pp. 15–28.

176. [1989] A "Dynamic" Proof of the Frobenius-Perron Theorem for Metzler Matrices. In T.W. Anderson, K.B. Atheya, and D.L. Iglehart (Eds.) *Probability, Statistics, and Mathematics: Papers in Honor of Samuel Karlin*. Boston, MA: Academic, pp. 17–26.

177. [1991] Certainty Equivalence and Inequivalence for Prices. In L.W. McKenzie and S. Zamagni (Eds.) *Value and Capital: Fifty Years Later*. Basingstoke, U.K.: Macmillan for the International Economic Association, pp. 41–63.

178. [1991] Cowles in the History of Economic Thought. In *Cowles Fiftieth Anniversary*. New Haven, CT: Cowles Foundation for Research in Economics, pp. 1–24.

179. [1991] The Dynamics of Technological Change. In Organization for Economic Co-operation and *Development, Technology and Productivity: The Challenge for Economic Policy*. Paris: OECD, pp. 473–476.

180. [1991] Panel Contribution: The Transition from Communism to an Alternative Economic Organisation. In A.B. Atkinson and R. Brunetta (Eds.) *Economics for the New Europe*. Basingstoke and London: Macmillan, in association with the International Economic Association, pp. 377–382.

181. [1991] Scale Returns in Communication and Elite Control of Organizations. *Journal of Law, Economics, and Organization* 7, Special Issue: 1–6.

182. [1991] Transition from socialism. *Estudios Economicos* 6: 5–22. El Colegio de Mexico.

183. [1992] Informational Equivalence of Signals. In P. Dasgupta, D. Gale, O. Hart, and E. Maskin (Eds.) *Economic Analysis of Markets and Games*. Cambridge, MA, and London: MIT, pp. 169–183.

184. [1992] Sex Differentiation in Annuities: Reflections on Utilitarianism and Inequality. In R. Selten (Ed.) *Rational Interaction*. Berlin: Springer-Verlag, pp. 333–336.

185. [1992] The Basic Economics of Arms Reduction. In W. Isard and C.H. Anderton (Eds.) *Economics of Arms Reduction and the Peace Process*. Amsterdam: Elsevier, Chapter 2, pp. 57–61.

186. [1992] Excellence and Equity in Higher Education. *Education Economics* 1: 5–12.

187. [1993] Economic Integration and the Future of the Nation-State. *Contemporary Policy Issues* XI: 1–6.

188. [1993] Contingent Valuation of Nonuse Values: Observations and Questions. In J. Hausman (Ed.) *Contingent Valuation: A Critical Assessment*. Amsterdam: North-Holland, Chapter XIV, pp. 479–484.

189. [1993] Does A Good Place Value News? In A.B. Atkinson (Ed.) *Alternatives to Capitalism: The Economics of Partnership*. New York: St. Martin's, Chapter 3, pp. 33–44.

190. [1993] (with J.E. Li) A Note on the Peace Dividend and Reallocation of Knowledge Skills. In J. Brauer and M. Chatterji (Eds.) *Economic Issues of Disarmament*. Basingstoke and London: Macmillan, Chapter 3, pp. 26–32.

191. [1994] Methodological individualism and social knowledge. *American Economic Review Papers and Proceedings* 84, 2: 1–9.

192. [1994] General Economic Theory and Income Distribution. In J.H. Bergstand, T.F. Cosimano, J.W. Houck, and R.G. Sheehan (Eds.) *The Changing Distribution of Income in an Open U.S. Economy*. Amsterdam, London, New York, and Tokyo: North Holland, 1994, Chapter 12, pp. 343–347.

193. [1994] The production and distribution of knowledge. In G. Silverberg and L. Soete (Eds.) *The Economics of Growth and Technical Change: Technologies, Nations, Agents*. Aldershot, U.K. and Brookfield, VT: Edward Elgar, Chapter 2, pp. 9–20.

194. [1994] (with T. Kehoe) Distinguished Fellow: Herbert Scarf's contributions to economics. *Journal of Economic Perspectives* 8: 161–181.

195. [1994] International peace-keeping forces: economics and politics. In M. Chatterji, H. Jager and A. Rima (Eds.) *The Economics of International Security*. Basingstoke: Macmillan, and New York: St. Martin's, pp. 81–86.

196. [1994] Information and the organization of industry. *Rivista internazionale di scienze sociali* 52: 111–124.

197. [1995] Foreword to M. McFaul and T. Perlmutter (Eds.) *Privatization, Conversion, Enterprise Reform in Russia*. Boulder, CO, San Francisco, CA, and Oxford: Westview.

198. [1995] A note on freedom and flexibility. In K. Basu, P. Pattanaik, and K. Suzumura (Eds.) *Choice, Welfare, and Development*. Oxford: Clarendon. pp. 7–16.

199. [1995] Some general observations on the economics of peace and war. *Peace Economics, Peace Science, and Public Policy* 2 (Winter): 1–8.

200. [1995] Information acquisition and the resolution of conflict. In K.J. Arrow, R.H. Mnookin, L. Ross, A. Tversky, and R. Wilson (Eds.) *Barriers to Conflict Resolution*. New York and London: Norton.

201. [1995] Economics as it is and as it is developing: a very rapid survey. In H. Albach and S. Rosenkranz (Eds.) *Intellectual Property Rights and Global Competition: Towards a New Synthesis*. Berlin: Edition Sigma, pp. 11–32.

202. [1995] The use of genetic and other medical information: ethical and market dilemmas. George Seltzer Distinguished Lecture, Industrial Relations Center, University of Minnesota.

203. [1995] Effet de serre et actualisation. *Revue de L'Energie* 471: 631–636.

204. [1995] (with D.W. Carlton and H.S. Sider) The competitive effects of line-of-business restrictions in telecommunications. *Managerial and Decision Economics* 16: 301–321.

205. [1996] Information, responsibility, and human services. In V.R. Fuchs (Ed.), *Individual and Social Responsibility: Child Care, Education, Medical Care and Long-Term Care in America.* Chicago and London: University of Chicago, Chapter 8, pp. 229–239.

206. [1996] Inequalities in income and wealth. In E. Malinvaud and M. Archer (Eds.) *The Study of the Tensions Between Human Equality and Social Inequalities from the Perspective of the Various Social Sciences.* Vatican City: Pontifical Academy of Social Sciences, pp. 115–124.

207. [1996] Comment on M. Kurz, "Rational preferences and rational beliefs." In K.J. Arrow, E. Colombatto, M. Perlman, and C. Schmidt (Eds.) *The Rational Foundations of Economic Behavior.* New York: St. Martin's, and Basingstoke and London: Macmillan, in association with the International Economic Association, pp 363–363.

208. [1996] The impact of operations research and decision theory on teaching and research in economics. In K.J. Arrow, R.W. Cottle, B.C. Eaves, and I. Olkin (Eds.) *Education in a Research University.* Stanford, CA: Stanford University, pp. 353–369.

209. [1996] The theory of risk-bearing: small and great risks. *Journal of Risk and Uncertainty* 12: 101–111.7.

210. [1996] (with J. Parikh and G. Pillet as Principal Lead Authors) Decision-making frameworks for addressing climate change. In J.P. Bruce, H. Lee, and E.F. Haites (Eds.) *Climate Change 1995: Economic and Social Dimensions of Climate Change*, Contribution of Working Group III to the Second Assessment of Intergovernmental Panel on Climate Change. Cambridge, UK, New York, and Melbourne: Cambridge University, pp. 53–78.

211. [1996] (with W.R. Cline, K-G. Mäler, M. Munasinghe, R. Squitieri, and J.E. Stiglitz as Principal Lead Authors) Intertemporal equity, discounting and economic efficiency. In J.P. Bruce, H. Lee, and E.F. Haites (Eds.) *Climate Change 1995: Economic and Social Dimensions of Climate Change*, Contribution of Working Group III to the Second Assessment

of Intergovernmental Panel on Climate Change. Cambridge, UK, New York, and Melbourne: Cambridge University, pp. 125–144.

212. [1996] The economics of information: a survey. *Empirica* 23: 119–128.

213. [1996] Elements of the economics of information; information and increasing returns. Chung-hua Series of Lectures by Invited Eminent Economists, No. 22: Nanking, Taipei, ROC: Institute of Economics, Academia Sinica.

214. [1996] Technical information and industrial structure. *Industrial and Corporate Change* 5: 645–652.

215. [1997] Economic growth for a small country. In A.W. Gray (Ed.) *International Perspectives on the Irish Economy*. Dublin: Indecon Economic Consultants, Chapter 1, pp. 1–8.

216. [1997] The benefits of education and the formation of preferences. In J.R. Behrman and N. Stacey (Eds.) *The Social Benefits of Education*. Ann Arbor, MI: University of Michigan, Chapter 2, pp. 11–16.

217. [1997] Invaluable goods. *Journal of Economic Literature* 35: 757–765.

218. [1997] The functions of social choice theory. In K.J. Arrow, A.K. Sen, and K. Suzumura, (Eds.) *Social Choice Re-examined*. Basingstoke and London: Macmillan in association with the International Economic Association, Vol. 1, pp. 3–9.

219. [1997] Kapitaltheorie als Erweiterung der Werttheorie. In K.J. Arrow, C. Bliss, and S. Zamagni, *John R. Hicks und sein "Value and Capital."* Dusseldorf: Verlag Wirtschaft und Finanzen, pp. 31–46.

220. [1998] Innovation and increasing returns to scale. In K.J. Arrow, Y-K Ng, and X. Yang, *Increasing Returns and Economic Progress*, Basingstoke, UK: Macmillan, and New York: St. Martin's, Chapter 18, pp. 403–408.

221. [1998] "What has economics to say about racial discrimination?" *Journal of Economic Perspectives* 12: 91–100.

222. [1998] The external costs of voting rules: a note on Guttman, Buchanan, and Tullock. *European Journal of Political Economy* 14: 219–222.

223. [1998] The place of institutions in the economy: a theoretical perspective. In Y. Hayami and M. Aoki (Eds.) *The Institutional Foundations of East Asian Economic Development*. Basingstoke and London: Macmillan, and New York: St Martin's in association with the International Economic Association, Chapter 2, pp. 39–48.

224. [1998] Inter-generational equity and the rate of discount in long-term social investment. In *International Economic Issues*, Vol. 4, *Economic Behavior and Design*, M. Sertel (Ed.). Basingstoke, UK: Macmillan, and New York: St. Martin's, Chapter 5, pp. 89–102.

225. [1999] Discounting, morality, and gaming. In P.R. Portney and J.P. Wyant (Eds.) *Discounting and Intergenerational Equity.* Washington, DC: Resources for the Future, Chapter 2, pp. 13–21.

226. [1999] (with F.H. Hahn) Notes on sequence economies, transaction costs, and uncertainty. *Journal of Economic Theory* 86: 203–218.

227. [1999] Amartya K. Sen's contributions to the study of social welfare. *Scandinavian Journal of Economics* 101: 163–172.

228. [1999] Team theory and distributed processing: surprise attack. *Information Systems Frontiers* 1: 11–13.

229. [1999] The economics of information. *Studi Economici* 54 (1): 5–14.

230. [1999] Comments on the commentaries. In J.E. Alt, M. Levi, and E. Ostrom (Eds.), *Competition and Cooperation: Conversations with Nobelists about Economics and Political Science.* New York: Russell Sage, pp. 51–65.

231. [1999] Reflections on political science. In J.E. Alt, M. Levi, and E. Ostrom (Eds.), *Competition and Cooperation: Conversations with Nobelists about Economics and Political Science.* New York: Russell Sage, pp. 321–325.

232. [2000] Economic transition: speed and scope. *Journal of Institutional and Theoretical Economics* 156: 10–18.

233. [2000] A comment on Cooper. *World Bank Research Observer* 15: 173–175.

234. [2000] Knowledge as a factor of production. In *Annual World Bank Conference on Development Economics 1999.* Washington, DC: International Bank for Reconstruction and Development, pp. 15–20.

235. [2001] Die Debatte uber Skalerntrage in "Economic Journal." In K.J. Arrow, S. Blankenburg, G.C. Harcourt, B. Schefold, and P. Sylos Labini, *Vademecum zu der Klassischen Debatte uber Kosten, Wettbewerb und Entwicklung,* Dusseldorf: Verlag Wirtschaft und Finanzen, pp. 47–56.

236. [2001] In memoriam: John C. Harsanyi. *Games and Economic Behavior* 36: 5–6.

237. [2001] The five most significant developments in economics of the twentieth century. *European Journal of the History of Economic Thought* 8: 298–304.

238. [2001] Reflections on the reflections. *Journal of Health Politics, Policy, and Law* 26: 1197–2003.

239. [2001] Entry, productivity, and investment. *Review of Economic Design* 6: 175–184.

240. [2001] Comment on "Developing Countries and the New Financial Architecture." In E. Malinvaud and L. Sabourin (Eds.) *Globalization: Ethical and Institutional Concerns.* Pontifical Academy of Social Sciences: Vatican City, pp. 306–310.

241. [2001] Economic anomalies (in Hebrew). *The Economic Quarterly* 48: 689–692.

242. [2002] Population, development, and human natures: a comment. *Environment and Development Economics* 7: 171–173.

243. [2002] Distributed information and the role of the state. In R.B. Freeman (Ed.) *Inequality around the World*. Basingstoke and New York: Palgrave Macmillan, Chapter 11, pp. 268–281.

244. [2002] An example of dynamic control of negative stock externalities. In B. Kristrom, P. Dasgupta and K.-G. Lofgren (Eds.) *Economic Theory for the Environment*. Cheltenham, UK, and Northampton, MA: Edward Elgar, Chapter 1, pp. 1–12.

245. [2003] (with P. Dasgupta and K.-G. Maler) The genuine savings criterion and the value of population. *Economic Theory* 21: 217–225.

246. [2003] (with P. Dasgupta and K.-G. Maler) Welfare economics in imperfect economies. In R. Arnott, B. Greenwald (Eds.) *Economics for an Imperfect World*. MA and London: MIT, Chapter 17, pp. 299–330.

247. [2003] (with P. Dasgupta and K.-G. Maler) Evaluating projects and assessing sustainable development in imperfect economies. *Environmental and Resource Economics* 26: 647–685.

248. [2003] General equilibrium and economic growth. In L. Basile, L. Basile, L.D'Apuzzo, M. Squillante and A.G.S. Ventre (Eds.) *Arrow*. Naples: La Citta del Sole, pp. 83–90.

249. [2004] Path dependence and competitive equilibrium. In T.W. Guinnane, W.A. Sundstrom, and W. Whatley (Eds.) *History Matters*. Stanford CA: Stanford University.

250. [2004] Is bounded rationality unboundedly rational? Some ruminations. In M. Augier and J.G. March (Eds.) *Models of a Man: Essays in Memory of Herbert A. Simon*. Cambridge, MA and London, pp. 47–55.

251. [2004] (with P. Dasgupta, L. Goulder, G. Daily, P. Ehrlich, G. Heal, S. Levin, K-G. Mäler, S. Schneider, D. Starrett, and B. Walker) Are we consuming too much? *Journal of Economic Perspectives* 18: 147–172.

252. [2004] Foreword. In M. Szenberg and L. Ramrattan (Eds.) *Reflections of Eminent Economists*. Cheltenham, UK, and Northampton, MA: Edward Elgar, pp. x–xii.

253. [2004] Speaking for the children and for the future. Vatican City: Pontifical Academy of Social Sciences. In M.A. Glendon (Ed.), *Inter-generational Solidarity, Welfare, and Human Ecology*, pp. 234–241.

254. [2005] John Holland and the evolution of economics. In L. Booker, S. Forrest, M. Mitchell, and R.L. Riolo (Eds.) *Perspectives on Adaptation in Natural and Artificial Systems.* Oxford and New York: Oxford University, Chapter 13, pp. 281–290.

255. [2005] Personal reflections on applied general equilibrium models. In T.J. Kehoe, T.N. Srinivasan, and J. Whaley (Eds.) *Frontiers in Applied General Equilibrium Theory.* Cambridge, UK, New York, Port Melbourne, Madrid, and Cape Town: Cambridge University, Chapter 1, pp. 13–23.

256. [2006] Winter on Schumpeter on the firm: some issues of intertemporal continuity. *Industrial and Corporate Change* 15: 143–144.

257. [2006] Freedom and social choice: notes from the margin. *Utilitas* 18: 52–60.

258. [2006] Foreword. In M. Szenberg, L. Ramrattan, and A.A. Gottesman (Eds.) *Samuelsonian Economics and the Twenty-first Century.* Oxford and New York: Oxford University, pp. xi–xiv.

259. [2006] Questions about a paradox. Chapter 54 in B. Weingast and D.A. Whitman (Eds.) *The Oxford Handbook of Political Economy,* Oxford and New York: Oxford University, pp. 971–979.

260. [2007] The macrocontext of the microeconomics of innovation. In E. Sheshinski, R.J. Strom and W.J. Baumel (Eds.) *Entrepreneurship, Innovation, and the Growth Mechanism of the Free-Enterprise Economies.* Princeton, NJ and Oxford: Princeton University, Chapter 2, pp. 20–27.

261. [2007] Eco(nomics/logy). Ecological Research 22: 8–9.

262. [2007] Global climate change: a challenge to policy. The Economists' Voice 4: 3, available at: www.bepress.com/ev/vol4/iss3/art2

263. [2007] (with G. Daily, P. Dasgupta, P. Ehrlich, L. Goulder, G. Heal, S. Levin, K.-G. Mäler, S. Schneider, D. Starrett, and B. Walker) Consumption, investment, and future well-being: reply to Daly et. al., *Conservation Biology* 21: 1363–1365.

264. [2007] (with A. Bensoussan, Q. Feng, and S.P. Sethi) Optimal savings and the value of population. *Proceedings of the National Academy of Sciences* 105, 43: 18421–18426.

265. [2009] A note on uncertainty and discounting in models of economic growth. *Journal of Risk and Uncertainty* 38: 87–94.

266. [2009] (with S. Levin) Intergenerational resource transfers with random offspring numbers. *Proceedings of the National Academy of Sciences* 106: 13702–13706.

267. [2009] (with P. Dasgupta) Conspicuous consumption and inconspicuous leisure. *Economic Journal* 119: F497–F516.

268. [2010] Economic theory and the financial crisis. In E. Michel-Kerjan and P. Slovic (Eds.) *The Irrational Economist*. New York: Public Affairs, pp. 183–191.

269. [2010] (with P. Dasgupta, L.H. Goulder, K. Mumford, and K. Oleson) China, the United States, and sustainability; perspectives based on comprehensive wealth. In G.E. Heal (Ed.) *Is Economic Growth Sustainable?* New York and London: Palgrave Macmillan. International Economic Association, 148.

270. [2010] The classification of social choice propositions. In K.J. Arrow, A.K. Sen, and K. Suzumura (Eds.) *Handbook of Social Choice and Welfare*, Volume 2. Amsterdam: Elsevier, Chapter 13, Part III, pp.24–27.

271. [2010] (with A. Bensoussan, Q. Feng, and S.P. Sethi) The genuine savings criterion and the value of population in an economy with endogenous fertility rate. In R. Boucekkine, N. Hritonenko, and Y. Yatsenko (Eds.) *Optimal Control of Age-Structured Populations in Economy, Demography, and the Environment.* Routledge: Abingdon, U.K., and New York, Chapter 1, pp. 20–44.

272. [2011] The responsibility of parents to children. In K.R. Monroe (Ed.) *Science, Ethics, and Politics.* Boulder, CO and London: Paradigm, pp. 126–134.

273. [2011] Credit instruments and information in general equilibrium. In P. Bridel (Ed.), *General Equilibrium Analysis: A Century After Walras.* Abingdon, U.K. and New York: Routledge, Chapter 10, pp. 102–108.

274. [2011] How growth can undermine growth: three examples. In O. de la Grandville (Ed.), *Frontiers of Economics and Globalization, Vol. 11: Economic Growth and Development.* Bingley, U.K: Emerald, Chapter 1, pp. 1–8.

275. [2012] (with P. Dasgupta, L.H. Goulder, K.J. Mumford, and K. Oleson) Sustainability and the measurement of wealth. *Environment and Development Economics* 17: 317–353.

276. [2012] Economic theory and the financial crisis. *Information Systems Frontiers* 14: 967–970.

277. [2013] (with P. Dasgupta, L.H. Goulder, K.J. Mumford, and K. Oleson) Sustainability and the measurement of wealth: further reflections. *Environment and Development Economics* 18, 4: 504.

278. [2013] Knowledge, belief, and the economic system. *WIFO Monatsberichte* 12: 943–951.

279. [2014] Is the market system an efficient bearer of risk? In T.J. Sargent and J. Vilmunen (Eds.) *Macroeconomics in the Service of Public Policy.* Oxford, U.K.: Oxford University, pp. 17–23.

280. [2014] (with M. Priebsch) Bliss, Catastrophe, and Rational Policy. *Environmental and Resource Economics* 58: 491–509.

281. [2014] (with P.R. Ehrlich and S. Levin) Some perspectives on linked ecosystems and socioeconomic systems. In S. Barrett, K.-G. Mäler, and E.S. Maskin *Environment and Development Economics: Essays in Honour of Sir Partha Dasgupta.* Oxford University Press Scholarship Online.

282. [2014] Conflict of values: a decision view. *Proceedings of the American Philosophical Society* 158: 25–30.

283. [2015] The economic system as trade in information. In C.E. Crangle, A. Garcia de las Sienra, and H.E. Longino (Eds.) *Foundations and Methods from Mathematics to Neuroscience: Essays Inspired by Patrick Suppes.* Stanford, CA: CSL Productions, pp. 93–98.

INDEX